Teach Yourself VISUALLY™
MORE
Windows® XP

Visual™

From
maranGraphics®

&

Wiley Publishing, Inc.

If you like
Teach Yourself VISUALLY
MORE Windows XP,
also see its companion:

Teach Yourself VISUALLY
Windows XP
ISBN: 0-7645-3619-2

Teach Yourself VISUALLY™ MORE Windows® XP

Published by
Wiley Publishing, Inc.
909 Third Avenue
New York, NY 10022

Published simultaneously in Canada

Copyright©2002 by maranGraphics Inc.
     5755 Coopers Avenue
     Mississauga, Ontario, Canada
     L4Z 1R9

Library of Congress Control Number: 2002108469

ISBN: 0-7645-3698-2

Manufactured in the United States of America

10 9 8 7 6 5 4 3 2 1

1K/RX/QY/QS/MG

Trademark Acknowledgments

maranGraphics Inc. has attempted to include trademark information for products, services and companies referred to in this guide. Although maranGraphics Inc. has made reasonable efforts in gathering this information, it cannot guarantee its accuracy.

The maranGraphics logo is a trademark or registered trademark of maranGraphics, Inc.. Wiley, the Wiley Publishing logo, Visual, the Visual logo, Simplified, Master VISUALLY, Teach Yourself VISUALLY, Visual Blueprint, In an Instant, Read Less - Learn More and related trade dress are trademarks or registered trademarks of Wiley Publishing, Inc. in the United States and other countries and may not be used without written permission. All other trademarks are the property of their respective owners. maranGraphics, Inc. and Wiley Publishing, Inc. are not associated with any product or vendor mentioned in this book.

maranGraphics has used their best efforts in preparing this book. As Web sites are constantly changing, some of the Web site addresses in this book may have moved or no longer exist. maranGraphics does not accept responsibility nor liability for losses or damages resulting from the information contained in this book. maranGraphics also does not support the views expressed in the Web sites contained in this book.

Important Numbers

For U.S. corporate orders, please call maranGraphics at 800-469-6616 or fax 905-890-9434.

For general information on our other products and services or to obtain technical support, please contact our Customer Care Department within the U.S. at 800-762-2974, outside the U.S. at 317-572-3993 or fax 317-572-4002.

Permissions

©2002 maranGraphics, Inc.
The 3-D illustrations are the copyright
of maranGraphics, Inc.

Wiley Publishing, Inc.   is a trademark of
                        Wiley Publishing, Inc.

U.S. Corporate Sales	U.S. Trade Sales
Contact maranGraphics at (800) 469-6616 or fax (905) 890-9434.	Contact Wiley at (800) 762-2974 or fax (317) 572-4002.

Some comments from our readers...

"I have to praise you and your company on the fine products you turn out. I have twelve of the *Teach Yourself VISUALLY* and *Simplified* books in my house. They were instrumental in helping me pass a difficult computer course. Thank you for creating books that are easy to follow."

   –Gordon Justin (Brielle, NJ)

"I commend your efforts and your success. I teach in an outreach program for the Dr. Eugene Clark Library in Lockhart, TX. Your *Teach Yourself VISUALLY* books are incredible and I use them in my computer classes. All my students love them!"

   –Michele Schalin (Lockhart, TX)

"Thank you so much for helping people like me learn about computers. The Maran family is just what the doctor ordered. Thank you, thank you, thank you."

   –Carol Moten (New Kensington, PA)

"I would like to take this time to compliment maranGraphics on creating such great books. Thank you for making it clear. Keep up the good work."

   –Kirk Santoro (Burbank, CA)

"I write to extend my thanks and appreciation for your books. They are clear, easy to follow, and straight to the point. Keep up the good work!"

   –Seward Kollie (Dakar, Senegal)

"What fantastic teaching books you have produced! Congratulations to you and your staff. You deserve the Nobel prize in Education in the Software category. Thanks for helping me to understand computers."

   –Bruno Tonon (Melbourne, Australia)

"Over time, I have bought a number of your 'Read Less-Learn More' books. For me, they are THE way to learn anything easily."

   –José A. Mazón (Cuba, NY)

"I was introduced to maranGraphics about four years ago and YOU ARE THE GREATEST THING THAT EVER HAPPENED TO INTRODUCTORY COMPUTER BOOKS!"

   –Glenn Nettleton (Huntsville, AL)

"Compliments To The Chef!! Your books are extraordinary! Or, simply put, Extra-Ordinary, meaning way above the rest! THANK YOU THANK YOU THANK YOU! for creating these."

   –Christine J. Manfrin (Castle Rock, CO)

"I'm a grandma who was pushed by an 11-year-old grandson to join the computer age. I found myself hopelessly confused and frustrated until I discovered the Visual series. I'm no expert by any means now, but I'm a lot further along than I would have been otherwise. Thank you!"

   –Carol Louthain (Logansport, IN)

"Thank you, thank you, thank you...for making it so easy for me to break into this high-tech world. I now own four of your books. I recommend them to anyone who is a beginner like myself. Now... if you could just do one for programming VCRs, it would make my day!"

   –Gay O'Donnell (Calgary, Alberta, Canada)

"You're marvelous! I am greatly in your debt."

   –Patrick Baird (Lacey, WA)

maranGraphics is a family-run business
located near Toronto, Canada.

At **maranGraphics**, we believe in producing great computer books—one book at a time.

Each maranGraphics book uses the award-winning communication process that we have been developing over the last 25 years. Using this process, we organize screen shots, text and illustrations in a way that makes it easy for you to learn new concepts and tasks.

We spend hours deciding the best way to perform each task, so you don't have to! Our clear, easy-to-follow screen shots and instructions walk you through each task from beginning to end.

Our detailed illustrations go hand-in-hand with the text to help reinforce the information. Each illustration is a labor of love—some take up to a week to draw!

We want to thank you for purchasing what we feel are the best computer books money can buy. We hope you enjoy using this book as much as we enjoyed creating it!

Sincerely,

The Maran Family

Please visit us on the Web at:
www.maran.com

CREDITS

Author:
Ruth Maran

Copy Development Director:
Wanda Lawrie

Copy Developers:
Raquel Scott
Megan Kirby

Project Manager:
Judy Maran

**Editing and
Screen Captures:**
Roxanne Van Damme
Roderick Anatalio
Norm Schumacher

Layout Designers:
Treena Lees
Sarah Jang

Illustrators:
Russ Marini
Steven Schaerer

**Screen Artist
and Illustrator:**
Darryl Grossi

Indexer:
Raquel Scott

**Wiley Vice President and
Executive Group Publisher:**
Richard Swadley

**Wiley Vice President
and Publisher:**
Barry Pruett

Wiley Editorial Support:
Jennifer Dorsey
Sandy Rodrigues
Lindsay Sandman

Post Production:
Robert Maran

ACKNOWLEDGMENTS

Thanks to the dedicated staff of maranGraphics, including
Roderick Anatalio, Darryl Grossi, Kelleigh Johnson,
Megan Kirby, Wanda Lawrie, Treena Lees,
Jill Maran, Judy Maran, Robert Maran, Ruth Maran,
Russ Marini, Steven Schaerer, Norm Schumacher,
Raquel Scott and Roxanne Van Damme.

Finally, to Richard Maran who originated
the easy-to-use graphic format of this guide.
Thank you for your inspiration and guidance.

TABLE OF CONTENTS

Chapter 1

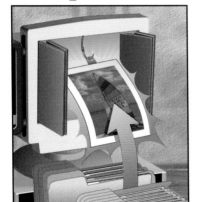

WORK WITH FILES

Chapter 2

USING WINDOWS ACCESSORIES

Chapter 3

Chapter 4

TABLE OF CONTENTS

Chapter 5

USING THE ACCESSIBILITY FEATURES

Chapter 6

CREATE MOVIES

Chapter 7

MANAGE MULTIPLE USERS

Chapter 8

WORK ON A NETWORK

Chapter 9

CONNECT COMPUTERS

TABLE OF CONTENTS

Chapter 10

BROWSE THE WEB

Chapter 11

EXCHANGE E-MAIL MESSAGES

Chapter 12

EXCHANGE INSTANT MESSAGES

Chapter 13

WORK WITH NEWSGROUPS

Chapter 14

MANAGE & TROUBLESHOOT YOUR COMPUTER

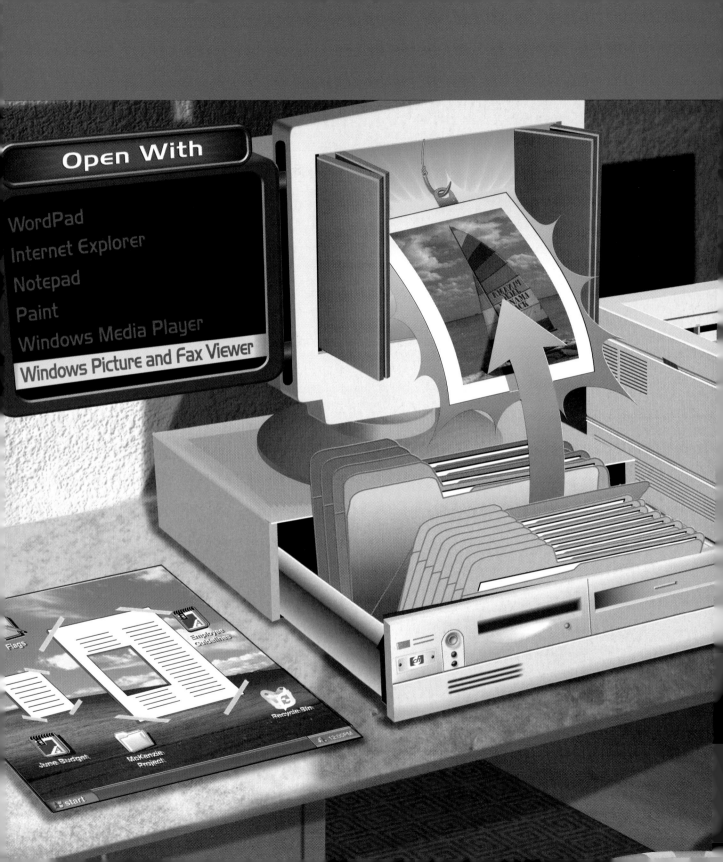

CHAPTER 1

Work With Files

This chapter teaches you how to work with the files on your computer more efficiently. Learn how to open a file in a specific program, put part of a file on the desktop, display file properties and more.

**Microsoft®
Windows® XP
is a program
that controls
the overall
activity of your
computer.**

Windows XP ensures
that all the hardware
and software on your
computer work
together smoothly
and efficiently.

Work With Files and Programs

Windows helps you work with the
files stored on your computer. You
can open files in specific programs,
display file properties and cancel
the printing of files. Windows also
includes programs you can use to
create text files, record sounds,
play DVD movies and create your
own movies.

Customize and Optimize Your Computer

Windows allows you to customize and
optimize your computer. You can add
Web content to your desktop, customize
the Start menu and set up user accounts.
Windows also allows you to use
accessibility features, change power
options and detect and repair disk errors.

Access the Internet

Windows allows you to browse
through information on the Web,
exchange electronic mail and
subscribe to newsgroups on the
Internet. You can also send
instant messages, share a
program and talk to another
person while viewing live video
of the person over the Internet.

PARTS OF THE WINDOWS XP SCREEN

The Windows XP screen displays various items that allow you to perform tasks in Windows.

DESKTOP
The background area of your screen.

TITLE BAR
Displays the name of an open window.

WINDOW
Displays the contents of a folder, file or other information.

MENU BAR
Provides access to lists of commands available in a window.

TOOLBAR
Contains buttons that provide quick access to frequently used commands.

ICON
An item on the desktop or in a window. An icon can represent an item such as a file or program.

RECYCLE BIN
Stores deleted files and allows you to recover them later.

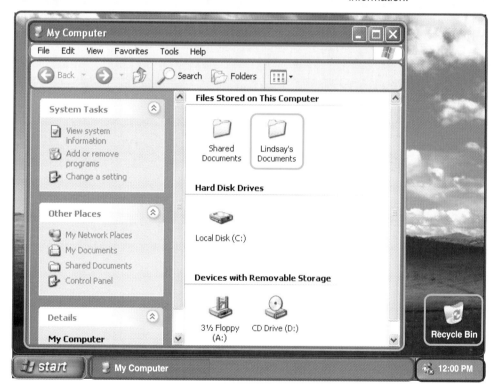

START BUTTON
Gives you quick access to programs, files, computer settings and help.

TASKBAR
Displays a button for each open window on your screen. You can use these buttons to switch between open windows.

NOTIFICATION AREA
Displays the current time and notification icons. Notification icons usually appear when events occur on your computer, such as when you print a file (🖨) or receive an e-mail message (📨).

VIEW PICTURES

You can view your pictures without opening an image editing program. Viewing a picture allows you to preview the picture in more detail.

By default, most pictures on your computer are stored in the My Pictures folder.

1 Double-click a picture you want to view.

■ The Windows Picture and Fax Viewer window appears, displaying the picture you selected.

2 To magnify or reduce the size of the picture, click one of the following buttons.

🔍 Zoom In

🔍 Zoom Out

3 To display the picture in a size that fits best in the window or at its actual size, click one of the following buttons.

🖼 Best Fit

◈ Actual Size

6

Can I view a slide show of pictures?

When viewing a picture in the Windows Picture and Fax Viewer window, you can click 🖳 to display a slide show of all the pictures in the same folder. To stop the slide show at any time, press the **Esc** key.

How can I make changes to a picture?

If you want to make changes to a picture you are viewing, you can open the picture in an image editing program. To open a picture in an image editing program and close the Windows Picture and Fax Viewer window, click 🖼 .

4 To rotate the picture 90 degrees, click one of the following buttons.

🔄 Rotate Clockwise

🔄 Rotate Counterclockwise

*Note: A dialog box may appear if rotating the picture may reduce its quality. Click **Yes** or **No** to specify if you want to rotate the picture.*

5 To print the picture, click 🖨 .

Note: The Photo Printing Wizard appears when you choose to print a picture. Follow the instructions in the wizard to print the picture.

6 To display other pictures in the same folder, click one of the following buttons to display the previous or next picture in the folder.

⏮ Previous Image

⏭ Next Image

7 When you finish viewing your pictures, click ✖ to close the Windows Picture and Fax Viewer window.

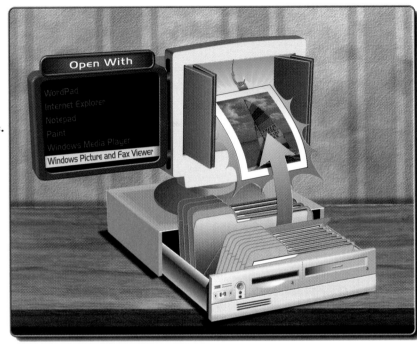

You can choose
the program on
your computer
that you want to
use to open a file.

For example, you
can choose to open a
picture in the Windows
Picture and Fax Viewer
so you can preview the
picture or in an image
editing program so you
can edit the picture.

OPEN A FILE IN A SPECIFIC PROGRAM

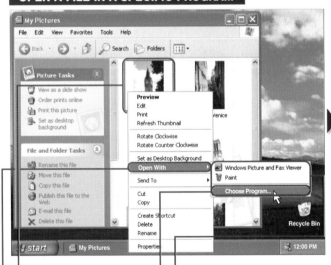

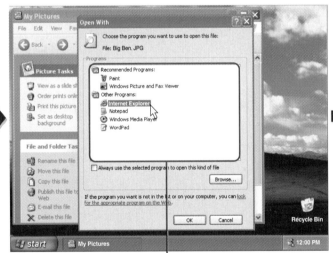

1 Right-click the file
you want to open in a
specific program. A
menu appears.

2 Click **Open With**.

*Note: If the Open With dialog
box appears, skip to step 4.*

■ A menu appears,
displaying a list of programs
you can use to open the file.
You can click a program in
the list to open the file using
that program.

3 To open the file in a
program that does not
appear in the list, click
Choose Program.

■ The Open With dialog
box appears.

■ This area lists the
programs available on your
computer. The programs
Windows recommends you
use to open the file appear
at the top of the list.

4 Click the program you
want to use to open the file.

Why does the Windows dialog box appear when I try to open a file?

If you try to open a file Windows does not recognize, a dialog box will appear, stating that Windows cannot open the file. To open the file, you must specify which program you want to use to open the file. Click the option you want to use to find a program to open the file (○ changes to ◉) and then click **OK**.

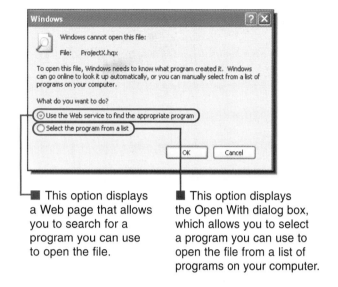

■ This option displays a Web page that allows you to search for a program you can use to open the file.

■ This option displays the Open With dialog box, which allows you to select a program you can use to open the file from a list of programs on your computer.

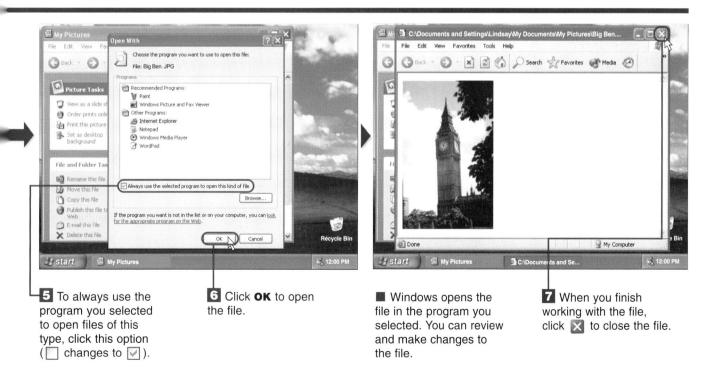

5 To always use the program you selected to open files of this type, click this option (☐ changes to ☑).

6 Click **OK** to open the file.

■ Windows opens the file in the program you selected. You can review and make changes to the file.

7 When you finish working with the file, click ✕ to close the file.

PUT PART OF A FILE ON THE DESKTOP

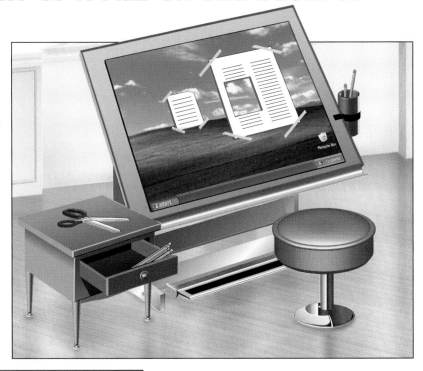

You can place frequently used information on your desktop to give you quick access to the information.

When you place part of a file on the desktop, Windows creates a file called a scrap.

Scraps are useful if you frequently add the same information to files, such as your name and address or company logo.

PUT PART OF A FILE ON THE DESKTOP

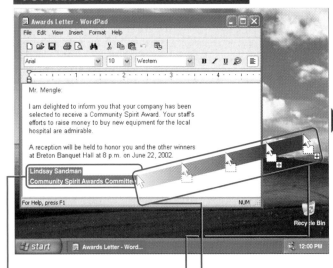

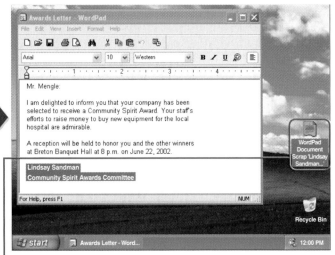

1 Open the file containing the information you want to place on your desktop. In this example, a WordPad file was opened.

2 Select the information you want to place on your desktop.

3 Position the mouse over the information.

4 Drag the information to a blank area on your desktop.

■ Windows creates a file called a scrap. The scrap stores a copy of the information you selected in the original file.

10

Why am I unable to create a scrap?

Scraps are only available for programs that allow you to drag and drop information to other programs. For example, you cannot create a scrap from a Microsoft Notepad file.

Can I rename or delete a scrap?

You can work with a scrap the same way you would work with any file on your computer.

Rename a Scrap

To rename a scrap, click the scrap on your desktop and then press the `F2` key. Type a new name for the scrap and then press the `Enter` key.

Delete a Scrap

To delete a scrap, click the scrap on your desktop and then press the `Delete` key. In the confirmation dialog box that appears, click **Yes** to delete the scrap.

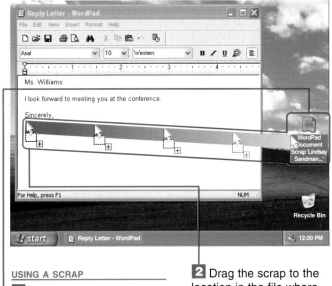

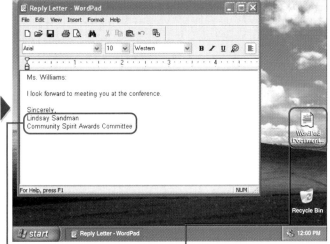

USING A SCRAP

1 To place the information from a scrap in a file, position the mouse ⌕ over the scrap.

2 Drag the scrap to the location in the file where you want the information to appear.

■ The information appears in the file.

■ The scrap remains on your desktop. You can place the information from the scrap in as many files as you want.

EXTRACT FILES FROM A COMPRESSED FOLDER

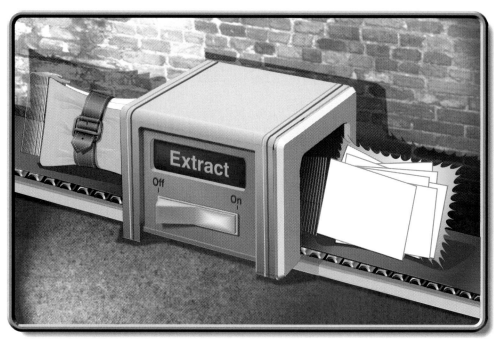

You can extract all the files from a compressed folder at once. Windows will create decompressed copies of the files that you can work with as you would work with any file on your computer.

Extracting files from a compressed folder is useful when you obtain compressed folders on the Internet. Files available on the Internet, such as programs and fonts, are often placed in a compressed folder to allow them to transfer over the Internet more quickly.

EXTRACT FILES FROM A COMPRESSED FOLDER

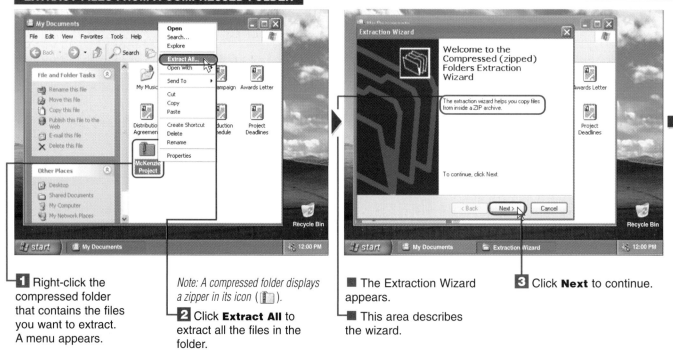

1 Right-click the compressed folder that contains the files you want to extract. A menu appears.

Note: A compressed folder displays a zipper in its icon ( ).

2 Click **Extract All** to extract all the files in the folder.

■ The Extraction Wizard appears.

■ This area describes the wizard.

3 Click **Next** to continue.

Can I extract a single file from a compressed folder?

Yes. To extract a single file from a compressed folder, double-click the compressed folder to open the folder. Then drag the file you want to extract to a new location outside the folder. Windows will create a decompressed copy of the file in the new location.

How do I delete a compressed folder?

If you no longer need a compressed folder after you extract the files, you can delete the folder. To delete a compressed folder, click the folder and then press the `Delete` key. In the confirmation dialog box that appears, click **Yes** to delete the folder. Windows will delete all the files and folders stored in the compressed folder.

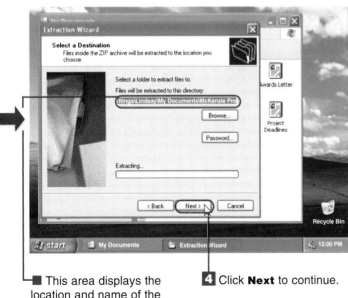

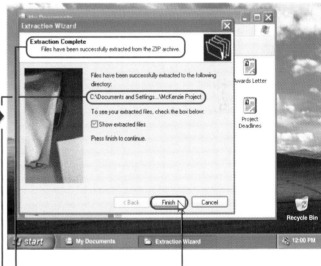

■ This area displays the location and name of the folder where Windows will place the extracted files.

4 Click **Next** to continue.

■ This message appears when the files have been successfully extracted.

■ This area indicates the location and name of the folder that contains the extracted files.

5 Click **Finish** to close the Extraction Wizard.

■ The contents of the new folder containing the extracted files will appear. The original compressed folder will remain on your computer.

ADD DESTINATIONS TO THE SEND TO MENU

You can add destinations to the Send To menu. The Send To menu allows you to quickly send copies of files and folders to other locations.

Adding a new destination to the Send To menu is useful if you frequently send files and folders to the same location.

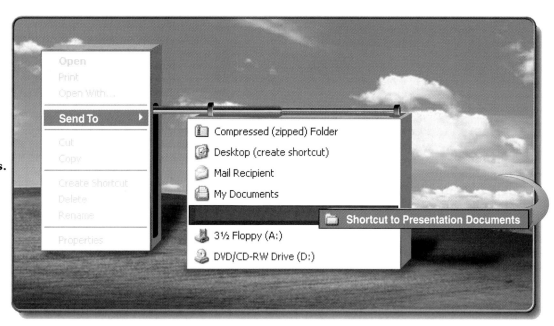

ADD DESTINATIONS TO THE SEND TO MENU

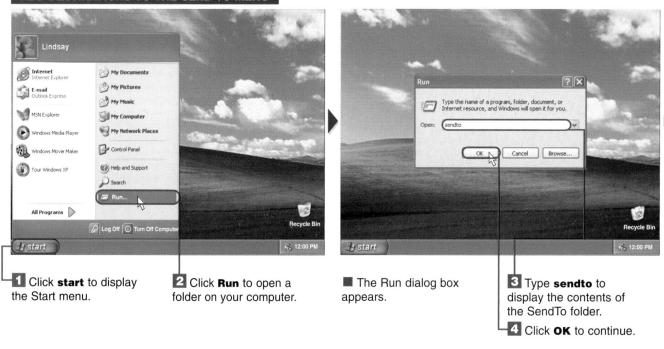

1 Click **start** to display the Start menu.

2 Click **Run** to open a folder on your computer.

■ The Run dialog box appears.

3 Type **sendto** to display the contents of the SendTo folder.

4 Click **OK** to continue.

What items automatically appear on the Send To menu?

By default, the Send To menu displays items that allow you to quickly send files and folders to your desktop, My Documents folder, floppy drive (A:) and recordable CD drive (D:). The Compressed (zipped) Folder item allows you to quickly create a compressed version of a folder. The Mail Recipient item allows you to quickly send a file in an e-mail message.

How do I rename or delete an item on the Send To menu?

Rename an Item

Perform steps **1** to **4** below to display the SendTo window. Click the item you want to rename and then press the **F2** key. Type a new name for the item and then press the **Enter** key.

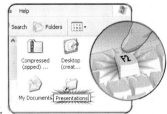

Delete an Item

Perform steps **1** to **4** below to display the SendTo window. Click the item you want to delete and then press the **Delete** key. In the confirmation dialog box that appears, click **Yes** to delete the item.

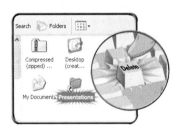

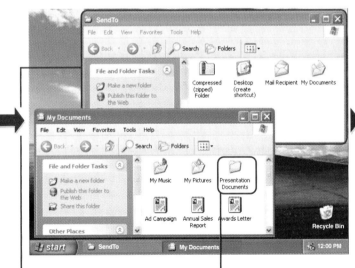

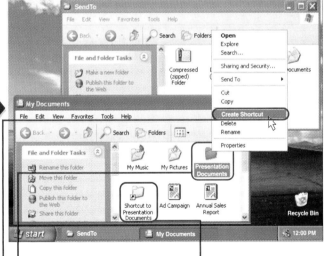

■ The SendTo window appears, displaying items that appear on the Send To menu.

5 In a different window or on the desktop, locate the item you want to add to the Send To menu.

*Note: In this example, the **Presentation Documents** folder will be added to the Send To menu.*

6 Right-click the item. A menu appears.

7 Click **Create Shortcut** to create a shortcut for the item.

■ A shortcut for the item appears. A shortcut displays an arrow (⤴) in its icon.

CONTINUED

ADD DESTINATIONS TO THE SEND TO MENU

Each item you add to the SendTo window will appear on the Send To menu.

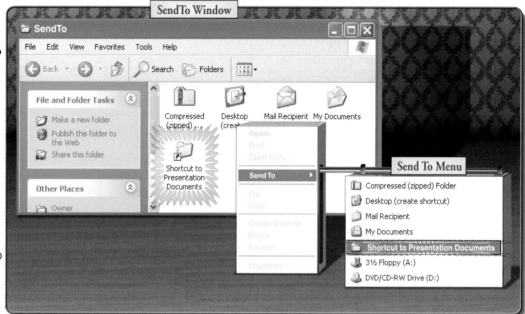

After you add an item to the Send To menu, you can use the menu to quickly send files and folders to the location.

ADD DESTINATIONS TO THE SEND TO MENU (CONTINUED)

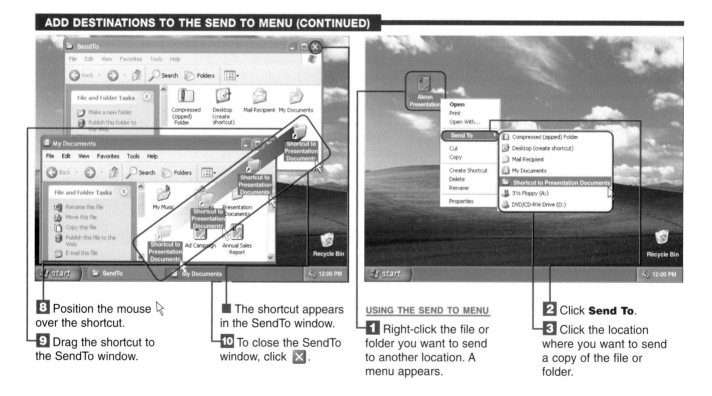

8 Position the mouse over the shortcut.

9 Drag the shortcut to the SendTo window.

■ The shortcut appears in the SendTo window.

10 To close the SendTo window, click ⊠.

USING THE SEND TO MENU

1 Right-click the file or folder you want to send to another location. A menu appears.

2 Click **Send To**.

3 Click the location where you want to send a copy of the file or folder.

You can create a copy
of all or part of your
screen. Copying all or
part of your screen is
useful if you are trying
to explain a computer
problem or procedure
and you want a visual
example to illustrate the
problem or procedure.

Copying the contents of
your screen is also useful
for keeping records of your
computer and program
settings.

COPY SCREEN OR WINDOW CONTENTS

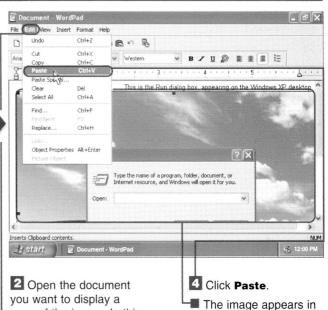

1 To copy the entire screen,
press the **Print Screen** key.

■ To copy just the active
window or dialog box, press
and hold down the **Alt** key
as you press the **Print
Screen** key.

*Note: The active window or
dialog box appears in front of
all other windows.*

■ Windows copies the
image of your screen.

2 Open the document
you want to display a
copy of the image. In this
example, a WordPad
document was opened.

3 Click **Edit**.

4 Click **Paste**.

■ The image appears in
the document.

DISPLAY THE STATUS BAR

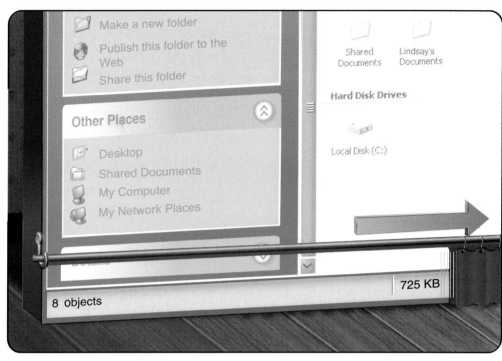

You can display the status bar at the bottom of a window. The status bar displays information about the items in a window.

8 objects

725 KB

DISPLAY THE STATUS BAR

1 Click **View**.

■ A check mark (✔) appears beside Status Bar if the status bar is currently displayed.

2 Click **Status Bar** to display the status bar.

■ The status bar appears at the bottom of the window.

■ The status bar usually displays the number of items and the total size of the items in a window.

Note: When you select a file in a window, the status bar usually displays the type of file, the date the file was last modified and the size of the file.

■ To once again hide the status bar, repeat steps **1** and **2**.

18

ARRANGE DESKTOP ITEMS

You can have Windows neatly arrange the items on your desktop.

Windows can arrange desktop items by name, size, type or the date the items were last modified.

ARRANGE DESKTOP ITEMS

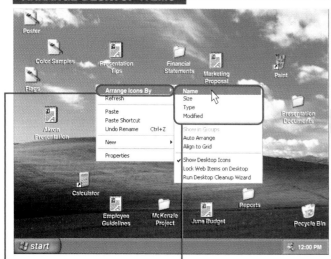

1 Right-click a blank area on your desktop. A menu appears.

2 Click **Arrange Icons By**.

3 Click the way you want to arrange the items on your desktop.

■ Windows arranges the items on your desktop. In this example, the desktop items are arranged by name.

■ Regardless of how you arrange items, Windows arranges files and folders separately.

ARRANGE OPEN WINDOWS

If you have several windows open on your screen, the contents of some windows may be hidden from view. You can arrange the windows so the contents of the windows are easier to work with.

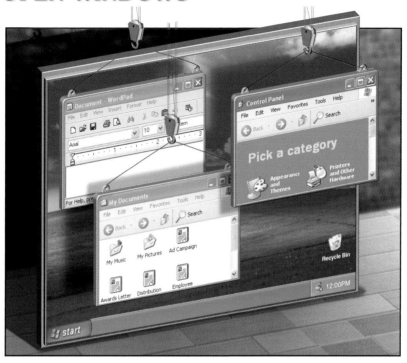

1 Right-click an empty area on the taskbar. A menu appears.

2 Click the way you want to arrange the open windows on your screen.

Note: Windows will not arrange windows you have minimized to buttons on the taskbar.

CASCADE WINDOWS

■ The windows neatly overlap each other. You can clearly see the title bar of each window.

■ You can click the title bar of the window you want to work with to make that window active. The window will appear in front of all the other windows.

How do I change back to the previous window arrangement?

To immediately change back to the previous window arrangement, right-click an empty area on the taskbar and then select **Undo Cascade** or **Undo Tile**.

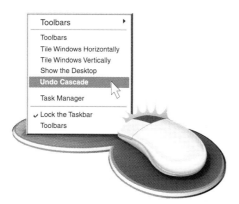

 Why can't I see a difference between horizontally and vertically tiled windows?

Horizontally and vertically tiled windows are displayed the same way on your screen when you have four or more windows open.

TILE WINDOWS HORIZONTALLY

■ The windows appear one above the other. You can view the contents of each window.

■ You can easily compare the contents of the windows and exchange information between the windows.

■ You can click anywhere in the window you want to work with to make that window active.

TILE WINDOWS VERTICALLY

■ The windows appear side by side. You can view the contents of each window.

■ You can easily compare the contents of the windows and exchange information between the windows.

■ You can click anywhere in the window you want to work with to make that window active.

DISPLAY FILE PROPERTIES

You can display the properties of a file to find out information about the file.

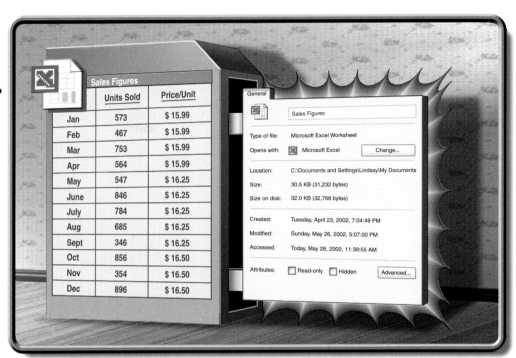

When displaying the properties of a file, you can find out information such as the type of file, the size of the file and the date and time the file was last changed.

DISPLAY FILE PROPERTIES

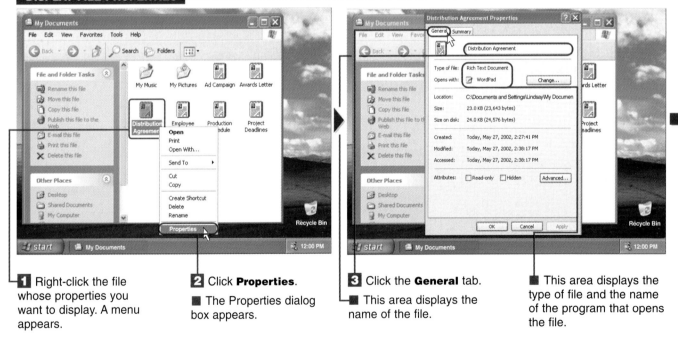

1 Right-click the file whose properties you want to display. A menu appears.

2 Click **Properties**.

■ The Properties dialog box appears.

3 Click the **General** tab.

■ This area displays the name of the file.

■ This area displays the type of file and the name of the program that opens the file.

Why is the amount of disk space required to store a file larger than the actual size of the file?

The amount of disk space required to store a file is determined by the number of clusters used to store the file. A cluster is the smallest amount of space that can be used to store a file on a hard drive. If the size of a file is smaller than one cluster, an entire cluster is still used to store the file.

What attributes are available for files?

Read-only

The Read-only attribute prevents people from saving changes they make to a file.

Hidden

The Hidden attribute hides and protects important files. To display hidden files, see page 64.

Archive

The Archive attribute appears if your computer uses the FAT file system. Some programs use this attribute to determine if a file needs to be backed up.

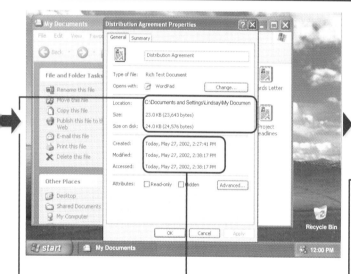

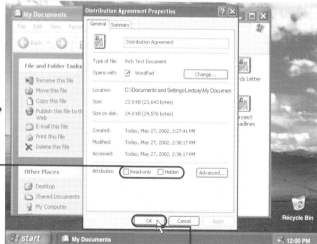

■ This area displays the location of the file on your computer, the size of the file and the amount of disk space required to store the file.

■ This area displays the date and time the file was created, last changed and last opened.

■ This area displays the attributes for the file. A check mark (✓) appears beside each attribute assigned to the file.

4 To turn an attribute on (☑) or off (☐), click the attribute.

5 When you finish reviewing the properties of the file, click **OK** to close the Properties dialog box.

DISPLAY FILE TYPES

You can view a list of the file types that are registered with Windows. Displaying the registered file types allows you to see which types of files you can work with in Windows.

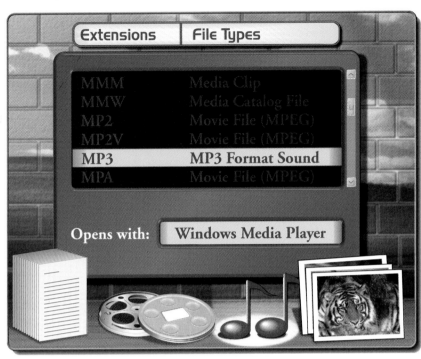

When a file type is registered, Windows can determine which program to use to open files of that type. Windows automatically recognizes over 250 types of files, including text, sound, image and movie files.

DISPLAY FILE TYPES

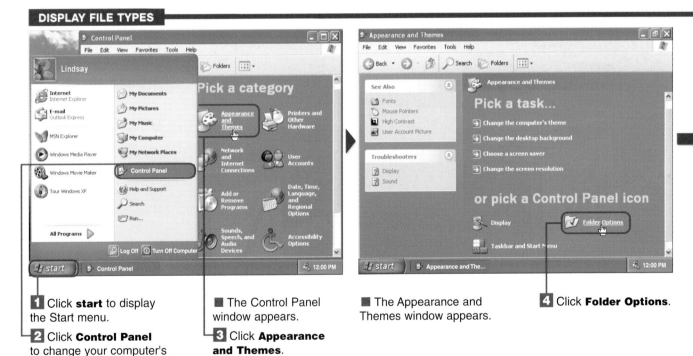

1 Click **start** to display the Start menu.

2 Click **Control Panel** to change your computer's settings.

■ The Control Panel window appears.

3 Click **Appearance and Themes**.

■ The Appearance and Themes window appears.

4 Click **Folder Options**.

How does Windows know which program to use to open a file?

Windows will use the file name extension of a file to determine which program to use to open the file. Each file name extension is associated with a specific program, as well as a specific file type. File name extensions are usually three letters that appear after the period at the end of a file name. For example, a file named Memo.txt will open in Notepad.

Why can't I see the file name extensions for my files?

By default, Windows does not display the file name extensions for registered file types. To have Windows display the file name extensions for all your files, perform steps **1** to **7** starting on page 64, selecting **Hide extensions for known file types** in step **6** (☑ changes to ☐).

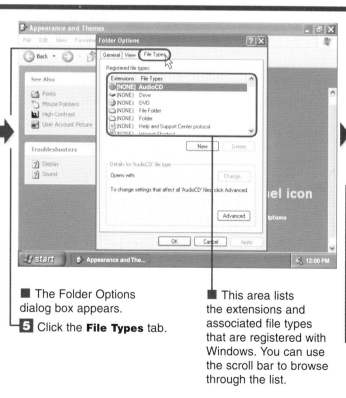

■ The Folder Options dialog box appears.

5 Click the **File Types** tab.

■ This area lists the extensions and associated file types that are registered with Windows. You can use the scroll bar to browse through the list.

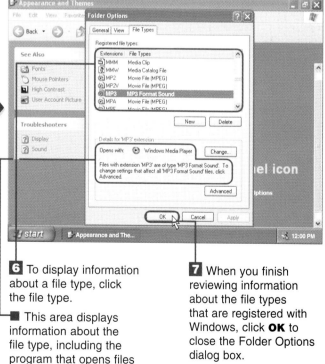

6 To display information about a file type, click the file type.

■ This area displays information about the file type, including the program that opens files of this type.

7 When you finish reviewing information about the file types that are registered with Windows, click **OK** to close the Folder Options dialog box.

PAUSE PRINTING

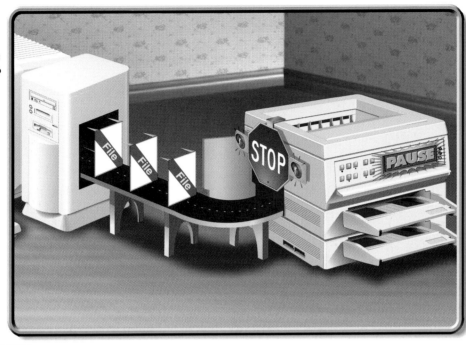

You can pause your printer to temporarily stop all the files waiting to print.

Pausing a printer is useful when you want to add more paper or change the toner for the printer.

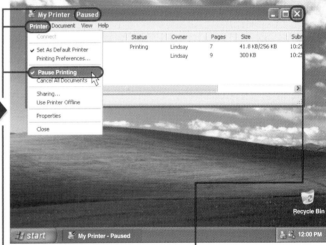

■ When you print files, a printer icon (🖨) appears in this area. The printer icon disappears when the files have finished printing.

1 Double-click the printer icon (🖨).

■ A window appears, displaying information about each file waiting to print.

2 Click **Printer**.

3 Click **Pause Printing** to pause the printing of all files.

■ When you pause printing, this area displays the word **Paused**.

4 When you finish viewing the information about the files waiting to print, click ✕ to close the window.

■ To resume printing at any time, repeat steps **1** to **4**.

CANCEL PRINTING

You can stop a file from printing. You may want to stop a file from printing if you accidentally selected the wrong file to print or if you want to make last-minute changes to the file.

CANCEL PRINTING

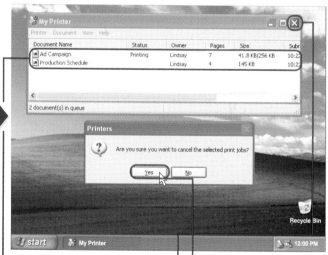

■ When you print files, a printer icon (🖨) appears in this area. The printer icon disappears when the files have finished printing.

1 Double-click the printer icon (🖨).

■ A window appears, displaying information about each file waiting to print.

2 Click the file you no longer want to print and then press the Delete key.

■ A confirmation dialog box appears.

3 Click **Yes** to cancel the printing of the file.

4 Click ✖ to close the window.

USING RUN TO START A PROGRAM

You can use the Run feature to quickly start a program. The Run feature is especially useful for programs that do not appear on the Start menu.

Programs that may not appear on the Start menu include MS-DOS programs, older Windows programs and advanced programs used to change the settings on your computer. For example, the System Configuration Utility (msconfig) allows you to change the setup of Windows and fix problems with your computer.

USING RUN TO START A PROGRAM

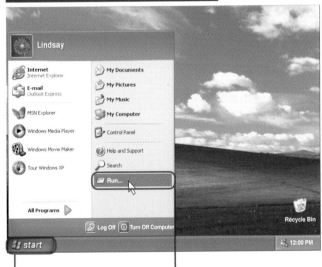

1 Click **start** to display the Start menu.

2 Click **Run** to start a program.

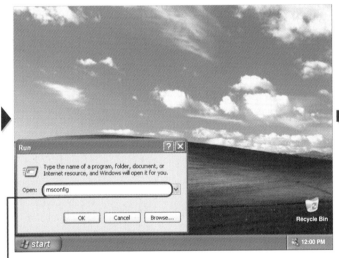

■ The Run dialog box appears.

3 Type the name of the program you want to start.

Note: Windows may display a list of programs when you begin typing the name of the program you want to start. If the program you want to start appears in the list, you can click the name of the program to select the program.

Can I use the Run feature to display a Web page?

Yes. To display a Web page, type the address of the Web page, such as www.yahoo.com, in the Run dialog box and then press the Enter key. Windows will start your Web browser and display the Web page you specified.

Is there another way I can quickly start a program?

You can add a program to the Start menu so you can quickly start the program at any time. Adding programs to the Start menu is useful for programs you will use often. To add a program to the Start menu, see page 92.

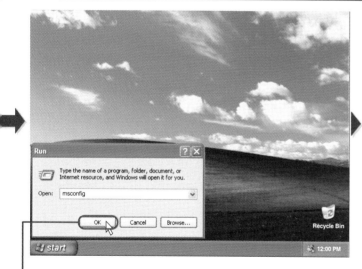

4 Click **OK** to start the program.

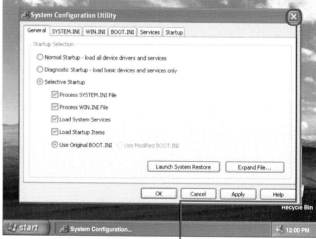

■ The program starts.

■ When you finish working with the program, click ☒ to close the program.

CHAPTER 2

Using Windows Accessories

You can use the accessories included with Windows XP to perform many tasks. In this chapter, you will learn how to use Windows accessories to insert special characters in your documents, record sounds and play DVD movies.

USING NOTEPAD

Notepad is an easy-to-use text editor that you can use to create and edit simple documents.

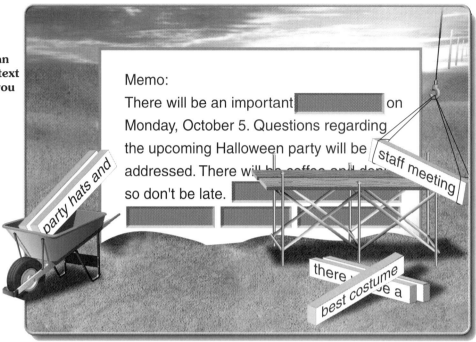

Memo:
There will be an important ▮▮▮▮▮ on Monday, October 5. Questions regarding the upcoming Halloween party will be addressed. There wi▮▮ ▮▮ ▮▮▮▮▮ ▮▮▮ ▮▮▮▮ so don't be late. ▮▮▮▮

party hats and

staff meeting

there ▮▮ ▮▮ a

best costume

Notepad is useful for creating small text documents that do not require formatting or graphics.

USING NOTEPAD

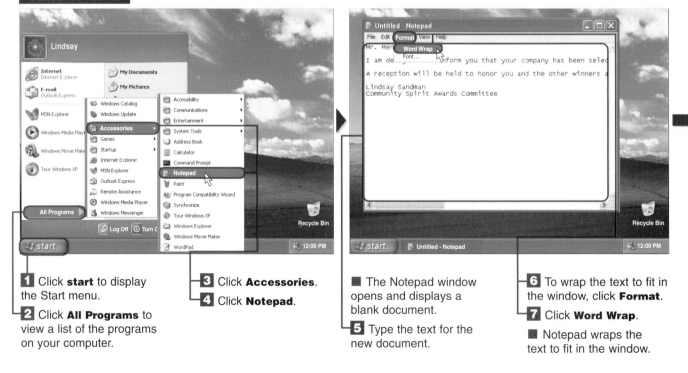

1 Click **start** to display the Start menu.

2 Click **All Programs** to view a list of the programs on your computer.

3 Click **Accessories**.

4 Click **Notepad**.

■ The Notepad window opens and displays a blank document.

5 Type the text for the new document.

6 To wrap the text to fit in the window, click **Format**.

7 Click **Word Wrap**.

■ Notepad wraps the text to fit in the window.

How do I open a Notepad document I have saved?

To open a Notepad document so you can review and edit the document, locate the document on your computer. By default, Notepad documents are stored in the My Documents folder and display the ▨ icon. You can double-click the document to open the document.

 Can Notepad automatically enter the time and date in a document?

If you type **.LOG** on the first line of a document, Notepad will add the current time and date to the end of the document each time you open the document. This is useful if you use Notepad to record information such as communications with clients or project updates and you want to log the current time and date for each entry.

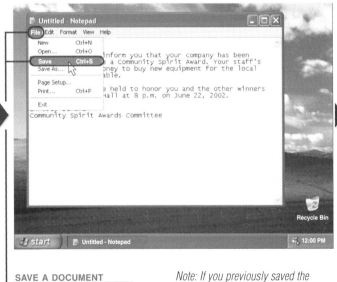

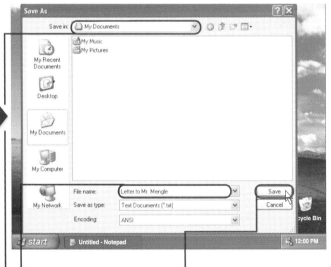

SAVE A DOCUMENT

8 Click **File**.

9 Click **Save**.

■ The Save As dialog box appears.

Note: If you previously saved the document, the Save As dialog box will not appear since you have already named the document.

10 Type a name for the document.

■ This area shows the location where Notepad will store the document. You can click this area to change the location.

11 Click **Save** to save the document.

12 When you finish working with the document, click ☒ to close the document.

USING CHARACTER MAP

You can use
Character Map
to include special
characters in your
documents that
are not available
on your keyboard.

Character map
offers many special
characters that you
can choose from,
including ©, é, ½
and ™. Each font
available in Character
Map provides a
different collection
of special characters.

USING CHARACTER MAP

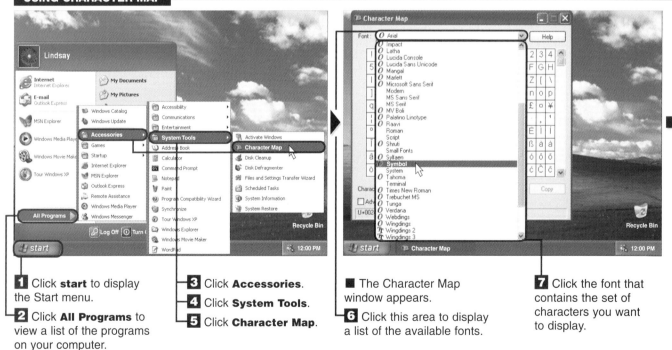

1 Click **start** to display
the Start menu.

2 Click **All Programs** to
view a list of the programs
on your computer.

3 Click **Accessories**.

4 Click **System Tools**.

5 Click **Character Map**.

■ The Character Map
window appears.

6 Click this area to display
a list of the available fonts.

7 Click the font that
contains the set of
characters you want
to display.

How can I quickly enter special characters in my documents?

Some special characters have a keystroke combination you can use to quickly add the characters to a document. For example, to enter the copyright symbol (©), press and hold down the Alt key as you enter **0169** using the numeric keypad on your keyboard. When you click a character in the Character Map window, the keystroke combination for the character appears in the bottom right corner of the window.

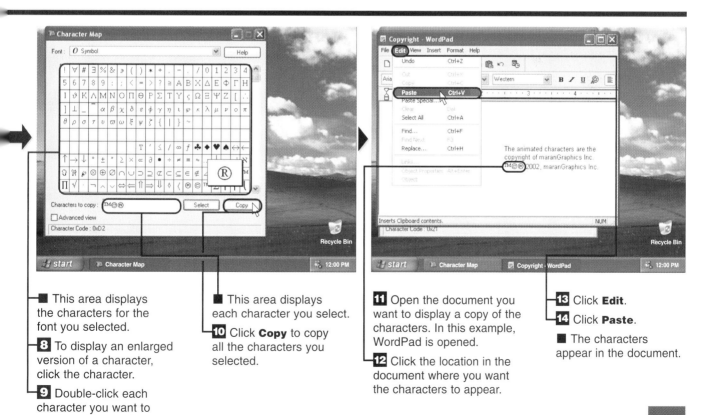

■ This area displays the characters for the font you selected.

8 To display an enlarged version of a character, click the character.

9 Double-click each character you want to use in a document.

■ This area displays each character you select.

10 Click **Copy** to copy all the characters you selected.

11 Open the document you want to display a copy of the characters. In this example, WordPad is opened.

12 Click the location in the document where you want the characters to appear.

13 Click **Edit**.

14 Click **Paste**.

■ The characters appear in the document.

35

USING SOUND RECORDER

You can use Sound Recorder to record, play and edit sounds on your computer.

You can record sounds from a microphone, CD player, stereo, VCR or any other sound device you can connect to your computer. You need a computer with sound capabilities to record and play sounds.

USING SOUND RECORDER

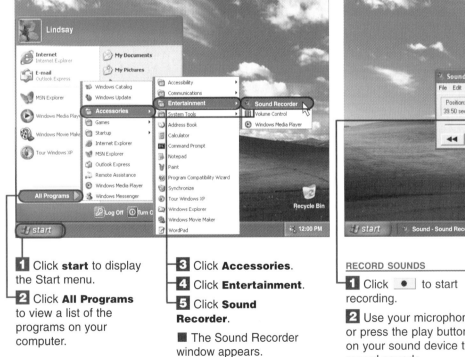

1 Click **start** to display the Start menu.

2 Click **All Programs** to view a list of the programs on your computer.

3 Click **Accessories**.

4 Click **Entertainment**.

5 Click **Sound Recorder**.

■ The Sound Recorder window appears.

RECORD SOUNDS

1 Click ● to start recording.

2 Use your microphone or press the play button on your sound device to record sounds.

3 Click ■ to stop recording.

36

How can I move to the beginning or end of a recording?

■ Click ◄◄ to move to the beginning of a recording.

■ Click ►► to move to the end of a recording.

■ You can also drag the slider (▯) to move to a specific position in a recording.

What sound effects can I add to a recording?

Sound Recorder has several sound effects you can use to change your recording. You can increase or decrease the volume of a recording, increase the speed of a recording to create a chipmunk effect or decrease the speed of a recording to create a spooky and mysterious effect. Sound Recorder also allows you to add an echo to a recording or play the recording in reverse.

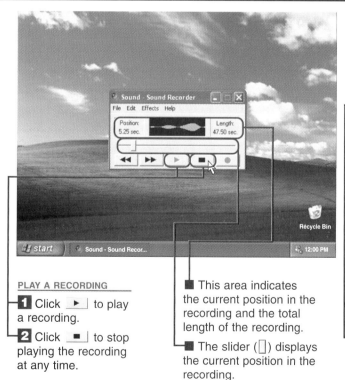

PLAY A RECORDING

1 Click ► to play a recording.

2 Click ■ to stop playing the recording at any time.

■ This area indicates the current position in the recording and the total length of the recording.

■ The slider (▯) displays the current position in the recording.

ADD SOUND EFFECTS

1 Click **Effects** to add a sound effect to a recording.

2 Click the sound effect you want to add.

Note: For more information on the sound effects you can add, see the top of this page.

■ To add other sound effects, repeat steps **1** and **2** for each sound effect.

CONTINUED

USING SOUND RECORDER

You can save a recording to store the recording for future use. You can also open a saved recording to once again play and edit the recording.

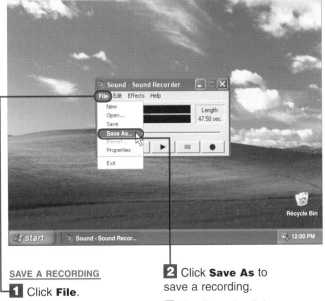

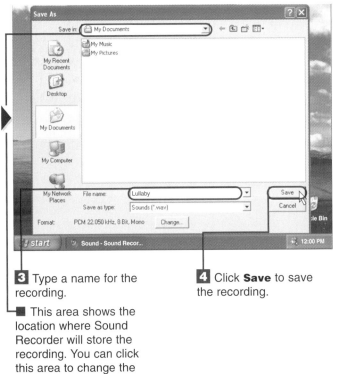

SAVE A RECORDING

1 Click **File**.

2 Click **Save As** to save a recording.

■ The Save As dialog box appears.

3 Type a name for the recording.

■ This area shows the location where Sound Recorder will store the recording. You can click this area to change the location.

4 Click **Save** to save the recording.

38

Can I play a recording in Windows Media Player?

Yes. Windows Media Player is a program that allows you to play media files, such as sound recordings. To play a recording in Windows Media Player, locate the recording on your computer. By default, recordings are stored in the My Documents folder and display the 🎵 icon. When you locate the recording you want to play, double-click the recording. Windows Media Player opens and plays the recording you selected.

 How can I perform more advanced sound recording and editing tasks?

Sound Recorder allows you to perform only basic sound recording and editing tasks. You can obtain a more sophisticated sound recording and editing program, such as Sound Forge or Cool Edit, on the Internet and at computer stores. These programs allow you to perform advanced sound editing tasks, such as reducing background noise and creating fade effects.

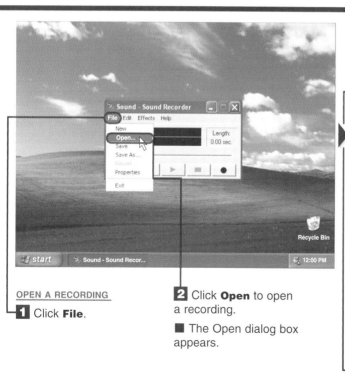

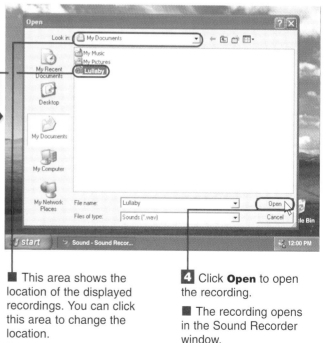

OPEN A RECORDING

1 Click **File**.

2 Click **Open** to open a recording.

■ The Open dialog box appears.

■ This area shows the location of the displayed recordings. You can click this area to change the location.

3 Click the recording you want to open.

4 Click **Open** to open the recording.

■ The recording opens in the Sound Recorder window.

USING MEDIA PLAYER TO PLAY A DVD MOVIE

You can use Windows Media Player to play DVD movies on your computer.

USING MEDIA PLAYER TO PLAY A DVD MOVIE

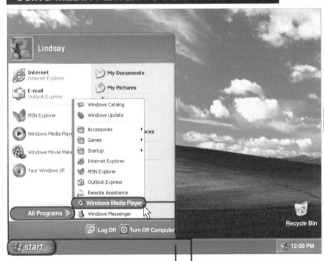

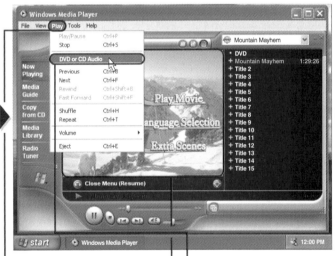

1 Insert a DVD into your DVD drive.

2 To prevent Windows from automatically playing the DVD, press and hold down the Shift key.

3 Click **start** to display the Start menu.

4 Click **All Programs** to view a list of the programs on your computer.

5 Click **Windows Media Player**.

■ The Windows Media Player window appears.

6 Position the mouse above the Windows Media Player window and click **Play**.

7 Click **DVD or CD Audio** to play the DVD.

■ The DVD plays in this area. A list of options allowing you to play the movie or access special features may appear. To select an option, you can click the option.

Does my computer require any special hardware or software to play DVD movies?

Before you can play DVD movies, your computer must have a DVD drive and a DVD decoder installed. A DVD decoder is software that allows your computer to play DVD movies. Your computer manufacturer may have installed a DVD decoder on your computer. If your computer does not have a DVD decoder installed, you can purchase DVD decoders that are compatible with Windows XP from companies such as InterVideo (www.intervideo.com) and CyberLink (www.gocyberlink.com).

How can I play a DVD movie using the entire screen?

To play a DVD movie using the entire screen, click ⬡ in the movie area. The ⬡ button is available only when the movie is playing. To once again display the movie in the Windows Media Player window, press the Esc key.

■ This area displays a list of the titles on the DVD. Each title represents a section of content on the DVD.

8 To display the chapters in a title, click the plus sign (⊕) beside the title (⊕ changes to ⊖).

■ The chapters in the title appear.

9 To play a specific title or chapter, double-click the title or chapter. The title or chapter is highlighted.

Note: The first title will usually play the entire movie.

10 To pause the play of the movie, click ⬤ (⬤ changes to ▶).

11 To stop the play of the movie, click ⬤.

Note: You can click ▶ to resume the play of the movie.

12 To adjust the volume, drag this slider (⬤) to a new position.

13 When you finish playing the DVD, click ✖ to close the Windows Media Player window.

USING THE COMMAND PROMPT

You can use the Command Prompt window to work with commands and run MS-DOS programs in Windows.

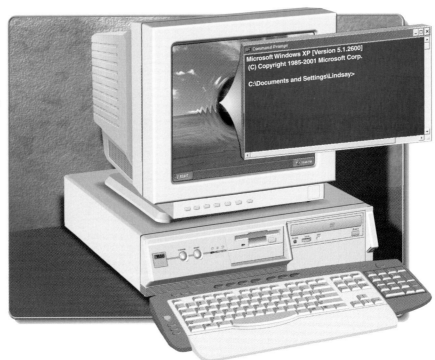

USING THE COMMAND PROMPT

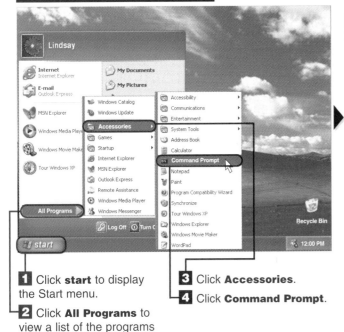

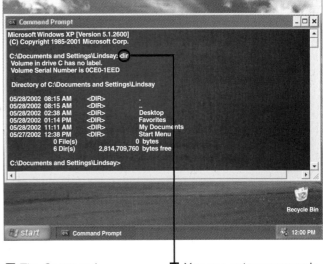

1 Click **start** to display the Start menu.

2 Click **All Programs** to view a list of the programs on your computer.

3 Click **Accessories**.

4 Click **Command Prompt**.

■ The Command Prompt window appears.

■ You can enter commands and start programs in the window. In this example, we type **dir** and then press the ⌴Enter⌴ key to list the contents of the current directory.

What commands can I use in the Command Prompt window?

To display a list of commands you can use, type **help** in the Command Prompt window and then press the Enter key. To find out how to use a specific command, type the name of the command followed by a space and **/?**. Then press the Enter key. For example, type **move /?** to find out how to use the move command.

C:\>help_

Can Windows run all MS-DOS programs?

Windows can run many MS-DOS programs without any problem. If Windows cannot run an MS-DOS program, a message may appear, indicating that the program is not suitable for use with Windows. Some MS-DOS programs, especially games, can run only when the Command Prompt window fills the entire screen.

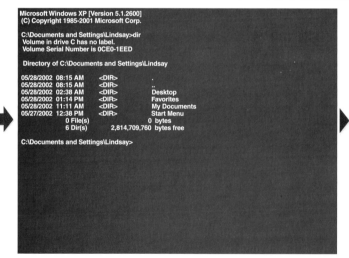

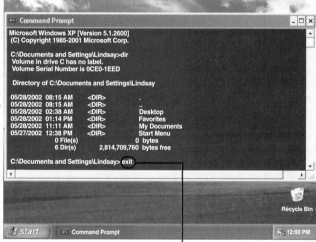

5 To have the Command Prompt window fill the entire screen, press and hold down the Alt key as you press the Enter key.

■ The Command Prompt window fills the entire screen.

6 To return the screen to a window, press and hold down the Alt key as you press the Enter key.

7 When you finish using the Command Prompt window, type **exit** and then press the Enter key to close the window.

CHAPTER 3

Customize Your Computer

You can change the appearance and behavior of Windows XP to suit your needs. This chapter teaches you how to add icons to the desktop, change the appearance of folders, adjust your keyboard settings and more.

CHANGE THE COLOR SETTING

You can change the number of colors displayed on your screen. More colors result in higher quality images.

You may want to display more colors on your screen when viewing photographs, watching movies or playing games on your computer.

CHANGE THE COLOR SETTING

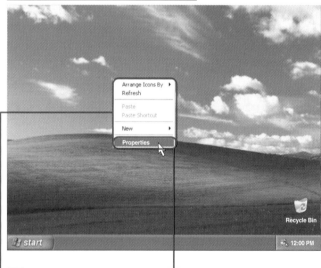

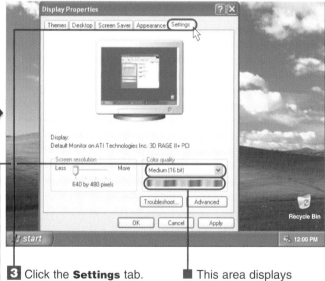

1 Right-click a blank area on your desktop. A menu appears.

2 Click **Properties**.

■ The Display Properties dialog box appears.

3 Click the **Settings** tab.

■ This area displays the current color setting.

■ This area displays the range of colors that the color setting allows Windows to display.

What color settings are available on my computer?

Windows usually offers three color settings. The color settings available on your computer depend on the capabilities of your monitor and video adapter.

Color Setting	Number of Colors
Medium (16 bit)	Displays more than 65,000 colors.
High (24 bit)	Displays more than 16 million colors.
Highest (32 bit)	Displays more than 4 billion colors.

Will changing the color setting affect my computer's performance?

Although your computer may work slightly faster at a lower color setting compared to a higher color setting, the difference in speed is minor.

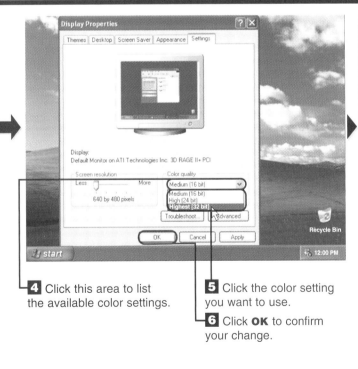

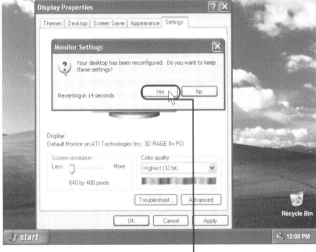

4 Click this area to list the available color settings.

5 Click the color setting you want to use.

6 Click **OK** to confirm your change.

■ Windows uses the new color setting you selected.

■ The Monitor Settings dialog box may appear, asking if you want to keep the new color setting.

7 Click **Yes** to keep the new color setting.

CHANGE VISUAL EFFECTS

You can change the visual effects that Windows uses when displaying items on your screen.

Transition effect for menus and tooltips

Enhances the way menus and tooltips appear and disappear on your screen. The Fade effect fades in menus and tooltips when they are displayed and dissolves them when they are closed. The Scroll effect slides menus and tooltips in and out.

Smooth edges of screen fonts

Smoothes the edges of fonts to make large text on your screen easier to read. The Standard smoothing method is ideal for desktop monitors, while the ClearType smoothing method is useful for most portable computers and other flat-screen monitors.

CHANGE VISUAL EFFECTS

1 Right-click a blank area on your desktop. A menu appears.

2 Click **Properties**.

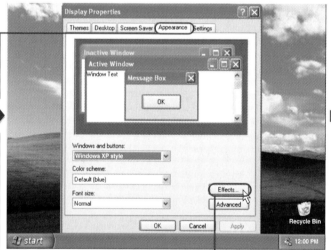

■ The Display Properties dialog box appears.

3 Click the **Appearance** tab.

4 Click **Effects** to change the visual effects for Windows.

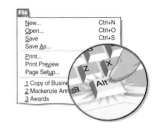

Use large icons

Displays large icons for items on the desktop and Start menu.

Show shadows under menus

Displays shadows under menus to give menus a three-dimensional appearance.

Show window contents while dragging

Displays the contents of a window while you move or resize the window. If you turn this option off, only the outline of a window you are moving or resizing will be displayed.

Hide underlined letters for keyboard navigation

Hides the underlined letters used to indicate keyboard shortcuts in menus until you press the `Alt` key.

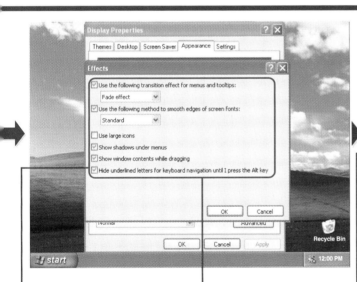

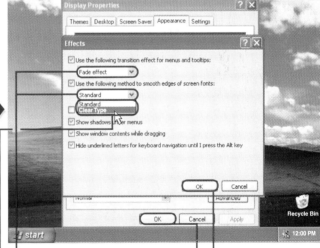

■ The Effects dialog box appears.

■ This area lists the visual effects that you can have Windows use. Windows uses each visual effect that displays a check mark (✓).

5 To turn a visual effect on (☑) or off (☐), click the effect.

6 If you selected to use a transition effect or to smooth the edges of screen fonts, you can click one of these areas to select the transition effect or smoothing method you want to use.

7 Click the transition effect or smoothing method you want to use.

8 Click **OK** to confirm your changes.

9 Click **OK** to close the Display Properties dialog box.

ADD DESKTOP ICONS

You can add icons to your desktop to give you quick access to features on your computer and files stored in commonly used locations.

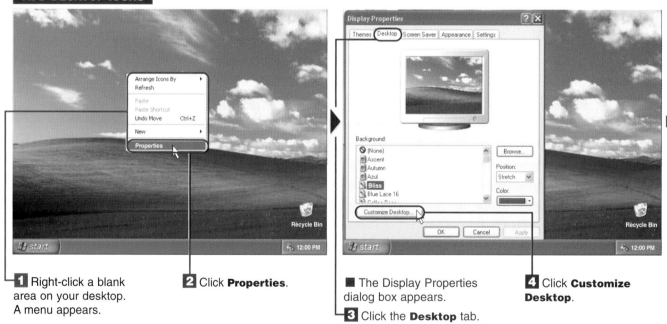

1 Right-click a blank area on your desktop. A menu appears.

2 Click **Properties**.

■ The Display Properties dialog box appears.

3 Click the **Desktop** tab.

4 Click **Customize Desktop**.

Which icons can I add to my desktop?

My Documents

Allows you to quickly access the My Documents folder, which provides a convenient place to store your documents.

My Computer

Allows you to quickly open the My Computer window to view the folders and files stored on your computer.

My Network Places

Allows you to quickly open the My Network Places window to view the folders and files available on your network.

Internet Explorer

Allows you to quickly open Internet Explorer so you can browse the Web.

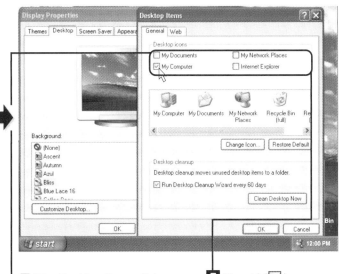

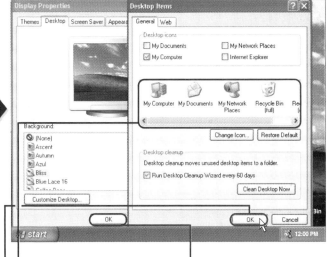

■ The Desktop Items dialog box appears.

■ Windows can display these items on your desktop. Each item that displays a check mark (✓) will appear on your desktop.

5 To add (☑) or remove (☐) a check mark from an item, click the item.

■ This area displays the icons used to represent items on your desktop.

6 Click **OK** to confirm your changes.

7 Click **OK** to close the Display Properties dialog box.

■ The icons for the items you selected appear on your desktop.

You can display a
Web page on your
desktop that you
frequently use.

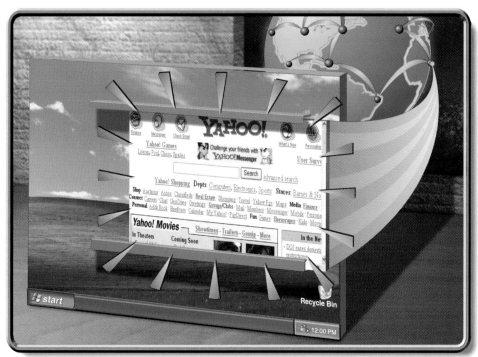

For example, you may
want to add a Web
page to your desktop
that displays the current
news or a search tool
such as Yahoo! or
Google that allows you
to search for topics of
interest on the Web.

ADD WEB CONTENT TO THE DESKTOP

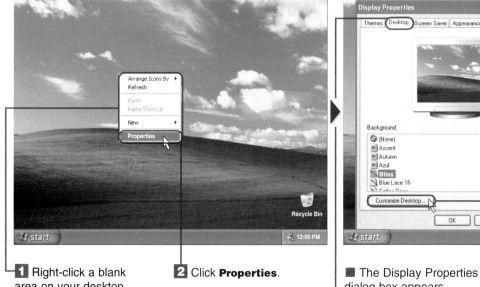

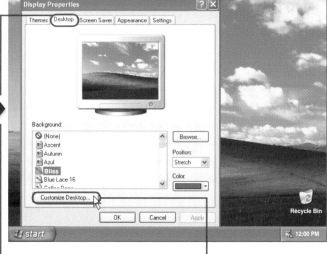

1 Right-click a blank
area on your desktop.
A menu appears.

2 Click **Properties**.

■ The Display Properties
dialog box appears.

3 Click the **Desktop** tab.

4 Click **Customize
Desktop**.

Where can I find other items that I can add to my desktop?

You can visit the Internet Explorer 4.0 Desktop Gallery Web site, which offers items such as a stock ticker and a weather map that you can add to your desktop. To visit the gallery, perform steps **1** to **6** below to display the New Desktop Item wizard and then click the **Visit Gallery** button. After you locate the item in the gallery that you want to add to your desktop, click the **Add to Active Desktop** button for the item and then follow the instructions on your screen.

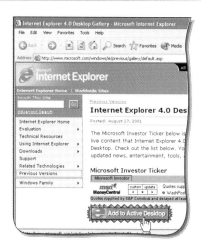

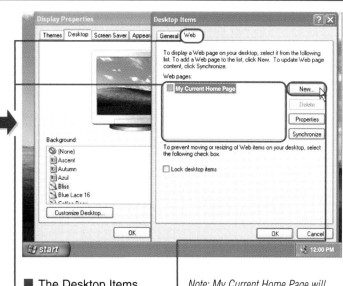

■ The Desktop Items dialog box appears.

5 Click the **Web** tab.

■ This area lists the Web pages you can display on your desktop.

Note: My Current Home Page will display your home page, which is the first Web page that appears when you start your Web browser. To display this Web page on your desktop, skip to step 10 on page 54.

6 To add a Web page to the list of Web pages, click **New**.

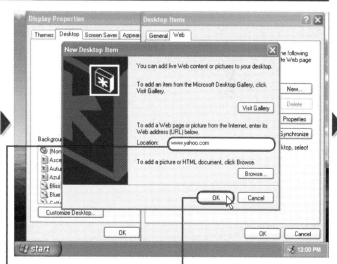

■ The New Desktop Item wizard appears.

7 Click this area and type the address of the Web page you want to display on your desktop.

8 Click **OK** to confirm the Web page address you typed.

Note: If you are not currently connected to the Internet, a dialog box will appear, allowing you to connect.

CONTINUED

ADD WEB CONTENT TO THE DESKTOP

When you add a Web page to your desktop, Windows makes the Web page available offline so the page appears on the desktop even when you are not connected to the Internet.

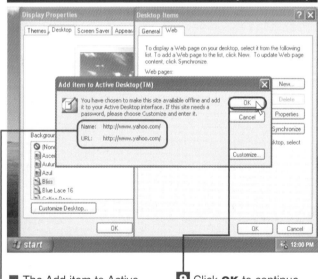

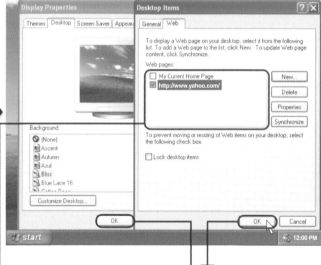

■ The Add item to Active Desktop dialog box appears.

■ This area displays the name and address of the Web page you specified.

9 Click **OK** to continue.

■ Windows copies the Web page to your computer.

■ The Web page appears in the list of Web pages you can display on your computer.

10 Each Web page that displays a check mark (✓) will appear on your desktop. To add (☑) or remove (☐) a check mark, click the box beside the Web page.

11 Click **OK** to confirm your changes.

12 Click **OK** to close the Display Properties dialog box.

How do I remove a Web page from my desktop?

To remove a Web page from your desktop, position the mouse ⌖ over the top edge of the Web page on the desktop. On the gray bar that appears, click ☒ to remove the Web page.

Will Windows update a Web page displayed on my desktop?

When you are connected to the Internet, Windows will usually update a Web page displayed on your desktop on a regular basis. Many Web pages, such as Web pages that report the news, contain information that must be updated regularly in order to continue being useful. If a Web page on your desktop does not update automatically, you can click a blank area on your desktop and then press the **F5** key to update the contents of the Web page.

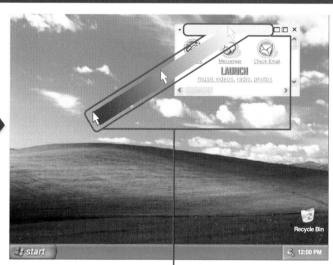

■ The Web page you selected appears on your desktop.

Note: Windows may automatically change the background color of the text for desktop items to make the text easier to read.

MOVE A WEB PAGE ON THE DESKTOP

1 Position the mouse ⌖ over the top edge of the Web page you want to move. A gray bar appears.

2 Drag the Web page to a new location on your desktop.

RESIZE A WEB PAGE ON THE DESKTOP

1 Position the mouse ⌖ over an edge of the Web page you want to resize (⌖ changes to ↕, ↔, ↖ or ↗).

2 Drag the edge of the Web page until the Web page displays the size you want.

CLEAN UP THE DESKTOP

You can use the Desktop Cleanup Wizard to clean up your desktop. The wizard will move shortcuts on your desktop that you use infrequently to a special folder called Unused Desktop Shortcuts.

A shortcut displays an arrow ( ) in its icon and provides a quick way of opening a file or program. Moving a shortcut to the Unused Desktop Shortcuts folder will not affect the original file or program.

Windows automatically runs the Desktop Cleanup Wizard every 60 days.

CLEAN UP THE DESKTOP

1 Right-click a blank area on your desktop. A menu appears.

2 Click **Arrange Icons By**.

3 Click **Run Desktop Cleanup Wizard**.

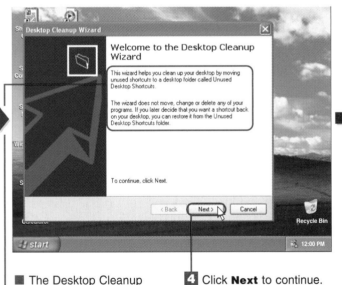

■ The Desktop Cleanup Wizard appears.

■ This area describes the wizard.

4 Click **Next** to continue.

Can I restore a shortcut to my desktop?

If you regret moving a shortcut to the Unused Desktop Shortcuts folder, you can move the shortcut back to your desktop. Double-click the Unused Desktop Shortcuts folder to open the folder. Click the shortcut you want to restore and then drag the shortcut to your desktop.

Can I delete the Unused Desktop Shortcuts folder?

Yes. You can delete the Unused Desktop Shortcuts folder to remove the folder and all the shortcuts in the folder from your desktop. To delete the Unused Desktop Shortcuts folder, click the folder and then press the `Delete` key. In the confirmation dialog box that appears, click **Yes** to delete the folder. The next time you run the Desktop Cleanup Wizard, the wizard will create a new Unused Desktop Shortcuts folder.

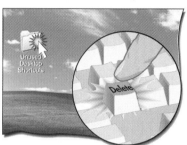

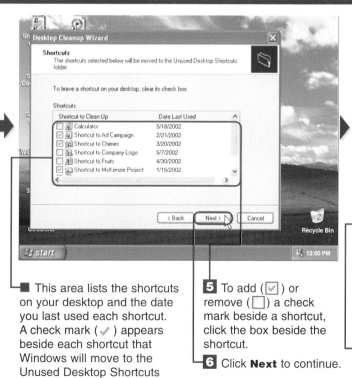

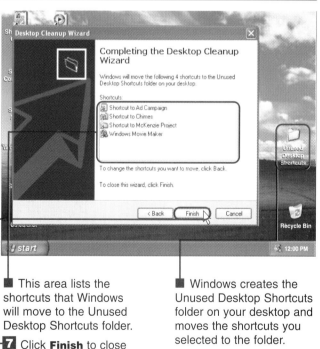

■ This area lists the shortcuts on your desktop and the date you last used each shortcut. A check mark (✓) appears beside each shortcut that Windows will move to the Unused Desktop Shortcuts folder.

5 To add (☑) or remove (☐) a check mark beside a shortcut, click the box beside the shortcut.

6 Click **Next** to continue.

■ This area lists the shortcuts that Windows will move to the Unused Desktop Shortcuts folder.

7 Click **Finish** to close the wizard.

■ Windows creates the Unused Desktop Shortcuts folder on your desktop and moves the shortcuts you selected to the folder.

CHANGE RECYCLE BIN PROPERTIES

You can change the properties of the Recycle Bin to specify the size of the Recycle Bin and how you want Windows to delete files on your computer.

The Recycle Bin stores files you delete and allows you to restore the files at any time.

CHANGE RECYCLE BIN PROPERTIES

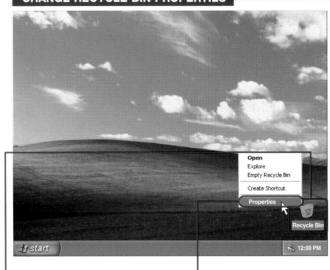

1 Right-click **Recycle Bin** on your desktop. A menu appears.

2 Click **Properties**.

■ The Recycle Bin Properties dialog box appears.

3 Click this option to use the same Recycle Bin settings for all the drives on your computer (○ changes to ◉).

4 Click this option if you want to permanently remove files you delete rather than send the files to the Recycle Bin (☐ changes to ☑).

Why would I change the storage size of the Recycle Bin?

By default, the Recycle Bin uses up to 10% of a hard drive's space to store deleted files. For example, on a 20 GB hard drive, the Recycle Bin can use as much as 2 GB. Reducing the storage size of the Recycle Bin can help conserve space on a drive.

Can I permanently delete a file without changing the Recycle Bin settings for all files?

To delete a file permanently, such as a confidential file, select the file and then press and hold down the Shift key as you press the Delete key. In the dialog box that appears, click **Yes** to confirm your deletion. Windows will permanently delete the file from your computer.

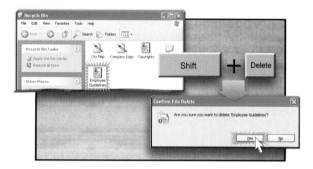

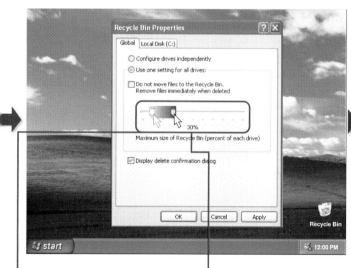

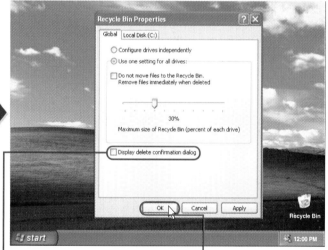

5 To change the storage size of the Recycle Bin, drag the slider ( ) in this area to a new location.

Note: The slider is not available if you chose to permanently remove files in step 4.

■ This area displays the percentage of the drive the Recycle Bin uses.

6 Click this option if you do not want a warning message to appear when you delete files (changes to).

7 Click **OK** to confirm all your changes.

CHANGE FOLDER APPEARANCE

You can change the template for a folder and the picture that appears on a folder's icon.

Template
Each folder template is designed to store a certain type of file, such as documents, pictures or videos. Each template offers specialized links you can select to perform common tasks in a folder. For example, a folder that uses the Pictures template will display links that allow you to perform tasks such as viewing pictures as a slide show and printing pictures.

Picture
Changing the picture that appears on a folder's icon can help you quickly identify the folder's contents.

CHANGE FOLDER APPEARANCE

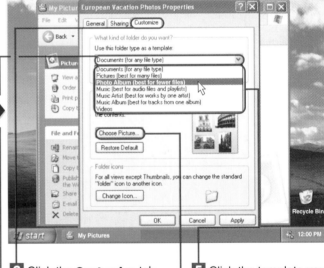

1 Right-click the folder you want to change. A menu appears.

Note: You cannot change the appearance of the My Documents, My Pictures or My Music folders.

2 Click **Properties**.

■ A Properties dialog box appears.

3 Click the **Customize** tab.

4 Click this area to list the templates available for the folder.

5 Click the template you want the folder to use.

6 To change the picture that appears on the folder's icon, click **Choose Picture**.

Why doesn't the picture I selected appear on the folder's icon?

You can see pictures on the icons of folders only when you display items in the Thumbnails view. To display items in a window in the Thumbnails view, select the **View** menu and then click **Thumbnails**.

How do I return a folder's icon to its original appearance?

To return a folder's icon to its original appearance, perform steps **1** to **3** below and then click the **Restore Default** button. Then click **OK**. By default, a folder's icon does not display a picture if the folder does not contain any pictures. If a folder contains pictures, the folder's icon will display up to four of the pictures in the folder.

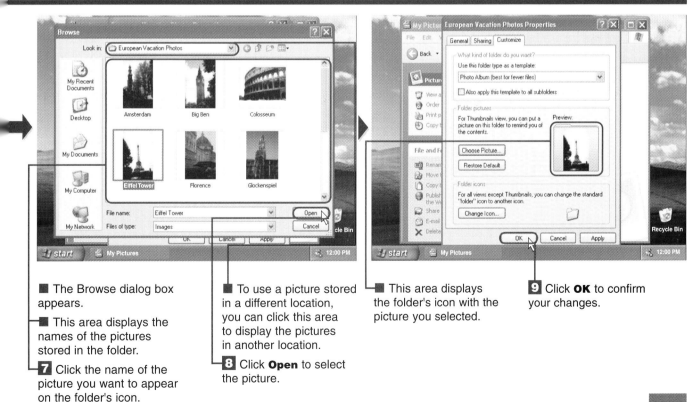

■ The Browse dialog box appears.

■ This area displays the names of the pictures stored in the folder.

7 Click the name of the picture you want to appear on the folder's icon.

■ To use a picture stored in a different location, you can click this area to display the pictures in another location.

8 Click **Open** to select the picture.

■ This area displays the folder's icon with the picture you selected.

9 Click **OK** to confirm your changes.

Windows provides several options you can select to change the way your folders look and act.

Tasks

You can choose to display a list of common tasks in folders or use Windows classic folders. When you show common tasks in folders, open windows display links that you can select to quickly perform common tasks. When you use Windows classic folders, the links do not appear.

CHANGE FOLDER OPTIONS

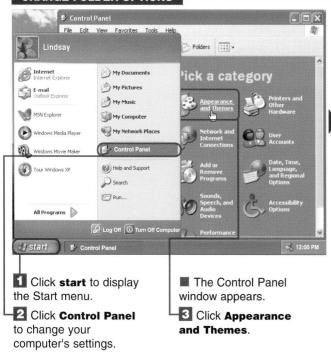

1 Click **start** to display the Start menu.

2 Click **Control Panel** to change your computer's settings.

■ The Control Panel window appears.

3 Click **Appearance and Themes**.

■ The Appearance and Themes window appears.

4 Click **Folder Options**.

Browse folders

You can choose to have each folder you open appear in the same window or in a new window. Opening folders in the same window reduces clutter on your desktop. Opening folders in new windows allows you to view the contents of several folders at once.

Click items

You can choose to open items using a single-click or a double-click. When you open items using a single-click, you can position the mouse over an item to select the item and click an item to open it. When you open items using a double-click, you can click an item to select the item or double-click an item to open it.

Underline icon titles

If you choose to open items using a single-click, you can have icon titles always appear underlined or appear underlined only when you position the mouse over an icon.

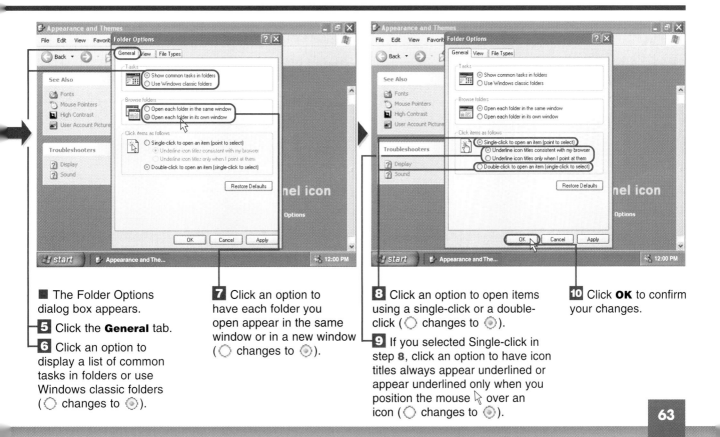

■ The Folder Options dialog box appears.

5 Click the **General** tab.

6 Click an option to display a list of common tasks in folders or use Windows classic folders (○ changes to ◉).

7 Click an option to have each folder you open appear in the same window or in a new window (○ changes to ◉).

8 Click an option to open items using a single-click or a double-click (○ changes to ◉).

9 If you selected Single-click in step **8**, click an option to have icon titles always appear underlined or appear underlined only when you position the mouse over an icon (○ changes to ◉).

10 Click **OK** to confirm your changes.

CHANGE FOLDER VIEW OPTIONS

You can customize the way Windows displays the contents of folders.

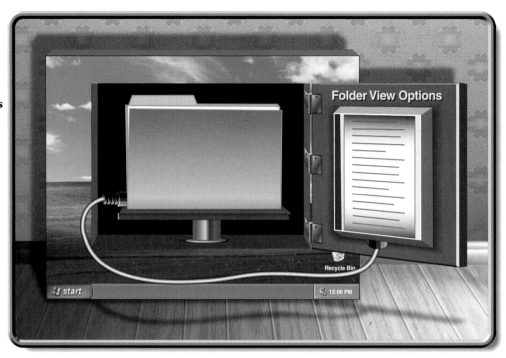

CHANGE FOLDER VIEW OPTIONS

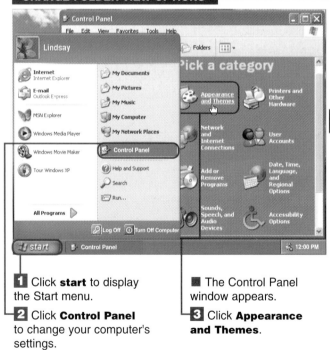

■ Click **start** to display the Start menu.

■ Click **Control Panel** to change your computer's settings.

■ The Control Panel window appears.

■ Click **Appearance and Themes**.

■ The Appearance and Themes window appears.

■ Click **Folder Options**.

■ The Folder Options dialog box appears.

**What are some of the folder
view options I can select?**

Display the full path
in the title bar

You can have Windows display
the location and name of an
open folder at the top of the
folder's window. For example,
C:\Reports\January indicates that
the **January** folder you have open
is located on your hard drive **(C:)**,
in a folder named **Reports**.

Hidden files
and folders

You can have Windows
hide or show hidden files
and folders. Hidden files are
usually program or system
files that you should not
change or delete. Hidden
files and folders will appear
dimmed.

Restore previous folder
windows at logon

You can have Windows
remember which folders you
leave open when you turn off
your computer and reopen the
folders the next time you turn
on your computer.

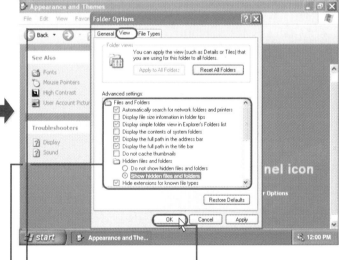

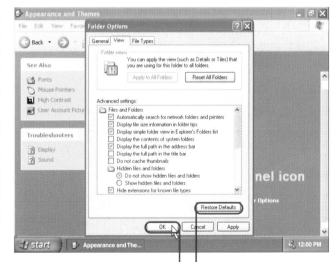

5 Click the **View** tab.

■ This area lists the folder
view options that you can
have Windows use. Windows
will use each option that
displays a check mark (✓).

6 To turn an option on (☑)
or off (☐), click the option.

*Note: When an option
displays a radio button (◉),
you can select only one of
several options. To select
an option, click the option
(○ changes to ◉).*

7 Click **OK** to confirm
your changes.

**RESTORE FOLDER VIEW
OPTIONS**

**You can restore the folder
view options that were
selected when you first
installed Windows.**

1 To redisplay the folder
view options, perform steps
1 to **5** starting on page 64.

2 Click **Restore
Defaults** to once again
use the original folder
view options.

3 Click **OK** to close
the Folder Options
dialog box.

CHANGE THE FORMAT OF NUMBERS, DATES AND TIMES

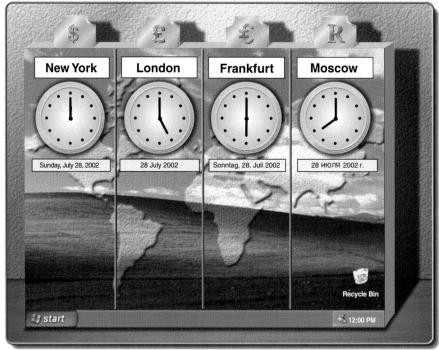

You can change the way numbers, currency, dates and times are displayed on your computer. This allows you to use the settings that are common to your language and region of the world.

New York	London	Frankfurt	Moscow
Sunday, July 28, 2002	28 July 2002	Sonntag, 28. Juli 2002	28 ИЮЛЯ 2002 г.

CHANGE THE FORMAT OF NUMBERS, DATES AND TIMES

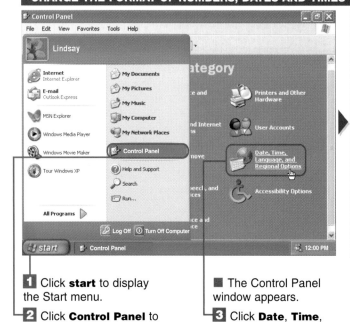

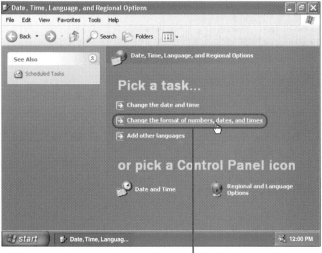

1 Click **start** to display the Start menu.

2 Click **Control Panel** to change your computer's settings.

■ The Control Panel window appears.

3 Click **Date**, **Time**, **Language**, and **Regional Options**.

■ The Date, Time, Language, and Regional Options window appears.

4 Click **Change the format of numbers**, **dates**, **and times**.

Why did **appear on my taskbar after I changed the format of numbers, currency, dates and times?**

When you change the format of numbers, currency, dates and times, the Language bar ( ) appears on your taskbar. If you want to enter text into a document in the language you selected in step **6** below, you can click to select the language. To remove the Language bar from your taskbar, see page 89.

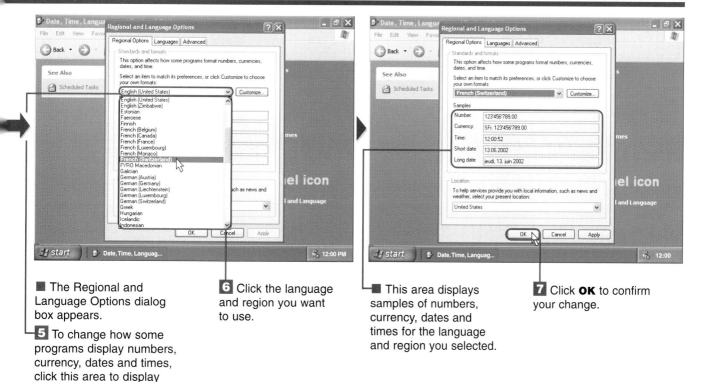

■ The Regional and Language Options dialog box appears.

5 To change how some programs display numbers, currency, dates and times, click this area to display a list of the available languages and regions.

6 Click the language and region you want to use.

■ This area displays samples of numbers, currency, dates and times for the language and region you selected.

7 Click **OK** to confirm your change.

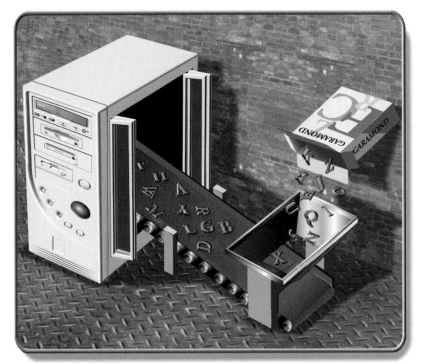

You can install extra fonts on your computer to give you more choices when creating documents.

You can obtain fonts on the Internet and at computer stores. When obtaining fonts, make sure you choose fonts designed for Windows.

Font files you obtain on the Internet are usually stored in compressed folders to reduce download time. You may need to extract the font files from the compressed folder before you can install the fonts. To extract files from a compressed folder, see page 12.

ADD FONTS

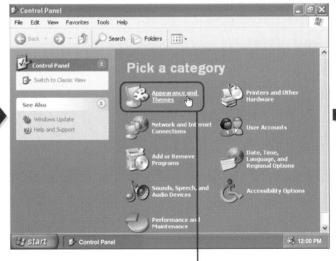

1 Click **start** to display the Start menu.

2 Click **Control Panel** to change your computer's settings.

■ The Control Panel window appears.

3 Click **Appearance and Themes**.

What types of fonts are included with Windows?

OpenType

OpenType fonts display the O icon. Most of the fonts included with Windows are OpenType fonts. An OpenType font generates characters using mathematical formulas so you can change the size of an OpenType font without distorting the font. An OpenType font will print exactly as it appears on your screen.

TrueType

TrueType fonts display the Tt icon. A TrueType font generates characters using mathematical formulas so you can change the size of a TrueType font without distorting the font. A TrueType font will print exactly as it appears on your screen.

System

System fonts display the A icon. Windows uses system fonts to display text in menus and dialog boxes.

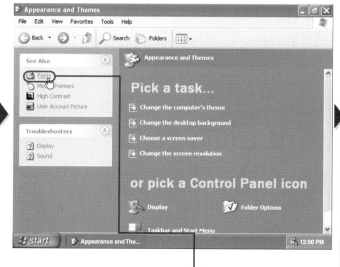

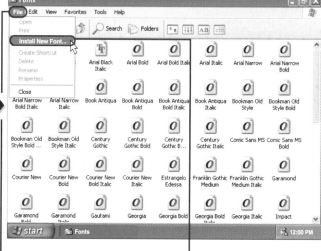

■ The Appearance and Themes window appears.

4 Click **Fonts** to add fonts to your computer.

■ The Fonts window appears. Each icon in the window represents a font installed on your computer.

5 To add fonts to your computer, click **File**.

6 Click **Install New Font**.

CONTINUED

ADD FONTS

When you add fonts to your computer, you will be able to use the fonts in all your programs.

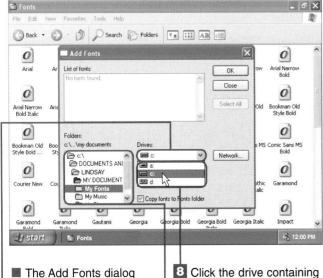

■ The Add Fonts dialog box appears.

7 Click this area to select the drive containing the fonts you want to add.

8 Click the drive containing the fonts.

■ This area lists the folders on the drive you selected.

9 Double-click the folder containing the fonts you want to add.

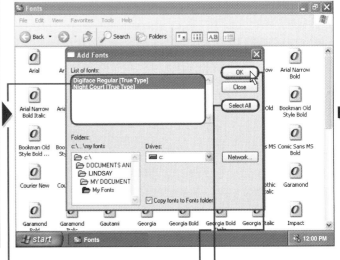

■ This area lists the fonts stored in the folder you selected.

10 Click the font you want to add to your computer.

11 To add more than one font, press and hold down the **Ctrl** key as you click each font you want to add.

■ To quickly select all the fonts in the current folder, click **Select All**.

12 Click **OK** to add the fonts you selected to your computer.

70

How do I delete a font from my computer?

To delete a font, perform steps **1** to **4** starting on page 68 to display the Fonts window. Click the font you want to delete and then press the Delete key. In the confirmation dialog box that appears, click **Yes** to delete the font. You should delete only fonts that you added to your computer.

How can I change the way Windows displays items in the Fonts window?

You can click one of the following buttons to change the way Windows displays items in the Fonts window.

	Display items as large icons.
	Display items as small icons in a list.
AB	Display how similar each item is to an item you select.
	Display information about each item.

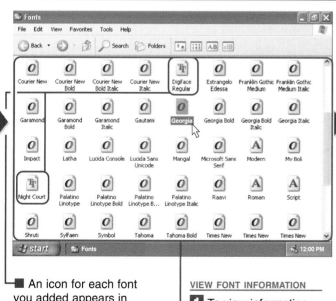

■ An icon for each font you added appears in the Fonts window.

VIEW FONT INFORMATION

1 To view information about a font, double-click the font.

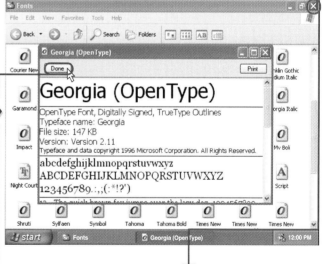

■ A window appears, displaying information about the font you selected and samples of the font in various sizes.

2 When you finish reviewing the information, click **Done** to close the window.

3 When you finish reviewing the fonts on your computer, click ⊠ to close the Fonts window.

CHANGE THE SYSTEM VOLUME

You can change the system volume to change the overall volume of sound on your computer. Changing the system volume will change the volume for all devices on your computer at once.

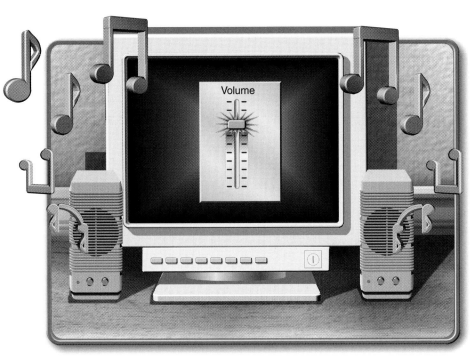

CHANGE THE SYSTEM VOLUME

1 Click **start** to display the Start menu.

2 Click **Control Panel** to change your computer's settings.

■ The Control Panel window appears.

3 Click **Sounds, Speech, and Audio Devices**.

■ The Sounds, Speech, and Audio Devices window appears.

4 Click **Adjust the system volume**.

How do I change the system volume using the speaker icon I added to the taskbar?

To change the system volume, click the speaker icon ( ) on the taskbar. If you cannot see the speaker icon ( ), click on the taskbar to display the speaker icon (changes to). In the Volume control box that appears, drag the volume slider ( ) up or down to increase or decrease the system volume. To turn the sound on ( ) or off ( ), click **Mute**.

Is there a quick way to change the speaker volume?

Many speakers have a volume dial that you can use to change the volume. Your speakers may also have a power button that you can use to turn the sound on or off.

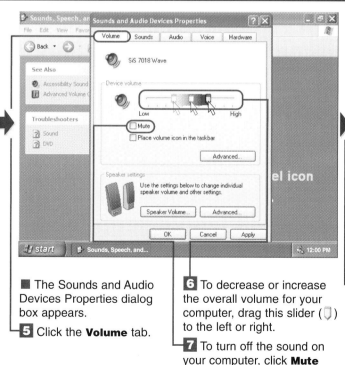

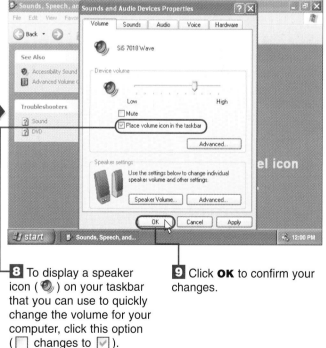

■ The Sounds and Audio Devices Properties dialog box appears.

5 Click the **Volume** tab.

6 To decrease or increase the overall volume for your computer, drag this slider ( ) to the left or right.

7 To turn off the sound on your computer, click **Mute** (changes to).

8 To display a speaker icon ( ) on your taskbar that you can use to quickly change the volume for your computer, click this option (changes to).

9 Click **OK** to confirm your changes.

RENAME OR DELETE A PRINTER

You can change
the name of a
printer to better
identify the printer.
You can also
delete a printer
you no longer use.

RENAME OR DELETE A PRINTER

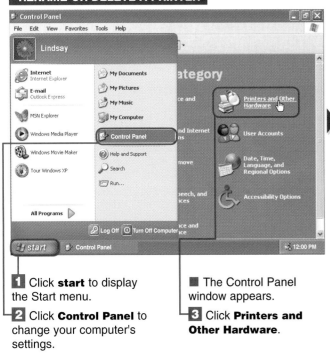

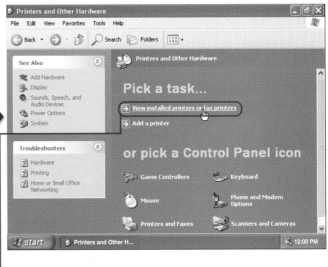

1 Click **start** to display
the Start menu.

2 Click **Control Panel** to
change your computer's
settings.

■ The Control Panel
window appears.

3 Click **Printers and
Other Hardware**.

■ The Printers and Other
Hardware window appears.

4 Click **View installed
printers or fax printers**.

■ The Printers and Faxes
window appears, displaying
an icon for each printer
installed on your computer.

74

Why is the Rename this printer option not available?

If the Rename this printer option is not available, you cannot rename the printer. For example, you may not be able to rename some printers on your network.

 Why did a warning message appear when I deleted a printer?

Windows displays a warning message when you delete your default printer. The default printer is the printer that automatically prints your documents and displays a check mark ( ) on its icon. If you have another printer installed on your computer, Windows will make this printer the new default printer.

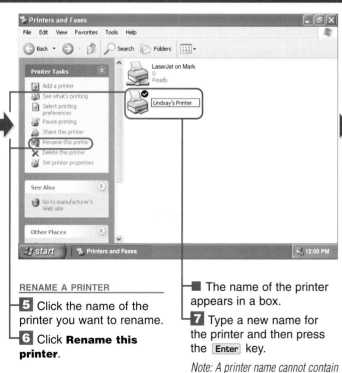

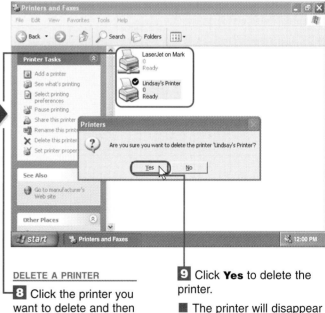

RENAME A PRINTER

5 Click the name of the printer you want to rename.

6 Click **Rename this printer**.

■ The name of the printer appears in a box.

7 Type a new name for the printer and then press the Enter key.

*Note: A printer name cannot contain the \ / : * ? " < > or | character.*

DELETE A PRINTER

8 Click the printer you want to delete and then press the Delete key.

■ A confirmation dialog box appears.

9 Click **Yes** to delete the printer.

■ The printer will disappear from the Printers and Faxes window.

You can change the
printing preferences
for a printer to specify
how you want the
printer to print all
your documents.

The available printing
preferences depend on
the printer you are using.

CHANGE PRINTING PREFERENCES

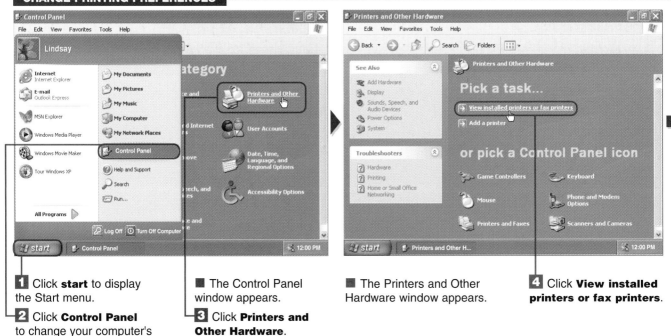

1 Click **start** to display
the Start menu.

2 Click **Control Panel**
to change your computer's
settings.

■ The Control Panel
window appears.

3 Click **Printers and
Other Hardware**.

■ The Printers and Other
Hardware window appears.

4 Click **View installed
printers or fax printers**.

What page orientations are available for my printed documents?

Portrait
Prints a document across the short side of a page and is used to print most documents.

Landscape
Prints a document across the long side of a page by rotating the document 90 degrees counterclockwise. The Landscape orientation is commonly used to print documents such as certificates and tables.

Rotated Landscape
Prints a document across the long side of a page by rotating the document 90 degrees clockwise.

How can I order the pages in my printed documents?

Front to Back
Prints each document so page 1 appears at the top of the printed pages.

Back to Front
Prints each document so page 1 appears at the bottom of the printed pages.

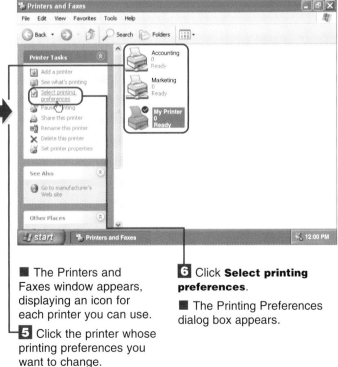

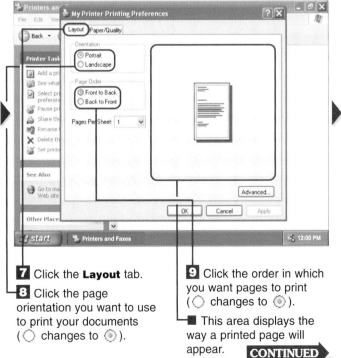

■ The Printers and Faxes window appears, displaying an icon for each printer you can use.

5 Click the printer whose printing preferences you want to change.

6 Click **Select printing preferences**.

■ The Printing Preferences dialog box appears.

7 Click the **Layout** tab.

8 Click the page orientation you want to use to print your documents (○ changes to ◉).

9 Click the order in which you want pages to print (○ changes to ◉).

■ This area displays the way a printed page will appear.

CONTINUED

CHANGE PRINTING PREFERENCES

When changing the printing preferences for all your documents, you can specify how many pages of a document you want to print on each sheet of paper.

CHANGE PRINTING PREFERENCES (CONTINUED)

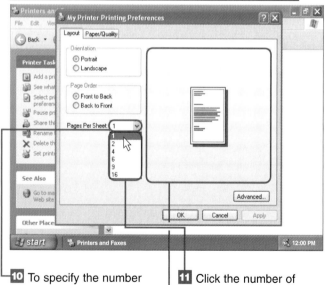

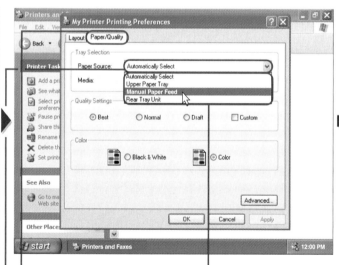

10 To specify the number of pages you want to print on each sheet of paper, click this area to display a list of options.

11 Click the number of pages you want to print on each sheet of paper.

■ This area displays the way a printed page will appear.

12 Click the **Paper/Quality** tab.

13 To specify where the paper you want to use is located in your printer, click this area to display a list of the available paper sources.

14 Click the paper source you want to use.

Note: The Automatically Select option instructs Windows to automatically select the appropriate paper source for the documents you print.

What types of material can I use to print my documents?

If your printer can print documents using specialty paper, you can select the type of material you want to use to print your documents. For example, you can select **Plain Paper** to print regular documents, **Glossy Photo Paper** to print high-quality photographs or **Transparency** to print transparencies for use with an overhead projector. The available types of material depend on the printer you are using.

What quality settings are available for my printed documents?

Best
Provides the highest print quality, but the lowest print speed. Ideal for printing the final copies of documents.

Normal
Provides good print quality by balancing print speed and print quality.

Draft
Provides the lowest print quality, but the fastest print speed. Ideal for printing rough drafts of documents.

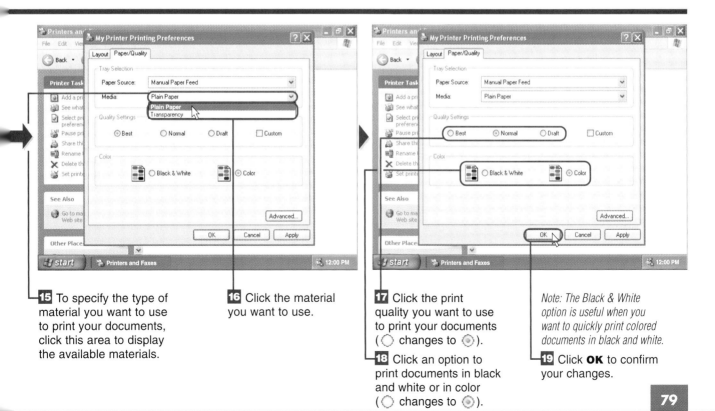

15 To specify the type of material you want to use to print your documents, click this area to display the available materials.

16 Click the material you want to use.

17 Click the print quality you want to use to print your documents (○ changes to ◉).

18 Click an option to print documents in black and white or in color (○ changes to ◉).

Note: The Black & White option is useful when you want to quickly print colored documents in black and white.

19 Click **OK** to confirm your changes.

CHANGE KEYBOARD SETTINGS

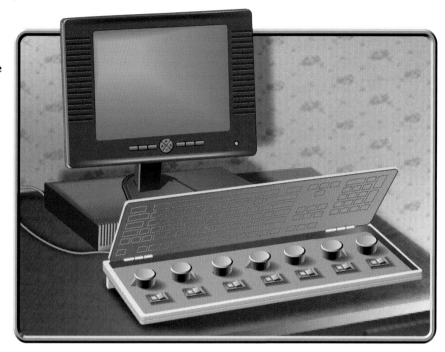

You can change the way your keyboard responds to the keys you type.

You can change how fast a character repeats when you hold down a key on your keyboard and how quickly the cursor, or insertion point, blinks.

CHANGE KEYBOARD SETTINGS

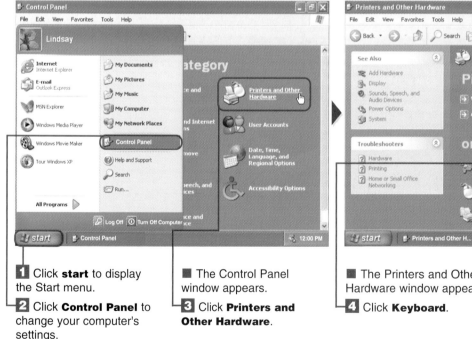

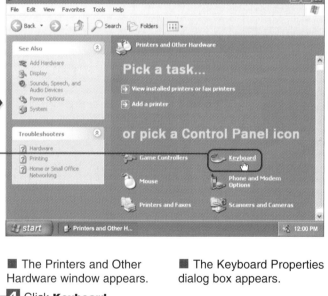

1 Click **start** to display the Start menu.

2 Click **Control Panel** to change your computer's settings.

■ The Control Panel window appears.

3 Click **Printers and Other Hardware**.

■ The Printers and Other Hardware window appears.

4 Click **Keyboard**.

■ The Keyboard Properties dialog box appears.

Why would I change the keyboard settings?

If you often accidentally hold down a key for too long, resulting in unwanted characters in a document, you may want to increase the amount of time you must hold down a key before the character starts repeating. If you often need to repeat characters in a document, you may want to increase the speed at which characters repeat. You may also want to increase the speed at which the cursor blinks to make the cursor easier to find on your screen or decrease the cursor blink rate if you find the cursor distracting.

I have trouble using my keyboard to type text in my documents. What can I do?

If you have limited mobility and difficulty using a keyboard, you can use On-Screen Keyboard to display a keyboard on your screen. This keyboard allows you to use your mouse or joystick to select characters you want to enter in a document. For more information on using On-Screen Keyboard, see page 106.

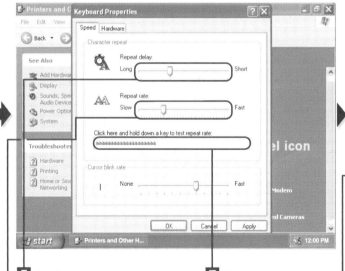

5 To change how long you must hold down a key before the character starts repeating, drag this slider ( ) to a new position.

6 To change how quickly characters repeat when you hold down a key, drag this slider ( ) to a new position.

7 To test the repeat delay and repeat rate settings, click this area and then press and hold down a key on your keyboard.

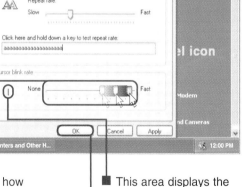

8 To change how quickly the cursor blinks, drag this slider ( ) to a new position.

Note: If you want the cursor to stop blinking and remain visible at all times, drag the slider to the left end of the bar.

■ This area displays the new cursor blink rate.

9 Click **OK** to confirm your changes.

You can use more than one monitor to expand your desktop area.

Using multiple monitors helps you more easily perform several tasks at once, such as working with a document while displaying a Web page. You can drag information between the monitors to set up items to suit your needs.

When using multiple monitors, one monitor will be your primary monitor. The primary monitor displays the Welcome screen that appears each time you turn on your computer. Most programs you open will also appear on the primary monitor.

USING MULTIPLE MONITORS

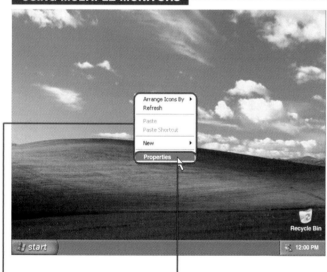

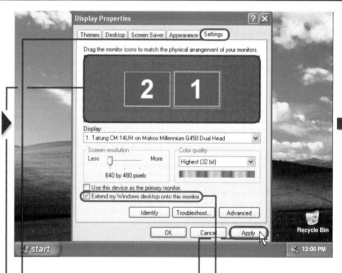

1 Right-click a blank area on your desktop. A menu appears.

2 Click **Properties**.

■ The Display Properties dialog box appears.

3 Click the **Settings** tab.

■ This area displays an icon for each monitor available on your computer.

4 To be able to use the second monitor, click the dimmed icon for the monitor.

5 Click **Extend my Windows desktop onto this monitor** (☐ changes to ☑).

6 Click **Apply** to apply your change.

How do I add a second monitor to my computer?

To add a second monitor, you need to install a second video adapter on your computer. A video adapter sends information from the computer to the monitor. Both video adapters must support the ability to work with multiple monitors. You can follow the manufacturer's instructions to install the second video adapter. When you turn on your computer, Windows will usually detect the new video adapter and automatically install the appropriate software.

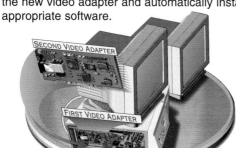

How do I determine which icon in the Display Properties dialog box represents which monitor?

In the Display Properties dialog box, click the **Identify** button. A large number will appear on the screen of each monitor, indicating which monitor corresponds to which icon.

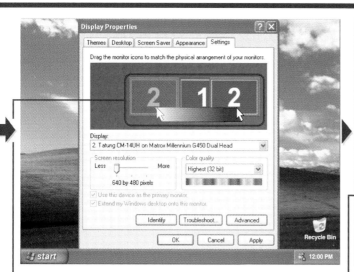

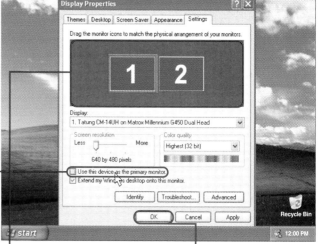

7 To change the arrangement of the icons to match the physical arrangement of your monitors, position the mouse over an icon and then drag the icon to a new position.

Note: The position of the icons determines the direction in which you will move items between the monitors.

8 To select the monitor you want to use as the primary monitor, click the icon for the monitor.

9 Click **Use this device as the primary monitor** (☐ changes to ☑).

Note: This option is unavailable if the monitor is already set as your primary monitor.

10 Click **OK** to confirm your changes.

■ If you no longer want to use a second monitor, perform step **1** to **5** (☑ changes to ☐ in step **5**). Then perform step **10**.

CHAPTER 4

Customize the Taskbar & Start Menu

This chapter shows you how to change the taskbar to suit your needs and work with the items on the Start menu.

MOVE OR RESIZE THE TASKBAR

You can move or resize the taskbar to suit your preferences.

By default, the taskbar is locked into position and cannot be moved or resized. You must unlock the taskbar before you can move or resize the taskbar.

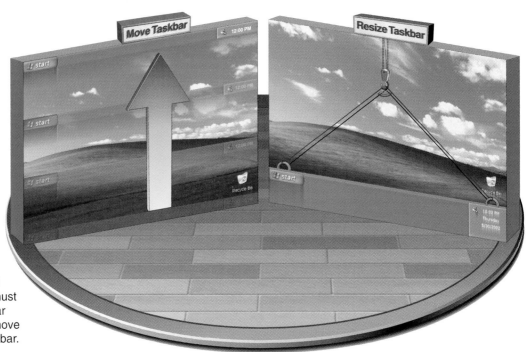

MOVE OR RESIZE THE TASKBAR

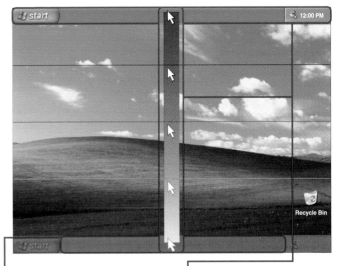

UNLOCK THE TASKBAR

■ The taskbar must be unlocked before you can move or resize the taskbar.

1 To unlock the taskbar, right-click an empty area on the taskbar. A menu appears.

■ A check mark (✔) appears beside Lock the Taskbar when the taskbar is locked.

2 Click **Lock the Taskbar** to unlock the taskbar.

Note: To once again lock the taskbar, repeat steps 1 and 2.

MOVE THE TASKBAR

1 Position the mouse over an empty area on the taskbar.

2 Drag the taskbar to the top, bottom, left or right edge of the screen.

■ The taskbar moves to the new location.

Why has my taskbar disappeared?

You may have accidentally resized the taskbar to a thin blue line at the edge of your screen. To display the taskbar, position the mouse ⇖ over the thin blue line at the edge of your screen (⇖ changes to ↕ or ↔). Then drag the mouse to increase the size of the taskbar.

How can I display all the information for a button on the taskbar?

A button on the taskbar displays three dots (...) if the button is too small to display the full name of the window it represents. To display all the information for a button, position the mouse ⇖ over the button. After a few seconds, a yellow box appears, displaying the full name of the window the button represents.

RESIZE THE TASKBAR

1 Position the mouse ⇖ over the edge of the taskbar (⇖ changes to ↕ or ↔).

2 Drag the mouse ↕ until the taskbar displays the size you want.

■ The taskbar changes to the new size.

ADD A TOOLBAR TO THE TASKBAR

Windows includes several toolbars that you can add to the taskbar. Toolbars provide quick access to files, Web pages and programs.

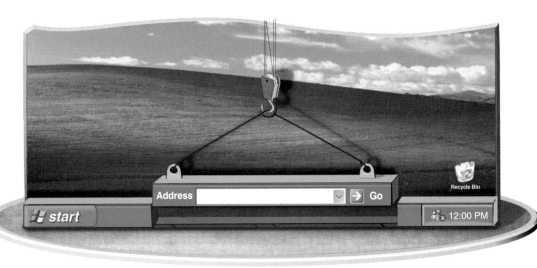

ADD A TOOLBAR TO THE TASKBAR

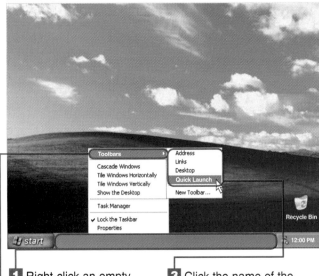

1 Right-click an empty area on the taskbar. A menu appears.

2 Click **Toolbars**.

3 Click the name of the toolbar you want to display.

Note: A toolbar with a check mark (✔) is currently displayed on the taskbar.

■ The toolbar you selected appears on the taskbar.

■ In this example, the Quick Launch toolbar appears.

What toolbars can I add to the taskbar?

Address

The Address toolbar provides an area where you can type a Web page address to quickly access the Web page without first opening your Web browser.

Links

The Links toolbar provides links that you can click to access useful Web pages.

Desktop

The Desktop toolbar contains all the items on your desktop and also provides easy access to common locations on your computer, such as the My Documents folder.

Quick Launch

The Quick Launch toolbar provides buttons you can click to quickly open Internet Explorer ( ), show the desktop ( ) or open Windows Media Player ( ).

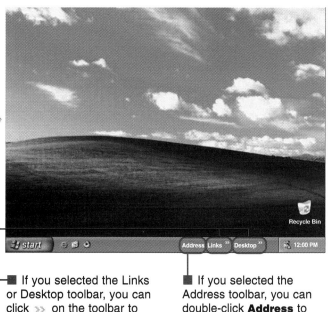

■ If you selected the Links or Desktop toolbar, you can click » on the toolbar to display a menu of the items on the toolbar.

■ If you selected the Address toolbar, you can double-click **Address** to fully display the toolbar.

*Note: If double-clicking **Address** does not fully display the toolbar, you need to first unlock the taskbar. To unlock the taskbar, see page 86.*

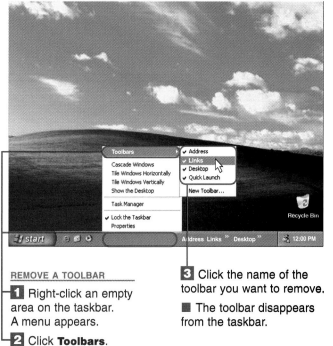

REMOVE A TOOLBAR

1 Right-click an empty area on the taskbar. A menu appears.

2 Click **Toolbars**.

3 Click the name of the toolbar you want to remove.

■ The toolbar disappears from the taskbar.

CHANGE THE TASKBAR SETTINGS

You can change the taskbar settings to suit your needs.

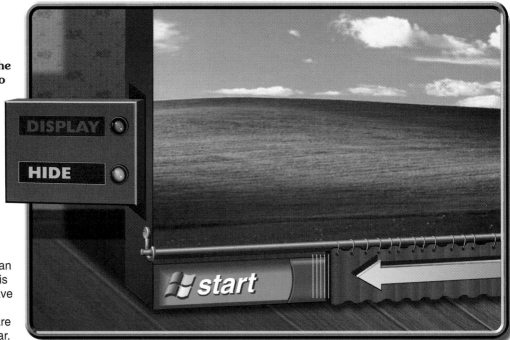

For example, you can ensure the taskbar is always visible or have Windows hide the taskbar when you are not using the taskbar.

CHANGE THE TASKBAR SETTINGS

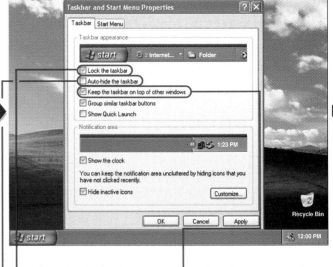

1 Right-click an empty area on the taskbar. A menu appears.

2 Click **Properties**.

■ The Taskbar and Start Menu Properties dialog box appears.

■ This option locks the taskbar so you cannot move or resize the taskbar.

■ This option hides the taskbar when you are not using the taskbar.

■ This option ensures the taskbar is always visible, even when a window fills the screen.

3 To turn an option on (✓) or off (☐), click the option.

How do I display the taskbar when the Auto-hide option is on?

To display the taskbar, position the mouse over the thin blue line at the edge of your screen where you last saw the taskbar. You can also press and hold down the `Ctrl` key and then press the `Esc` key to display the taskbar and the Start menu at any time.

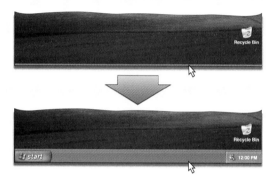

How do I display hidden notification icons?

When notification icons are hidden on the taskbar, an arrow (◀) appears next to the notification area on the right side of the taskbar. To display the hidden notification icons, click ◀ . To once again hide the notification icons, click ▶ .

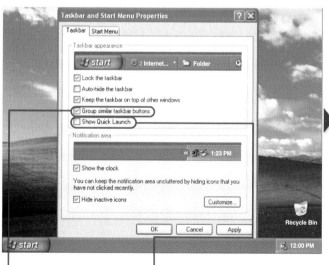

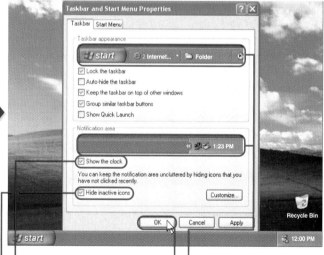

■ This option groups similar taskbar buttons. If the taskbar becomes crowded, this option will display all the buttons for a program as a single button.

■ This option displays the Quick Launch toolbar on the taskbar. The Quick Launch toolbar gives you quick access to Internet Explorer, your desktop and Windows Media Player.

4 To turn an option on (☑) or off (☐), click the option.

■ This option displays the time on the taskbar.

■ This option hides notification icons on the taskbar that you have not recently used.

5 To turn an option on (☑) or off (☐), click the option.

■ These areas display a preview of the changes you have made.

6 Click **OK** to confirm your changes.

ADD OR REMOVE A PROGRAM ON THE START MENU

You can add programs to the Start menu so you can quickly open the programs. You can also remove programs you no longer want to appear on the Start menu.

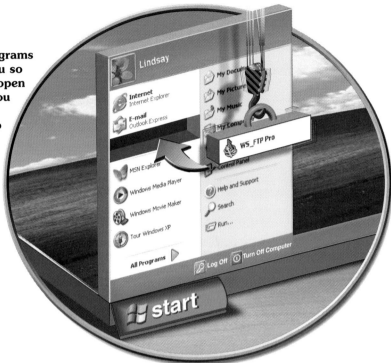

Most programs designed for Windows will automatically appear on the Start menu when you install the programs. If a program does not automatically appear on the Start menu, you can add the program to the Start menu yourself.

Removing programs you do not need or rarely use reduces clutter on the Start menu.

ADD A PROGRAM TO THE START MENU

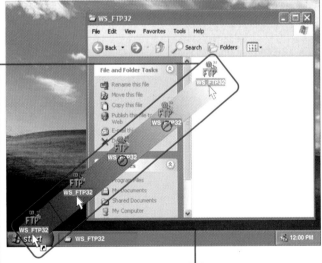

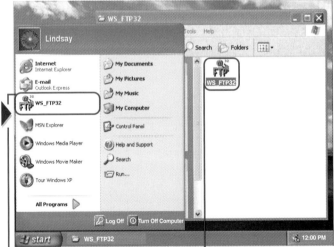

1 Locate the program on your computer that you want to add to the Start menu.

2 Position the mouse ▷ over the program.

3 Drag the program to the start button.

■ Windows places a shortcut to the program on the Start menu.

■ The program remains in its original location on your computer.

Note: To move the program to a different location on the Start menu, see page 94 to rearrange programs on the Start menu.

Can I add files to the Start menu?

Yes. You can add files to the Start menu the same way you add programs to the Start menu. Adding files to the Start menu will give you quick access to files you frequently use.

How do I restore a program I accidentally removed from the Start menu?

You can use the Recycle Bin to restore a program you accidentally removed from the Start menu.

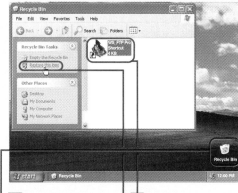

1 Double-click **Recycle Bin** on your desktop to display all the files you have deleted.

2 Click the deleted program you want to restore.

3 Click **Restore this item** to add the program to the Start menu again.

REMOVE A PROGRAM FROM THE START MENU

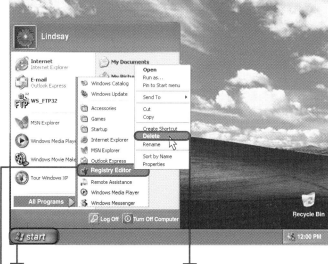

1 Click **start** to display the Start menu.

2 Locate the program you want to remove from the Start menu.

3 Right-click the program. A menu appears.

4 Click **Delete** to remove the program from the Start menu.

Note: You may need to click ***Remove from This List*** *instead of* ***Delete*** *in step **4**.*

■ A confirmation dialog box may appear.

5 Click **Yes** to remove the program from the Start menu.

Note: When you remove a program from the Start menu, Windows does not delete the program from your computer.

93

REARRANGE PROGRAMS ON THE START MENU

You can rearrange the programs on the Start menu to customize the menu to suit your preferences.

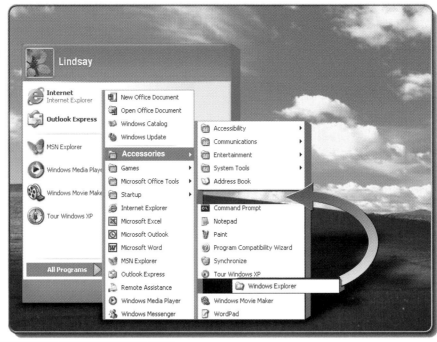

You cannot rearrange some items on the Start menu.

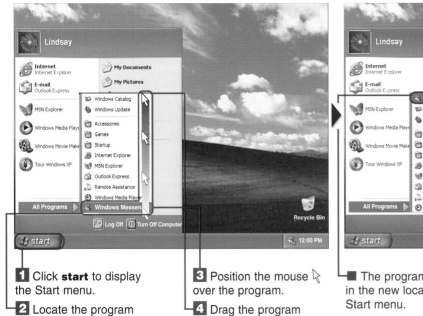

1 Click **start** to display the Start menu.

2 Locate the program you want to move to a new location on the Start menu.

3 Position the mouse over the program.

4 Drag the program to a new location.

Note: A black line indicates where the program will appear.

■ The program appears in the new location on the Start menu.

■ The program disappears from its original location on the Start menu.

You can pin a program to the top of the Start menu to provide a quick way of opening a program you use regularly.

Pinning a program to the top of the Start menu does not remove the program from its original location on the Start menu.

PIN A PROGRAM TO THE TOP OF THE START MENU

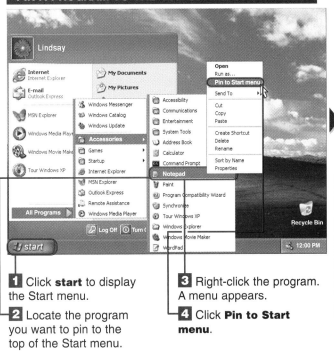

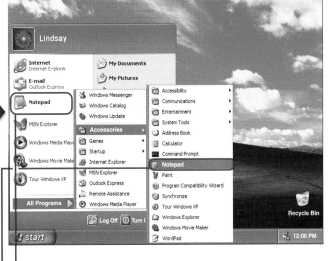

1 Click **start** to display the Start menu.

2 Locate the program you want to pin to the top of the Start menu.

3 Right-click the program. A menu appears.

4 Click **Pin to Start menu**.

■ The program appears at the top of the Start menu.

■ The program also remains in its original location.

*Note: To unpin a program from the top of the Start menu, repeat steps 1 to 4, except select **Unpin from Start menu** in step 4.*

ADD A SUBMENU TO THE START MENU

You can add a new submenu to the Start menu to better organize the programs on the Start menu.

ADD A SUBMENU TO THE START MENU

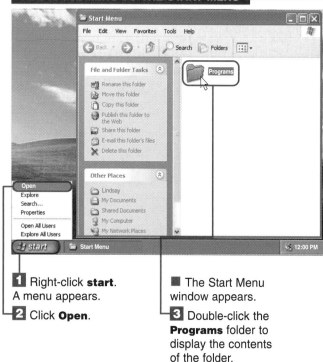

1 Right-click **start**. A menu appears.

2 Click **Open**.

■ The Start Menu window appears.

3 Double-click the **Programs** folder to display the contents of the folder.

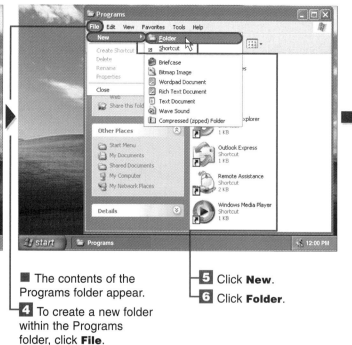

■ The contents of the Programs folder appear.

4 To create a new folder within the Programs folder, click **File**.

5 Click **New**.

6 Click **Folder**.

How do I add programs to the new submenu I created?

You can move programs from other locations on the Start menu to the new submenu. To rearrange programs on the Start menu, see page 94. If the program you want to add to the submenu does not currently appear on the Start menu, you will need to first add the program to the Start menu. To add a program to the Start menu, see page 92.

Can I remove a submenu I added to the Start menu?

Yes. To remove a submenu you added to the Start menu, perform steps **1** to **3** below to display the contents of the Programs folder. Click the folder for the submenu you want to remove and then press the Delete key. In the confirmation dialog box that appears, click **Yes** to delete the folder. The submenu will no longer appear on the Start menu.

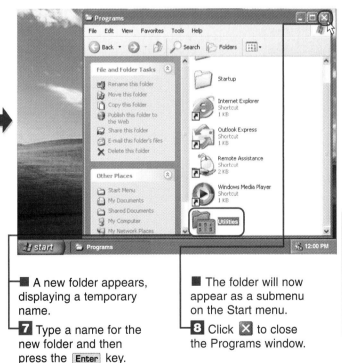

■ A new folder appears, displaying a temporary name.

7 Type a name for the new folder and then press the Enter key.

■ The folder will now appear as a submenu on the Start menu.

8 Click ✕ to close the Programs window.

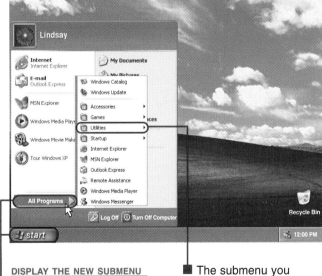

DISPLAY THE NEW SUBMENU

1 Click **start** to display the Start menu.

2 Click **All Programs** to view a list of the programs on your computer.

■ The submenu you created appears on the All Programs menu.

Note: To close the Start menu without selecting an item, click outside the menu area.

CUSTOMIZE THE START MENU

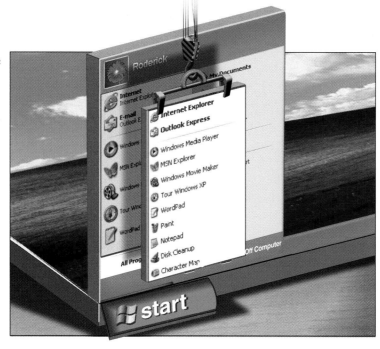

You can customize the appearance of the Start menu and the way the Start menu works.

For example, you can change the size of the icons that appear beside programs on the Start menu. You can also change the number of recently used programs that appear on the Start menu.

CUSTOMIZE THE START MENU

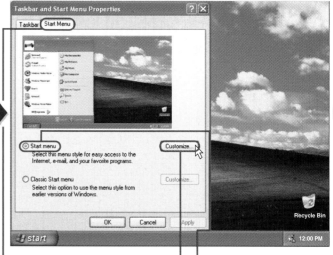

1 Right-click the **start** button. A menu appears.

2 Click **Properties**.

■ The Taskbar and Start Menu Properties dialog box appears.

3 Click the **Start Menu** tab.

4 Click **Start menu** to use the Start menu designed for Windows XP (○ changes to ◉).

5 Click **Customize** to personalize the Start menu.

Can I have the Start menu resemble the style used in previous versions of Windows?

Yes. If you prefer the style of Start menu used in previous versions of Windows, you can have Windows use the classic Start menu style. To use the classic Start menu style, perform steps **1** to **4** below, except select **Classic Start menu** in step **4**. Then press the Enter key.

How can I clear the list of recently used programs that appears on the Start menu?

To clear the list of recently used programs, perform steps **1** to **5** below to display the Customize Start Menu dialog box. Click the **Clear List** button to remove all the programs from the list of recently used programs. Windows will not remove the programs from your computer.

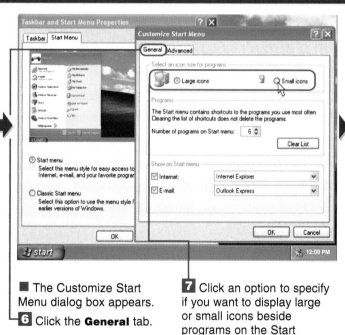

■ The Customize Start Menu dialog box appears.

6 Click the **General** tab.

7 Click an option to specify if you want to display large or small icons beside programs on the Start menu (○ changes to ◉).

■ This area displays the number of recently used programs that can appear on the Start menu.

Note: By default, Windows displays up to six recently used programs on the Start menu.

8 To change the maximum number of recently used programs that can appear on the Start menu, double-click this area and type a new number.

CONTINUED ▶

CUSTOMIZE THE START MENU

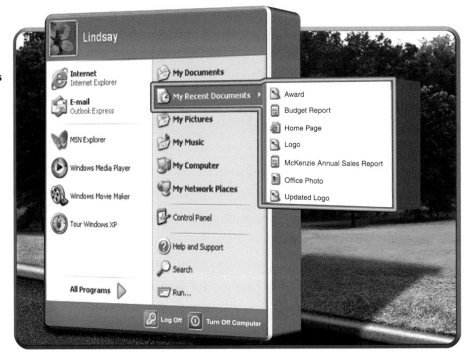

You can have Windows display a list of your most recently opened documents on the Start menu to provide quick access to these documents.

The Start menu will list your most recently opened documents on the My Recent Documents submenu.

CUSTOMIZE THE START MENU (CONTINUED)

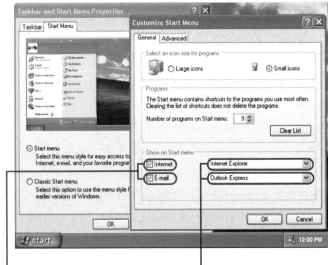

9 These options display shortcuts to your Web browser and e-mail program at the top of the Start menu. You can click an option to turn the option on (☑) or off (☐).

■ These areas display the Web browser and e-mail program Windows will start when you click the shortcuts at the top of the Start menu.

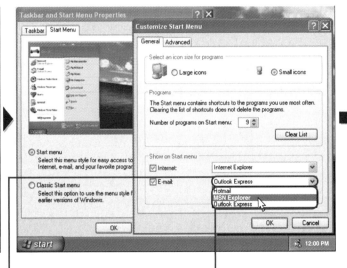

10 To change the Web browser or e-mail program that Windows will start when you click the shortcuts at the top of the Start menu, click the appropriate area to display a list of programs.

11 Click the program you want to use.

How do I start my Web browser and e-mail program if I removed the shortcuts to the programs from the top of the Start menu?

The Start menu offers the All Programs menu, which gives you access to all the programs installed on your computer. To start your Web browser or e-mail program, click **start**, select **All Programs** and then click your Web browser or e-mail program in the list of programs that appears.

How can I clear the list of recently opened documents that appears on the Start menu?

To clear the list of recently opened documents, perform steps **1** to **5** on page 98 to display the Customize Start Menu dialog box and then perform step **12** below. Click the **Clear List** button to remove all the documents from the list of recently opened documents. Windows will not remove the documents from your computer.

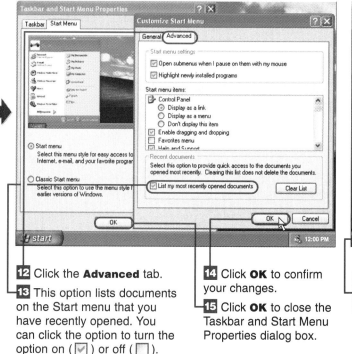

12 Click the **Advanced** tab.

13 This option lists documents on the Start menu that you have recently opened. You can click the option to turn the option on (☑) or off (☐).

14 Click **OK** to confirm your changes.

15 Click **OK** to close the Taskbar and Start Menu Properties dialog box.

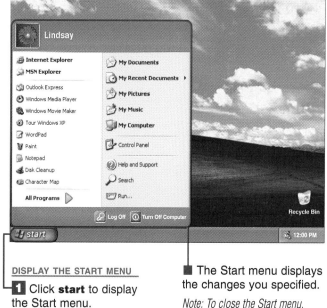

DISPLAY THE START MENU

1 Click **start** to display the Start menu.

■ The Start menu displays the changes you specified.

Note: To close the Start menu, click an area outside the menu.

CHAPTER 5

Using the Accessibility Features

You can use the accessibility features included with Windows XP to set up your computer to meet your vision, hearing or mobility needs. Read this chapter to learn more.

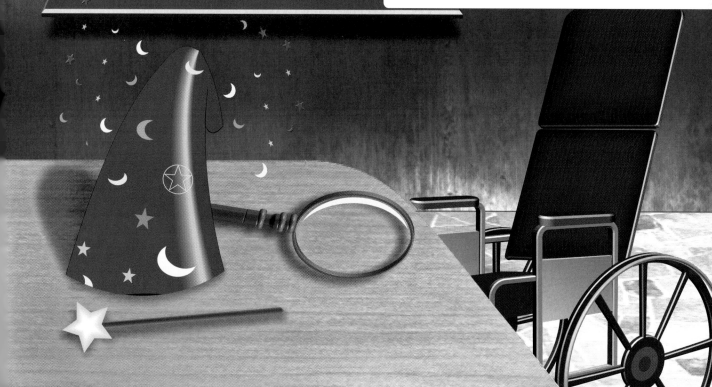

USING MAGNIFIER

If you have difficulty reading the information displayed on your screen, you can use Magnifier to display an enlarged view of the screen.

Magnifier provides only basic features and is suitable for people with minor visual impairments. If you need a magnification program with more advanced features, visit the Microsoft Accessibility Web site at www.microsoft.com/enable for information about programs you can use.

USING MAGNIFIER

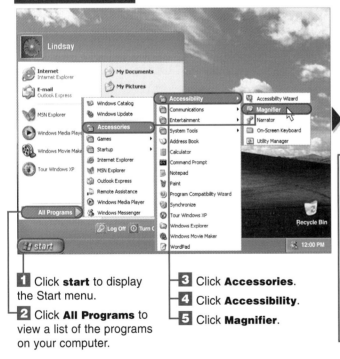

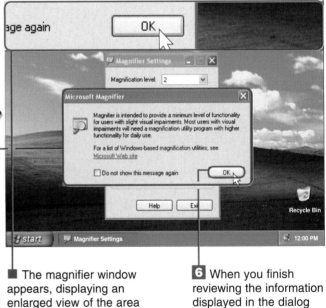

1 Click **start** to display the Start menu.

2 Click **All Programs** to view a list of the programs on your computer.

3 Click **Accessories**.

4 Click **Accessibility**.

5 Click **Magnifier**.

■ The magnifier window appears, displaying an enlarged view of the area surrounding the mouse.

■ The Microsoft Magnifier dialog box also appears, indicating that Magnifier may help people with minor visual impairments.

6 When you finish reviewing the information displayed in the dialog box, click **OK** to close the dialog box.

How can I change the size of the magnifier window?

To change the size of the magnifier window, position the mouse ⤢ over the bottom edge of the window (⤢ changes to ↕). Then drag the edge of the window until the window displays the size you want.

Is there another way I can make the screen easier to read?

Yes. You can change the colors displayed in the magnifier window to their complementary colors. For example, white changes to black and blue changes to yellow. In the Magnifier Settings window, click the **Invert colors** option to change colors to their complementary colors (☐ changes to ☑).

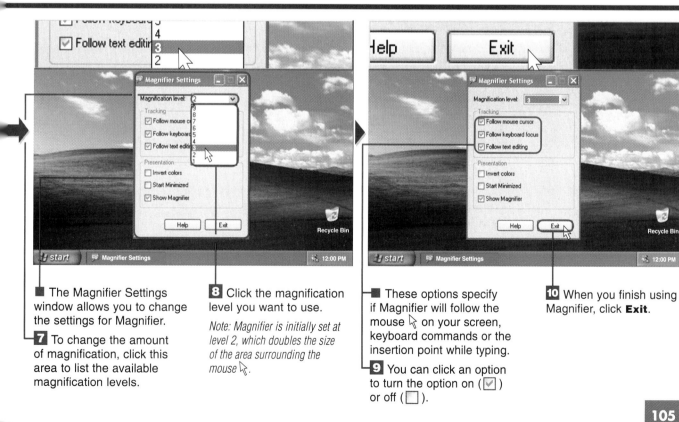

■ The Magnifier Settings window allows you to change the settings for Magnifier.

7 To change the amount of magnification, click this area to list the available magnification levels.

8 Click the magnification level you want to use.

Note: Magnifier is initially set at level 2, which doubles the size of the area surrounding the mouse ⤢.

■ These options specify if Magnifier will follow the mouse ⤢ on your screen, keyboard commands or the insertion point while typing.

9 You can click an option to turn the option on (☑) or off (☐).

10 When you finish using Magnifier, click **Exit**.

USING ON-SCREEN KEYBOARD

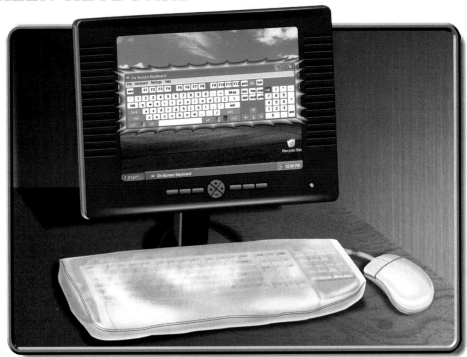

If you have limited mobility and have difficulty using a conventional keyboard, you can display a keyboard on your screen. This keyboard allows you to use your mouse or joystick to type.

On-Screen Keyboard provides only basic features and is suitable for people with minor mobility impairments. If you need a program with more advanced features, visit the Microsoft Accessibility Web site at www.microsoft.com/enable for information about programs you can use.

USING ON-SCREEN KEYBOARD

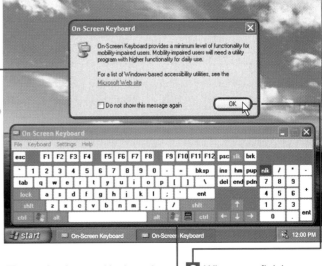

1 Click **start** to display the Start menu.

2 Click **All Programs** to view a list of the programs on your computer.

3 Click **Accessories**.

4 Click **Accessibility**.

5 Click **On-Screen Keyboard**.

■ The On-Screen Keyboard dialog box appears, stating that the on-screen keyboard provides minimal help for people with mobility impairments.

6 When you finish reviewing the information in the dialog box, click **OK** to close the dialog box.

■ The On-Screen Keyboard window also appears.

What typing modes are available for On-Screen Keyboard?

On-Screen Keyboard offers three typing modes you can choose from to type characters in a document.

Click to select	**Hover to select**	**Joystick or key to select**
You can use a mouse or joystick to click each keyboard character you want to type. This option is turned on by default.	You can use a mouse or joystick to position the mouse over a keyboard character until Windows types the character for you.	You can press the **Spacebar** on your keyboard to have Windows scan the on-screen keyboard and highlight each row of keys. When Windows highlights the row containing the keyboard character you want, you can press the **Spacebar** to select the row. Windows then scans the row and highlights each keyboard character so you can press the **Spacebar** to select the character you want to type.

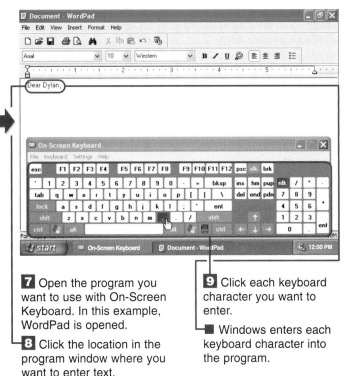

7 Open the program you want to use with On-Screen Keyboard. In this example, WordPad is opened.

8 Click the location in the program window where you want to enter text.

9 Click each keyboard character you want to enter.

■ Windows enters each keyboard character into the program.

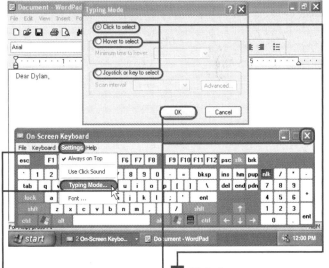

CHANGE THE TYPING MODE

1 To change the way you select characters on the on-screen keyboard, click **Settings**.

2 Click **Typing Mode**.

■ The Typing Mode dialog box appears.

3 Click the way you want to select characters (○ changes to ◉).

4 Click **OK** to confirm your change.

■ When you finish using On-Screen Keyboard, click ☒ to close the program.

107

USING NARRATOR

If you have difficulty seeing the information displayed on your screen, you can have Narrator read aloud the items on the screen.

To use Narrator, your computer must have sound capabilities.

Narrator provides only basic features and is suitable for people with minor visual impairments. If you need a screen reader program with more advanced features, visit the Microsoft Accessibility Web site at www.microsoft.com/enable for information about programs you can use.

USING NARRATOR

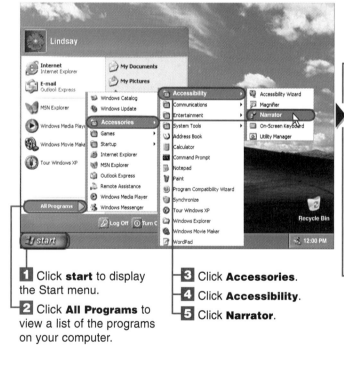

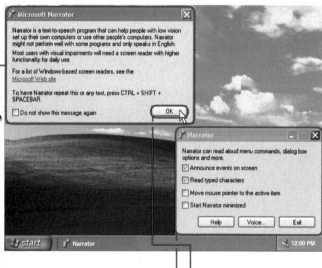

1 Click **start** to display the Start menu.

2 Click **All Programs** to view a list of the programs on your computer.

3 Click **Accessories**.

4 Click **Accessibility**.

5 Click **Narrator**.

■ The Microsoft Narrator dialog box appears, indicating that Narrator may help people with minor visual impairments.

Note: Narrator immediately begins describing the contents of the dialog box.

6 When you finish reviewing the information displayed in the dialog box, click **OK** to close the dialog box.

■ The Narrator window also appears.

What keyboard keys can I use to control the information Narrator reads?

To have Narrator:	Press:
Read the title bar of a window	Alt + Home
Read the status bar of a window	Alt + End
Repeat a selected item	Ctrl + Shift + Enter
Repeat the contents of the active window or dialog box	Ctrl + Shift +Spacebar
Stop speaking temporarily	Ctrl

 Can Narrator read aloud the information displayed in any program on my computer?

Narrator will read aloud information when you work with Notepad, WordPad, Internet Explorer and items in the Control Panel or on the desktop. Narrator may not be able to read aloud the information in some programs on your computer.

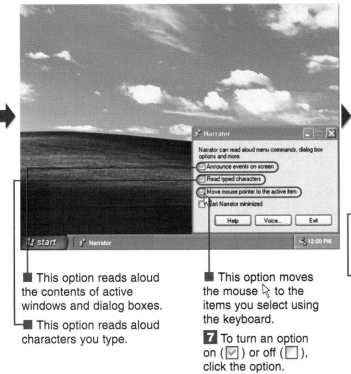

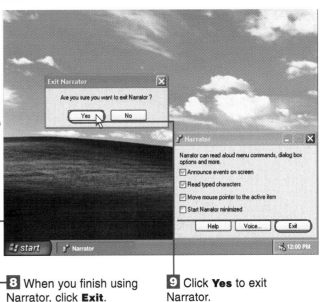

■ This option reads aloud the contents of active windows and dialog boxes.

■ This option reads aloud characters you type.

■ This option moves the mouse to the items you select using the keyboard.

7 To turn an option on (☑) or off (☐), click the option.

8 When you finish using Narrator, click **Exit**.

■ A dialog box appears, confirming that you want to exit Narrator.

9 Click **Yes** to exit Narrator.

USING THE ACCESSIBILITY WIZARD

You can use the
Accessibility Wizard
to help you set up
Windows to meet
your vision, hearing
and mobility needs.

The Accessibility
Wizard provides only
basic assistance for
people with special needs.
If you need programs
with more advanced
features, visit the Microsoft
Accessibility Web site at
www.microsoft.com/enable
for information about
programs you can use.

USING THE ACCESSIBILITY WIZARD

1 Click **start** to display
the Start menu.

2 Click **All Programs** to
view a list of the programs
on your computer.

3 Click **Accessories**.

4 Click **Accessibility**.

5 Click **Accessibility
Wizard**.

■ The Accessibility
Wizard appears.

■ This area displays
information about the
wizard.

6 Click **Next** to continue.

What options can I select to change the size of text and other items on my screen?

Change the font size

Increases the size of text in title bars, menus and other items. This option does not increase the size of text inside windows.

Switch to a lower screen resolution

Switches your computer to a lower screen resolution, which will increase the size of items on your screen, including the text inside windows. This option is available only if your screen displays a resolution of 1024x768 or higher.

Use Microsoft Magnifier

Displays an enlarged view of the area surrounding the mouse ⌖ in a window at the top of your screen.

Disable personalized menus

If you use the Classic Start menu, this option disables personalized menus to ensure Windows will not hide items you do not frequently use on the Start menu. For information on the Classic Start menu, see the top of page 99.

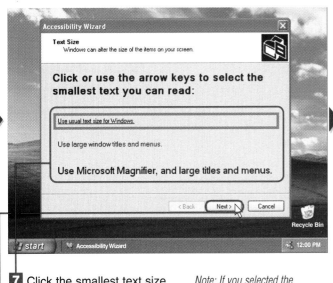

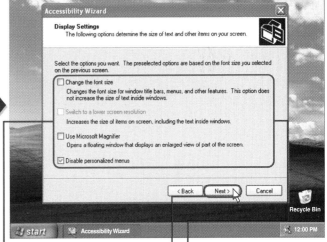

7 Click the smallest text size you can read. A blue border appears around your selection.

8 Click **Next** to continue.

■ The wizard immediately changes the size of text in title bars, menus and other items on your screen to match the text size you selected.

Note: If you selected the largest text size, Magnifier starts and displays an enlarged view of the area surrounding the mouse ⌖ at the top of your screen. For information on using Magnifier, see page 104.

■ The wizard offers options that can change the size of text and other items on your screen.

Note: The wizard automatically selects options based on the text size you selected in step **7**. *For information on the options, see the top of this page.*

9 To turn an option on (☑) or off (☐), click the option.

10 Click **Next** to continue.

CONTINUED

USING THE ACCESSIBILITY WIZARD

The Accessibility Wizard displays a list of statements and asks you to select each statement that applies to you. The statements you select will help the wizard determine which accessibility options may benefit you the most when using Windows.

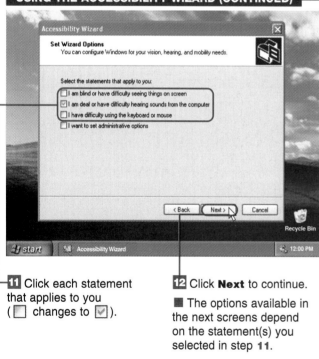

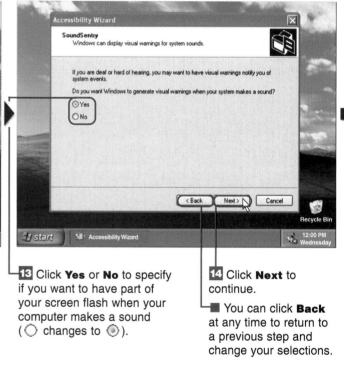

11 Click each statement that applies to you (☐ changes to ☑).

12 Click **Next** to continue.

■ The options available in the next screens depend on the statement(s) you selected in step **11**.

13 Click **Yes** or **No** to specify if you want to have part of your screen flash when your computer makes a sound (○ changes to ◉).

14 Click **Next** to continue.

■ You can click **Back** at any time to return to a previous step and change your selections.

What are some of the accessibility options I can select to meet my vision, hearing and mobility needs?

Vision

✔ Increase the size of scroll bars, window borders and icons on your desktop.

✔ Use a high contrast color scheme to make text easier to read.

✔ Change the size and color of the mouse ⟍ .

✔ Change the speed at which the cursor blinks and the width of the cursor.

Hearing

✔ Have part of your screen flash when your computer makes a sound.

✔ Display captions for speech and sounds in programs that support this feature.

Mobility

✔ You can press the **Shift**, **Ctrl** or **Alt** key and have that key remain active while you press another key.

✔ Have Windows ignore repeated keystrokes.

✔ Use the numeric keypad on your keyboard to control the mouse ⟍ .

✔ Switch the functions of the left and right mouse buttons to set up the mouse to work with the hand you prefer.

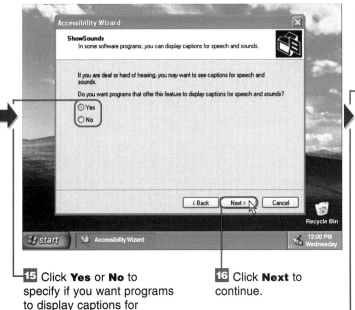

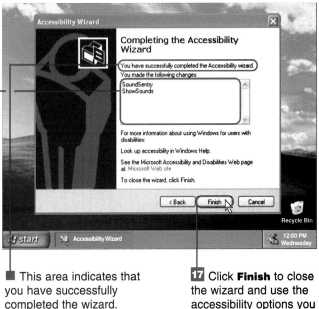

15 Click **Yes** or **No** to specify if you want programs to display captions for speech and sounds (○ changes to ◉).

Note: Some programs do not support this feature.

16 Click **Next** to continue.

■ This area indicates that you have successfully completed the wizard.

■ This area displays the changes you have made.

17 Click **Finish** to close the wizard and use the accessibility options you selected.

USING THE ACCESSIBILITY OPTIONS

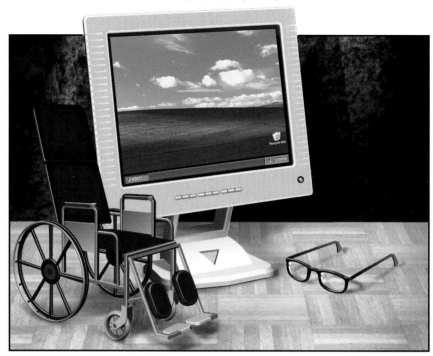

If you have vision, hearing or mobility impairments, Windows offers many accessibility options that you can select to make your computer easier to use.

The accessibility options that Windows offers are intended to provide only basic assistance for people with special needs. If you need programs with more advanced features, visit the Microsoft Accessibility Web site at www.microsoft.com/enable for information about programs you can use.

USING THE ACCESSIBILITY OPTIONS

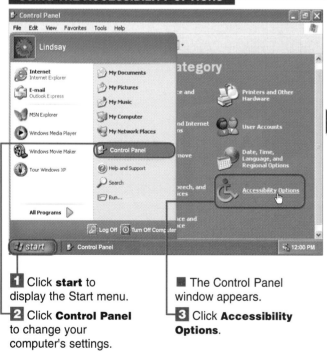

1 Click **start** to display the Start menu.

2 Click **Control Panel** to change your computer's settings.

■ The Control Panel window appears.

3 Click **Accessibility Options**.

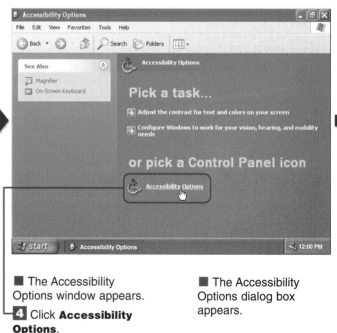

■ The Accessibility Options window appears.

4 Click **Accessibility Options**.

■ The Accessibility Options dialog box appears.

Why did StickyKeys stop working?

Windows automatically turns off StickyKeys when the Shift, Ctrl, Alt or Windows logo (▣) key and another key are pressed at the same time. If you share your computer with a person who does not have difficulty pressing two keys at the same time, this allows the person to automatically turn off StickyKeys.

Can I use keyboard shortcuts to turn on accessibility options?

Yes. You can use keyboard shortcuts to quickly turn on or off the accessibility options for your keyboard. When you use a keyboard shortcut to turn on an accessibility option, a confirmation dialog box appears. Click **OK** in the dialog box to turn on the option.

Accessibility Option	Keyboard Shortcut
StickyKeys	Press the Shift key 5 times.
FilterKeys	Press and hold down the **right** Shift key for 8 seconds.
ToggleKeys	Press and hold down the Num Lock key for 5 seconds.

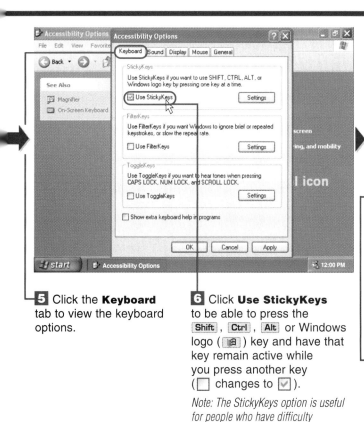

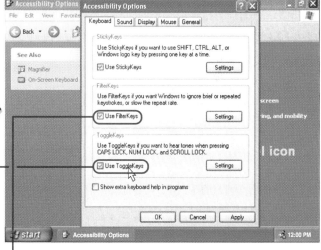

5 Click the **Keyboard** tab to view the keyboard options.

6 Click **Use StickyKeys** to be able to press the Shift, Ctrl, Alt or Windows logo (▣) key and have that key remain active while you press another key (☐ changes to ☑).

Note: The StickyKeys option is useful for people who have difficulty pressing two keys at the same time.

7 Click **Use FilterKeys** to have Windows ignore brief or repeated keystrokes (☐ changes to ☑).

8 Click **Use ToggleKeys** to play a sound when you press the Caps Lock, Num Lock or Scroll Lock key (☐ changes to ☑).

Note: The ToggleKeys option plays a high-pitched sound when you turn on a key and a low-pitched sound when you turn off a key.

CONTINUED

USING THE ACCESSIBILITY OPTIONS

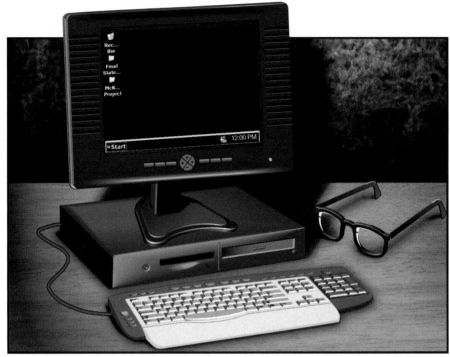

Windows offers accessibility options that can help people who have difficulty hearing computer sounds, seeing items on the screen and using a mouse.

USING THE ACCESSIBILITY OPTIONS (CONTINUED)

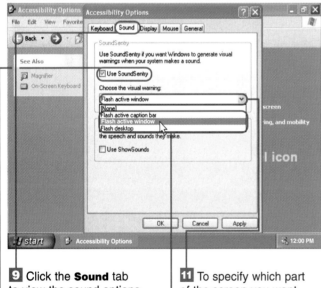

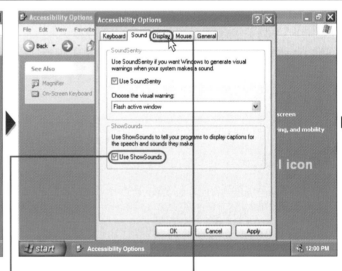

9 Click the **Sound** tab to view the sound options.

10 Click **Use SoundSentry** to have part of your screen flash when your computer makes a sound (☐ changes to ☑).

11 To specify which part of the screen you want Windows to flash, click this area to display a list of options.

12 Click the part of the screen you want Windows to flash.

13 Click **Use ShowSounds** to display captions for speech and sounds your programs make (☐ changes to ☑).

14 Click the **Display** tab to view the display options.

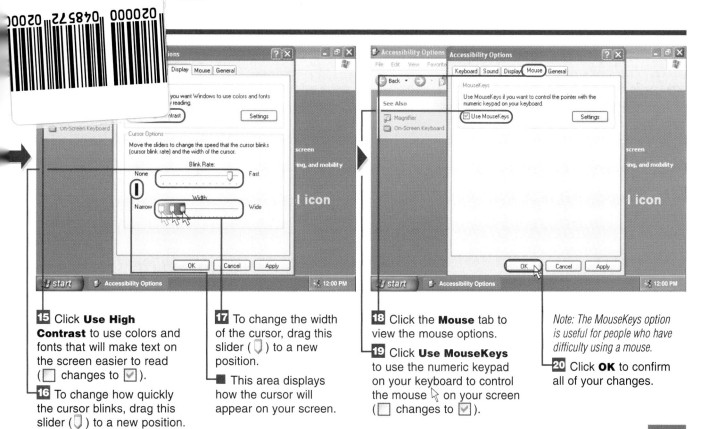

After I turn on the MouseKeys option, how can I control the mouse  ?

You must use the keys on the numeric keypad located on the right side of your keyboard to control the mouse . To use the numeric keypad to control the mouse , the Num Lock light must be on. To turn on the light, press the **Num Lock** key on your keyboard.

Mouse Action	Keys to Press on the Numeric Keypad
Move left or right	Press ← or →.
Move up or down	Press ↑ or ↓.
Move diagonally	Press the **Home**, **End**, **PgUp** or **PgDn** key.
Click	Press **5**.
Double-click	Press the plus sign (+).
Right-click	Press the minus sign (-) and then press **5**. Then press slash (/).
Drag and drop	Press the **Ins** key to begin dragging an item. Press the **↑**, **↓**, **←** or **→** key to move the item. Press the **Del** key to drop the item.

15 Click **Use High Contrast** to use colors and fonts that will make text on the screen easier to read (☐ changes to ☑).

16 To change how quickly the cursor blinks, drag this slider (◖) to a new position.

17 To change the width of the cursor, drag this slider (◖) to a new position.

■ This area displays how the cursor will appear on your screen.

18 Click the **Mouse** tab to view the mouse options.

19 Click **Use MouseKeys** to use the numeric keypad on your keyboard to control the mouse on your screen (☐ changes to ☑).

Note: The MouseKeys option is useful for people who have difficulty using a mouse.

20 Click **OK** to confirm all of your changes.

USING UTILITY MANAGER

Utility Manager allows you to control the accessibility programs included with Windows.

You can use Utility Manager to immediately start or stop an accessibility program or set up an accessibility program to start automatically.

Accessibility programs can help make a computer easier to use for people with vision, hearing or mobility impairments.

USING UTILITY MANAGER

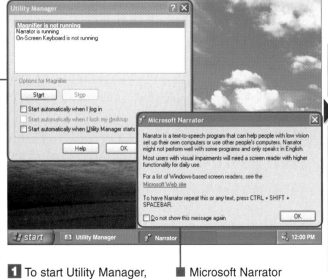

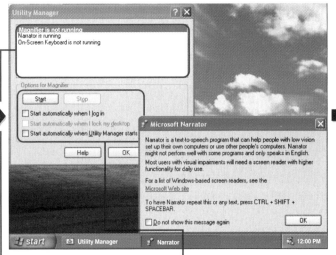

1 To start Utility Manager, press and hold down the Windows logo key ( ) as you press the **U** key.

■ The Utility Manager dialog box appears.

■ Microsoft Narrator starts automatically when you start Utility Manager.

■ This area displays the name of each accessibility program and whether each program is running or not running.

■ This area displays the options that are turned on or off for the currently selected accessibility program.

Note: To select another accessibility program, click the name of the program.

118

What accessibility programs can Utility Manager control?

Magnifier

Magnifier displays an enlarged view of the area surrounding the mouse. Magnifier is useful if you have difficulty seeing the information displayed on your screen. For more information on using Magnifier, see page 104.

Narrator

Narrator reads aloud the items on your screen, such as the contents of active windows and dialog boxes. Narrator is useful if you have difficulty reading the information displayed on your screen. For more information on using Narrator, see page 108.

On-Screen Keyboard

On-Screen Keyboard displays a keyboard on your screen. On-Screen Keyboard allows you to use your mouse or joystick to select the characters you want to enter in a document. This accessibility program is useful if you have difficulty using a conventional keyboard. For more information on using On-Screen Keyboard, see page 106.

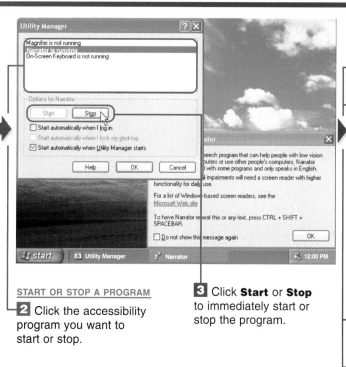

START OR STOP A PROGRAM

2 Click the accessibility program you want to start or stop.

3 Click **Start** or **Stop** to immediately start or stop the program.

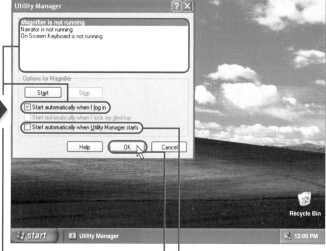

START A PROGRAM AUTOMATICALLY

4 Click the accessibility program you want to start automatically.

■ This option starts the program automatically each time you log on to Windows.

■ This option starts the program automatically each time you start Utility Manager.

5 To turn an option on (☑) or off (☐), click the option.

6 Click **OK** to confirm your changes.

PLAYING

Bike Video

MUSIC OR NARRATION

SOFT   LOUD

SOFT   LOUD

SOUND FROM VIDEO CLIPS

CHAPTER 6

Create Movies

Read this chapter to find out how to use Windows Movie Maker to create and work with movies on your computer. You will learn how to record video, trim video clips and add music and narration to your movies.

RECORD A VIDEO

You can use Windows Movie Maker to record a video from your video camera onto your computer. Recording a video onto your computer allows you to view and edit the video on the computer.

You can also record video from a Web camera, television broadcast, VCR or DVD player onto your computer.

Before you start recording, make sure your video camera or other video source is properly connected to your computer and turned on. Also make sure the tape or other media is at the point where you want to begin recording.

RECORD A VIDEO

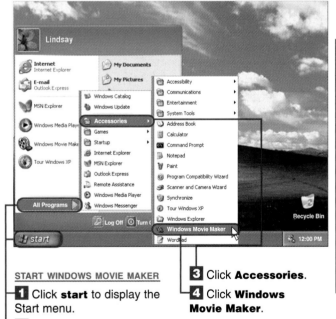

START WINDOWS MOVIE MAKER

1 Click **start** to display the Start menu.

2 Click **All Programs** to view a list of the programs on your computer.

3 Click **Accessories**.

4 Click **Windows Movie Maker**.

■ The Windows Movie Maker window appears.

RECORD A VIDEO

1 Click **Record** to record a video onto your computer.

Note: A dialog box appears if your computer may not provide acceptable performance when recording from a high-speed device, such as a digital video camera. Click **Yes** *to record using the device.*

Why am I unable to record video from my digital video camera?

Your digital video camera may need to be in a specific mode to record video onto your computer. For example, some digital video cameras must be in the VTR mode to record video.

What should I consider when selecting a quality setting to record my video?

A higher quality setting produces a higher quality video, but results in a larger file size. A video with a larger file size takes up more space on your computer and will take longer to transfer over the Internet. Also, some computers may not be able to properly play a higher quality video.

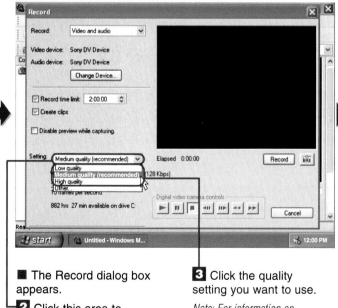

■ The Record dialog box appears.

2 Click this area to display a list of the quality settings you can use to record the video.

3 Click the quality setting you want to use.

Note: For information on selecting a quality setting, see the top of this page.

4 Click ▶ to begin playing the video.

Note: You can also press the play button on your video camera or other video source to begin playing the video.

■ This area displays the video.

5 Click **Record** to start recording the video onto your computer.

CONTINUED

RECORD A VIDEO

Windows automatically stores each video you record in the My Videos folder on your computer.

Windows creates the My Videos folder the first time you start Windows Movie Maker. The My Videos folder is stored in the My Documents folder.

RECORD A VIDEO (CONTINUED)

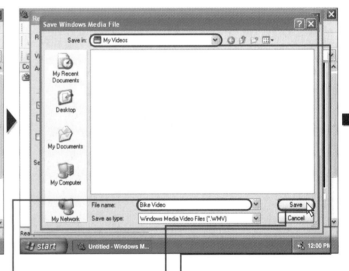

■ The word **Recording** flashes in this area when you are recording.

■ This area displays the time that has passed since you started recording the video.

6 Click **Stop** when you want to stop recording the video.

Note: You may have to press the stop button on your video camera or other video source to stop the video.

■ The Save Windows Media File dialog box appears.

7 Type a name for your video.

■ This area shows the location where Windows Movie Maker will store your video. You can click this area to change the location.

8 Click **Save** to save the video.

■ Windows Movie Maker creates the clips for your video.

How does Windows Movie Maker organize the videos I record?

Collections

Each time you record a video, Windows Movie Maker creates a collection to store all the clips for the video. Each collection appears as a folder ( ) in the Windows Movie Maker window.

Video Clips

Windows Movie Maker automatically breaks up a video you record into smaller, more manageable segments, called video clips. A video clip is created each time Windows detects a different sequence in a video, such as when you turn on your video camera or when you switch from pause to record.

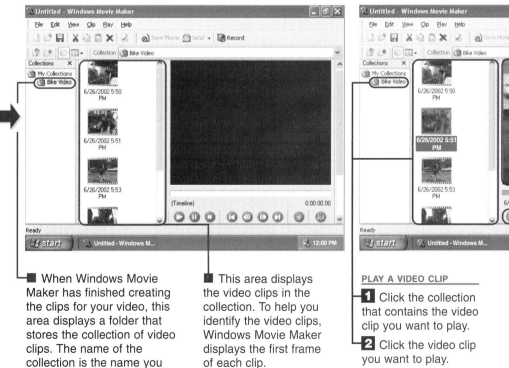

■ When Windows Movie Maker has finished creating the clips for your video, this area displays a folder that stores the collection of video clips. The name of the collection is the name you specified in step **7**.

■ This area displays the video clips in the collection. To help you identify the video clips, Windows Movie Maker displays the first frame of each clip.

PLAY A VIDEO CLIP

1 Click the collection that contains the video clip you want to play.

2 Click the video clip you want to play.

3 Click to play the video clip.

■ The video clip plays in this area.

IMPORT A VIDEO

You can import a video into Windows Movie Maker so you can edit the video to create your own movies.

You can import videos you obtain on the Internet, videos you create using a video editing program or videos you receive in e-mail messages from other people.

IMPORT A VIDEO

1 Click **File**.

2 Click **Import**.

■ The Select the File to Import dialog box appears.

■ This area shows the location of the displayed files. You can click this area to change the location.

3 Click the video you want to import.

4 Click **Open** to import the video.

■ Windows Movie Maker imports the video and breaks up the video into smaller, more manageable segments, called clips.

What types of videos can I import into Windows Movie Maker?

Windows Movie Maker can import many types of videos, including movie files (.mpeg, .mpg, m1v, .mp2, .mpa, .mpe), video files (.asf, .avi, .wmv) and Windows media files (.asf, .wm, .wma, .wmv). The extension at the end of a file name indicates the type of video, such as birthdayparty.avi. To display file name extensions for all the files on your computer, see page 64.

After I import a video into Windows Movie Maker, can I delete the original video from my computer?

You should not delete, move or rename the original video after importing a video into Windows Movie Maker. Windows Movie Maker will not store a copy of a video you import, but will refer to the original video on your computer. If you delete, move or rename the original video, you may not be able to work with the video in Windows Movie Maker.

■ When Windows Movie Maker has finished creating the clips for your video, this area displays a folder that stores the collection of video clips. The name of the collection is the name of the video you imported.

■ This area displays the video clips in the collection. To help you identify the video clips, Windows Movie Maker displays the first frame of each clip.

PLAY A VIDEO CLIP

1 Click the collection that contains the video clip you want to play.

2 Click the video clip you want to play.

3 Click [▶] to play the video clip.

■ The video clip plays in this area.

ADD A VIDEO CLIP TO THE STORYBOARD

You must add each video clip you want to include in your movie to the storyboard.

The storyboard displays the order in which video clips will play in your movie.

ADD A VIDEO CLIP TO THE STORYBOARD

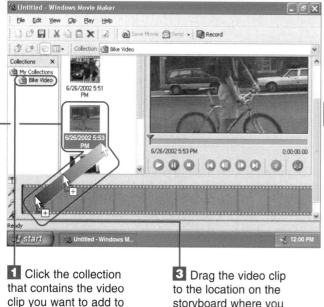

1 Click the collection that contains the video clip you want to add to the storyboard.

2 Position the mouse over the video clip you want to add.

3 Drag the video clip to the location on the storyboard where you want the video clip to play in your movie.

Note: You can add a video clip before, after or between any existing video clips on the storyboard.

■ The video clip appears on the storyboard.

■ You can repeat steps **1** to **3** for each video clip you want to add to the storyboard.

REMOVE A VIDEO CLIP

1 Click the video clip on the storyboard that you want to remove. Then press the Delete key.

Note: Deleting a video clip from the storyboard will not remove the video clip from Windows Movie Maker.

PREVIEW A MOVIE

You can preview all the video clips you have added to the storyboard as a movie.

PREVIEW A MOVIE

1 Click a blank area on the storyboard.

2 Click ▶ to preview all the video clips you have added to the storyboard as a movie.

■ The movie plays in this area.

■ A white border appears around the video clip that is currently playing.

■ This slider (▼) indicates the progress of the movie.

3 To pause or stop the movie, click ⏸ or ⏹ .

Note: To once again play the movie, click ▶ .

RENAME A VIDEO CLIP

You can rename a video clip to better describe the contents of the video clip.

You can rename collections the same way you rename video clips. A collection stores video clips in Windows Movie Maker.

RENAME A VIDEO CLIP

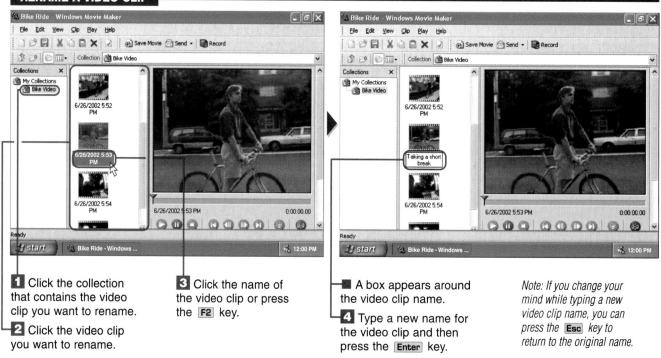

1 Click the collection that contains the video clip you want to rename.

2 Click the video clip you want to rename.

3 Click the name of the video clip or press the F2 key.

■ A box appears around the video clip name.

4 Type a new name for the video clip and then press the Enter key.

Note: If you change your mind while typing a new video clip name, you can press the Esc key to return to the original name.

DELETE A VIDEO CLIP

You can delete a video clip you no longer want to use in your movies. Deleting video clips can help reduce clutter in your list of video clips.

If you added a video clip to the storyboard, deleting the video clip from a collection will not remove the video clip from the storyboard.

You can delete collections the same way you delete video clips. A collection stores video clips in Windows Movie Maker. Deleting a collection will remove the collection and all the video clips stored in the collection.

DELETE A VIDEO CLIP

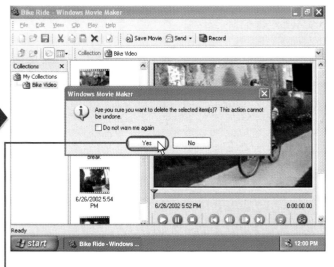

1 Click the collection that contains the video clip you want to delete.

2 Click the video clip you want to delete.

3 Click [X] or press the Delete key to delete the video clip.

■ A dialog box appears, confirming that you want to delete the video clip.

4 Click **Yes** to permanently delete the video clip.

■ The video clip disappears from the Windows Movie Maker window.

TRIM A VIDEO CLIP

You can trim a video clip on the storyboard to remove the parts of the clip you do not want to play in your movie.

You can trim the beginning of a video clip, the end of a video clip, or both. Trimming a video clip on the storyboard will not affect the original video clip.

Trimming video clips will reduce the length and file size of a movie. A movie with a smaller file size will take up less storage space on your computer and transfer more quickly over the Internet.

TRIM A VIDEO CLIP

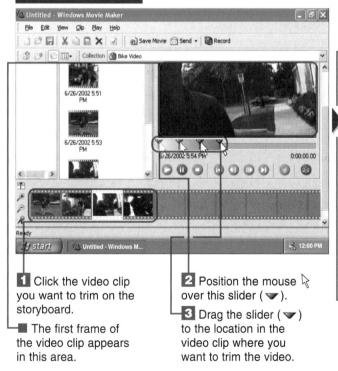

1 Click the video clip you want to trim on the storyboard.

■ The first frame of the video clip appears in this area.

2 Position the mouse over this slider (▼).

3 Drag the slider (▼) to the location in the video clip where you want to trim the video.

4 Click **Clip**.

5 Click **Set Start Trim Point** to remove the video before the slider (▼).

■ Click **Set End Trim Point** to remove the video after the slider (▼).

Note: To remove trim points you set for a video clip, click the video clip on the storyboard and then perform steps 4 and 5, selecting Clear Trim Points in step 5.

CREATE A TRANSITION

You can create a smooth transition from one video clip to another in your movie. The first video clip will fade out as the following video clip fades in.

CREATE A TRANSITION

1 Click ▦ to display the video clips on the storyboard in the timeline view (▦ changes to ▦).

2 To create a transition between two video clips, position the mouse ▷ over the second video clip.

3 Drag the video clip so it overlaps the first video clip.

■ The amount of overlap between the two video clips determines the length of the transition.

■ To once again display the video clips in the storyboard view, click ▦.

Note: To remove a transition, perform steps 1 and 2. Then drag the video clip to the right until the video clips no longer overlap.

ADD MUSIC TO A MOVIE

You can add music to a movie to enhance the movie.

The music you add to a movie will not replace the sound from the video clips in the movie.

You can download music from the Internet, copy songs from a music CD or record your own music using a sound recording program.

ADD MUSIC TO A MOVIE

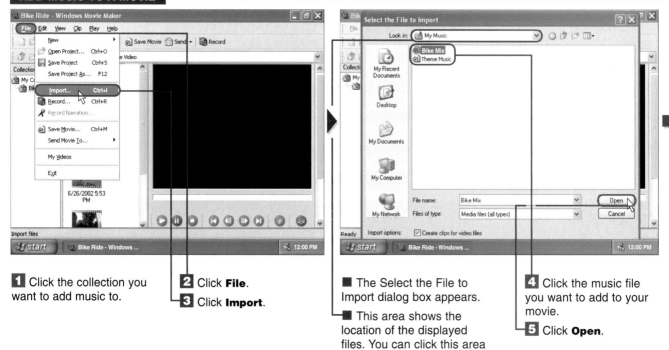

1 Click the collection you want to add music to.

2 Click **File**.

3 Click **Import**.

■ The Select the File to Import dialog box appears.

■ This area shows the location of the displayed files. You can click this area to change the location.

4 Click the music file you want to add to your movie.

5 Click **Open**.

Can I change when the music I added to a movie will start playing?

Yes. To change when music will start playing in a movie, click 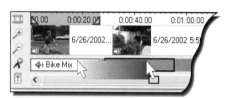 to display the video clips on the storyboard in the timeline view (changes to). Position the mouse over the sound clip for the music below the timeline and then drag the sound clip to a new location. To once again display the video clips in the storyboard view, click.

How do I remove music I added to a movie?

If you no longer want to play music you added to a movie, click to display the video clips on the storyboard in the timeline view (changes to). Click the sound clip for the music below the timeline and then press the Delete key. Removing the sound clip from the timeline will not remove the sound clip from Windows Movie Maker. To once again display the video clips in the storyboard view, click.

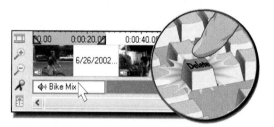

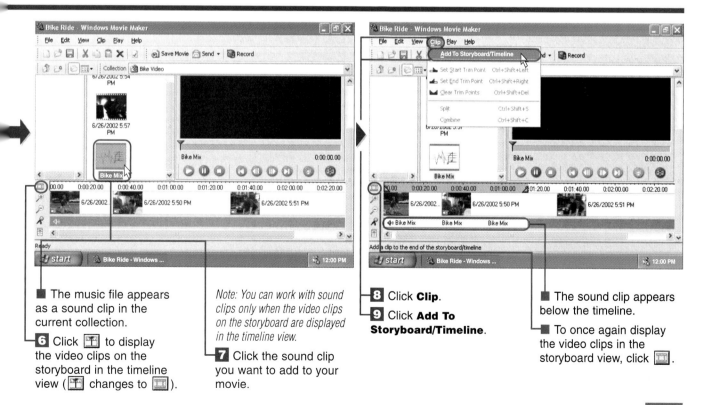

■ The music file appears as a sound clip in the current collection.

Note: You can work with sound clips only when the video clips on the storyboard are displayed in the timeline view.

6 Click to display the video clips on the storyboard in the timeline view (changes to).

7 Click the sound clip you want to add to your movie.

8 Click **Clip**.

9 Click **Add To Storyboard/Timeline**.

■ The sound clip appears below the timeline.

■ To once again display the video clips in the storyboard view, click.

RECORD NARRATION

You can record narration for a movie. Recording narration allows you to add your comments to a home movie or presentation.

Jim is demonstrating the experimental XP51 bicycle. It has been streamlined and features better braking with a more comfortable riding position.

You need a computer with sound capabilities and a microphone to record narration.

RECORD NARRATION

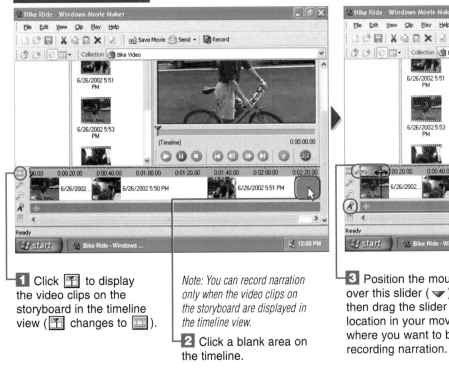

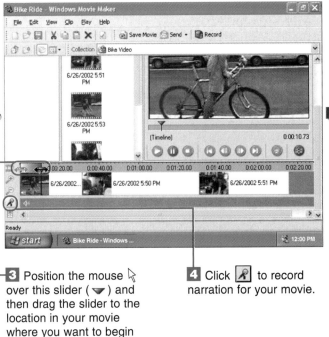

1 Click 🖽 to display the video clips on the storyboard in the timeline view (🖽 changes to 🎞️).

Note: You can record narration only when the video clips on the storyboard are displayed in the timeline view.

2 Click a blank area on the timeline.

3 Position the mouse ⌖ over this slider (▾) and then drag the slider to the location in your movie where you want to begin recording narration.

4 Click 🎙️ to record narration for your movie.

Can I change when narration will start playing?

Yes. To change when narration will start playing in a movie, click to display the video clips on the storyboard in the timeline view (changes to). Position the mouse over the sound clip for the narration below the timeline and then drag the sound clip to a new location. To once again display the video clips in the storyboard view, click .

How can I remove narration from a movie?

If you no longer want to include narration in a movie, click to display the video clips on the storyboard in the timeline view (changes to). Click the sound clip for the narration below the timeline and then press the Delete key. Removing the sound clip from the timeline will not remove the sound clip from Windows Movie Maker. To once again display the video clips in the storyboard view, click .

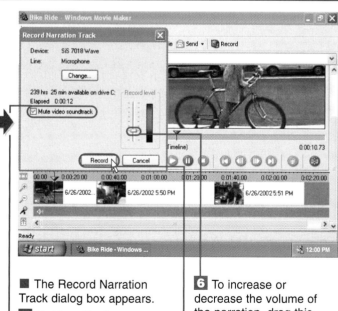

■ The Record Narration Track dialog box appears.

5 If video clips in your movie contain sound, you can click this option so you do not hear the sound while recording the narration (☐ changes to ☑).

6 To increase or decrease the volume of the narration, drag this slider (☐) up or down.

7 Click **Record** to start recording the narration.

8 Speak into your microphone to record the narration.

■ This area displays the time that has passed since you started recording the narration.

■ This area displays the movie as you record the narration.

9 Click **Stop** when you want to stop recording the narration.

CONTINUED

RECORD NARRATION

When you finish recording your narration, Windows Movie Maker allows you to save the narration as a sound file on your computer.

RECORD NARRATION (CONTINUED)

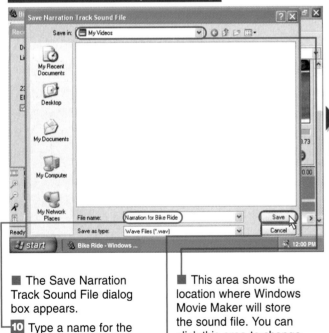

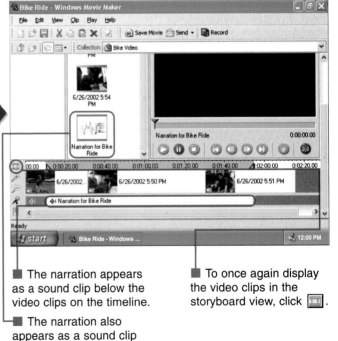

■ The Save Narration Track Sound File dialog box appears.

10 Type a name for the sound file.

■ This area shows the location where Windows Movie Maker will store the sound file. You can click this area to change the location.

11 Click **Save** to save the sound file.

■ The narration appears as a sound clip below the video clips on the timeline.

■ The narration also appears as a sound clip in the current collection.

■ To once again display the video clips in the storyboard view, click [ ].

CHANGE SOUND LEVELS

You can change the sound levels in a movie to make the music or narration you added to the movie play louder or softer than the sound from the video clips.

For example, you may want to change the sound levels so the music you added plays softly in the background of the movie. By default, music or narration you add to a movie will play at the same sound level as the sound from the video clips.

CHANGE SOUND LEVELS

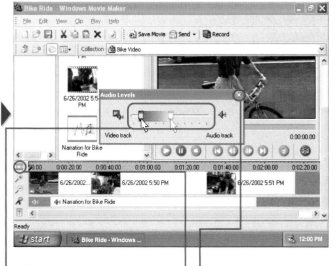

1 Click 🎬 to display the video clips on the storyboard in the timeline view (🎬 changes to 🎬).

Note: You can work with sound in a movie only when the video clips on the storyboard are displayed in the timeline view.

2 Click 🎬 to change the sound levels in the movie.

■ The Audio Levels dialog box appears.

3 Drag the slider (🔲) left or right to adjust the sound levels.

Note: To increase the volume of the video clips and reduce the volume of the music or narration, drag the slider to the left. To increase the volume of the music or narration and reduce the volume of the video clips, drag the slider to the right.

4 Click ✖ to close the Audio Levels dialog box.

■ To once again display the video clips in the storyboard view, click 🎬.

SAVE A MOVIE

After you finish creating your movie, you can save the movie on your computer.

Saving a movie allows you to play the movie at any time and share the movie with other people.

You cannot make changes to a movie you have saved.

SAVE A MOVIE

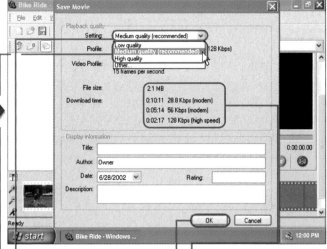

1 Click **Save Movie** to save the video clips on the storyboard as a movie.

Note: If you added music or narration to the movie, Windows Movie Maker will save the sounds with the movie.

■ The Save Movie dialog box appears.

2 Click this area to display a list of the quality settings you can use to save the movie.

3 Click the quality setting you want to use.

Note: You should not select a higher quality setting than you used to record your video.

■ This area displays the file size of the movie and the estimated amount of time the movie will take to transfer over the Internet using three different types of Internet connections.

4 Click **OK** to continue.

How can I share a movie with other people?

After you save a movie, you can share the movie with other people by sending the movie in e-mail messages or distributing copies of the movie on recordable CDs. You can also publish the movie on the Web to allow people to view the movie from any location around the world.

How can I later play a movie I have saved?

Windows automatically stores your movies in the My Videos folder, which is stored in the My Documents folder. You can double-click a movie in the My Videos folder to play the movie. Windows Media Player will open and play the movie.

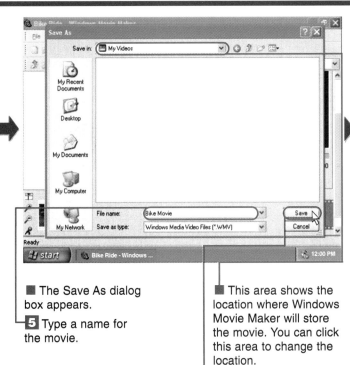

■ The Save As dialog box appears.

5 Type a name for the movie.

■ This area shows the location where Windows Movie Maker will store the movie. You can click this area to change the location.

6 Click **Save** to save the movie.

■ A dialog box appears when Windows Movie Maker has finished saving your movie.

7 Click **Yes** or **No** to specify if you want to watch the movie now.

Note: If you select **Yes**, Windows Media Player will open and play your movie.

CHAPTER 7

Manage Multiple Users

If you share your computer with one or more people, you can create a separate user account for each person. In this chapter, you will learn how to create and manage user accounts on your computer.

CREATE A USER ACCOUNT

If you share your computer with other people, you can create a separate user account for each person.

You must have a computer administrator account to create a user account.

CREATE A USER ACCOUNT

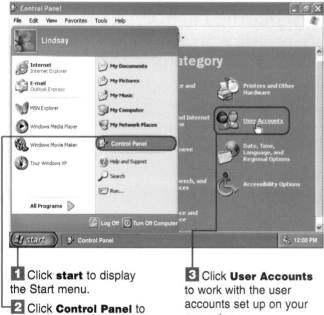

1 Click **start** to display the Start menu.

2 Click **Control Panel** to change your computer's settings.

■ The Control Panel window appears.

3 Click **User Accounts** to work with the user accounts set up on your computer.

■ The User Accounts window appears.

■ This area displays the user accounts set up on your computer. Windows automatically creates the Owner and Guest accounts.

■ The Owner account is a computer administrator account. The Guest account allows a person without a user account to use the computer.

Note: If user accounts were created when Windows was installed on your computer, the first user account created replaced the Owner account.

4 Click **Create a new account**.

144

Will Windows keep my personal files separate from the files of other users?

Yes. Windows will keep your personal files separate from the personal files created by other users. For example, your My Documents folder displays only the files you have created. Internet Explorer also keeps your lists of recently visited Web pages and favorite Web pages separate from the lists of other users.

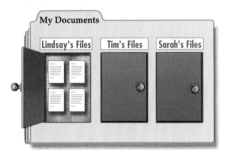

How do I log on to Windows using a new user account?

When you turn on your computer, the Welcome screen appears. The Welcome screen displays the user accounts that are set up on your computer and allows you to select the account you want to use. To log on to Windows using a new user account, click the name of the account.

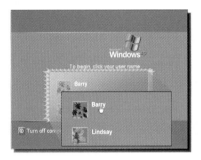

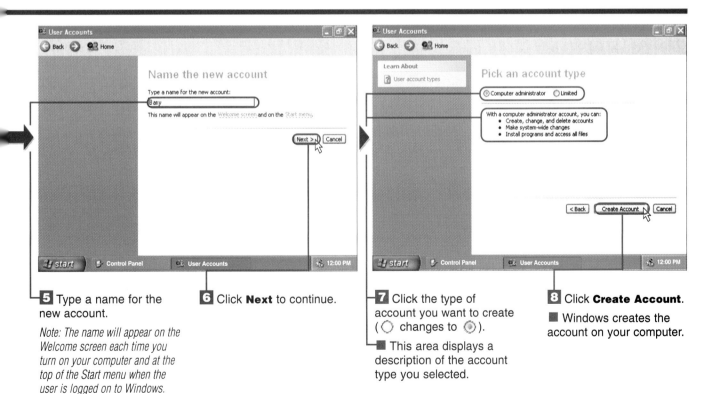

5 Type a name for the new account.

Note: The name will appear on the Welcome screen each time you turn on your computer and at the top of the Start menu when the user is logged on to Windows.

6 Click **Next** to continue.

7 Click the type of account you want to create (○ changes to ◉).

■ This area displays a description of the account type you selected.

8 Click **Create Account**.

■ Windows creates the account on your computer.

CHANGE THE NAME OF A USER ACCOUNT

You can change the name of your user account to personalize the account. For example, you may want to use a nickname instead of your real name.

CHANGE THE NAME OF A USER ACCOUNT

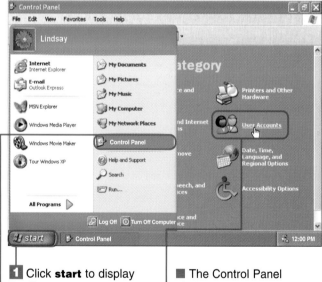

1 Click **start** to display the Start menu.

2 Click **Control Panel** to change your computer's settings.

■ The Control Panel window appears.

3 Click **User Accounts** to work with the user accounts set up on your computer.

■ The User Accounts window appears.

■ This area displays the user accounts that are set up on your computer.

4 Click the account you want to use a different name.

Why can't I change the name of my user account?

If you have a limited account, you cannot change the name of your own account or any other account set up on your computer. Only a person with a computer administrator account can change the name of user accounts. You may want to ask someone with a computer administrator account set up on your computer to change your account name for you. For more information on the types of user accounts, see the top of page 151.

Can I change the name of the Guest account?

No. You cannot change the name of the Guest account. The Guest account allows a person who does not have a user account set up on your computer to use the computer. For more information on the Guest account, see page 152.

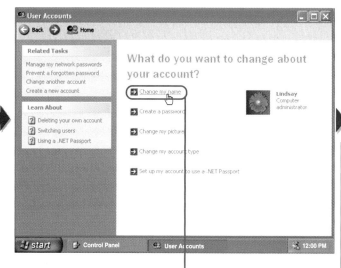

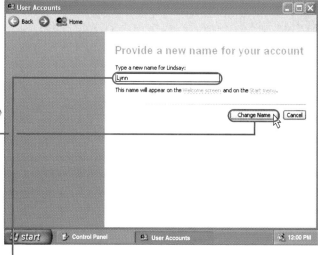

■ A list of tasks that you can perform to change the account appears.

5 Click **Change my name**.

Note: If you are changing the name of another user's account, click ***Change the name***.

6 Type a new name for the account.

7 Click **Change Name** to change the name of the account.

■ The new name for the account will appear on the Welcome screen each time you turn on your computer and at the top of the Start menu when you are logged on to Windows.

CHANGE THE PICTURE FOR A USER ACCOUNT

You can select a different picture for your user account to better suit your personality or interests.

If you have a computer administrator account, you can change the picture for any account set up on your computer. If you have a limited account, you can change the picture for only your own account.

CHANGE THE PICTURE FOR A USER ACCOUNT

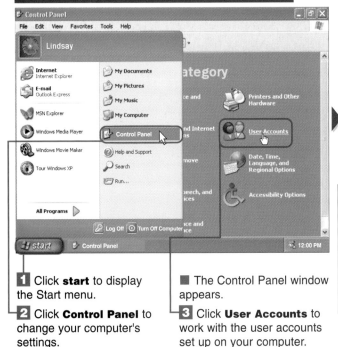

1 Click **start** to display the Start menu.

2 Click **Control Panel** to change your computer's settings.

■ The Control Panel window appears.

3 Click **User Accounts** to work with the user accounts set up on your computer.

■ The User Accounts window appears.

■ If you have a computer administrator account, this area displays the accounts that are set up on your computer. The picture for each account appears beside each account name.

■ If you have a limited account, skip to step **5**.

4 Click the account you want to use a different picture.

Where will the new picture for a user account appear?

When you select a new picture for a user account, the new picture will appear on the Welcome screen each time you turn on your computer. The Welcome screen displays all the user accounts that are set up on your computer and allows you to select the account you want to use. The new picture will also appear at the top of the Start menu when the user is logged on to Windows.

How can I use a picture stored on my computer for a user account?

When viewing the available pictures for a user account in the User Accounts window, click **Browse for more pictures**. In the Open dialog box that appears, locate the picture you want to use for the user account and then double-click the picture to use the picture.

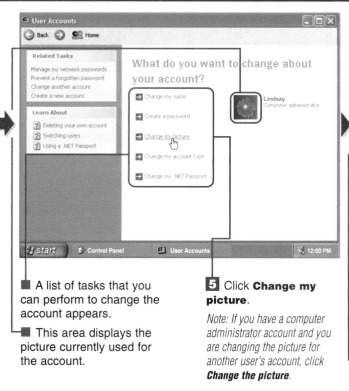

■ A list of tasks that you can perform to change the account appears.

■ This area displays the picture currently used for the account.

5 Click **Change my picture**.

Note: If you have a computer administrator account and you are changing the picture for another user's account, click ***Change the picture***.

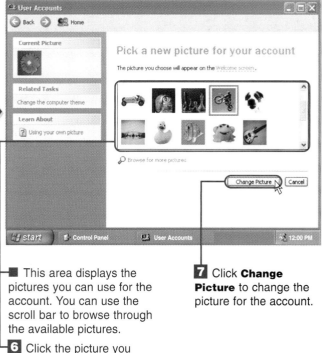

■ This area displays the pictures you can use for the account. You can use the scroll bar to browse through the available pictures.

6 Click the picture you want to use.

7 Click **Change Picture** to change the picture for the account.

CHANGE THE ACCOUNT TYPE FOR A USER ACCOUNT

You can change
the type of account
assigned to a user.
Changing the type
of account will give
a user more or less
access to information
and features on your
computer.

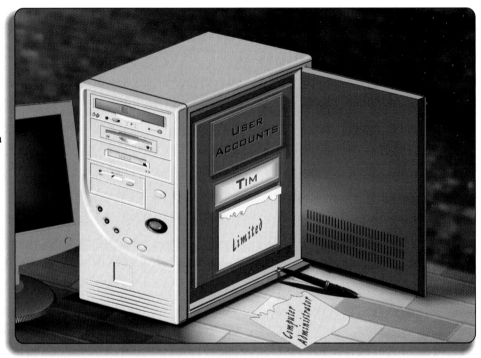

You must have a
computer administrator
account to change the
account type for a user.

CHANGE THE ACCOUNT TYPE FOR A USER ACCOUNT

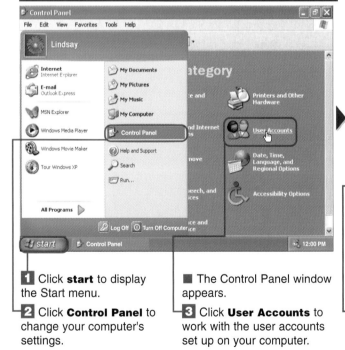

1 Click **start** to display
the Start menu.

2 Click **Control Panel** to
change your computer's
settings.

■ The Control Panel window
appears.

3 Click **User Accounts** to
work with the user accounts
set up on your computer.

■ The User Accounts window
appears.

■ This area displays the
accounts that are set up on
your computer. The type of
each account appears below
each account name.

4 Click the account you
want to change.

*Note: You cannot change the
account type for the Guest
account, which allows a person
without a user account to use
your computer.*

What types of accounts are available?

Computer Administrator

As a computer administrator, you can perform any task on the computer. For example, you can create and change all user accounts as well as install programs and hardware. In most cases, you can also view the personal files of all other users set up on the computer.

Limited

As a limited user, you can perform only certain tasks on the computer. For example, you can create and change your password, change your account picture and change some computer settings, but you cannot delete important files. If the computer uses the NTFS file system, you will also not be able to view the personal files of any other user set up on the computer. For more information about file systems, see page 284.

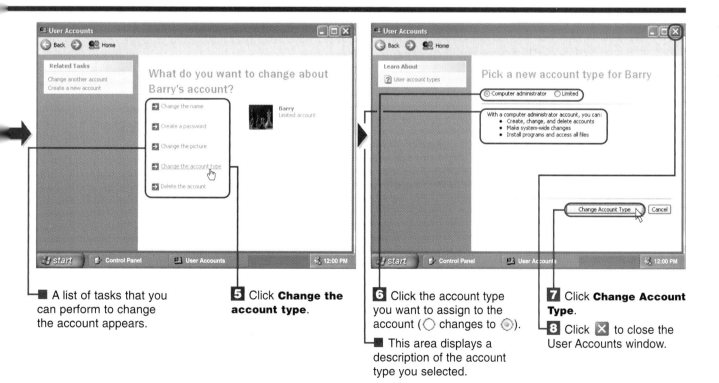

■ A list of tasks that you can perform to change the account appears.

5 Click **Change the account type**.

6 Click the account type you want to assign to the account (○ changes to ⦿).

■ This area displays a description of the account type you selected.

7 Click **Change Account Type**.

8 Click ✕ to close the User Accounts window.

TURN ON THE GUEST ACCOUNT

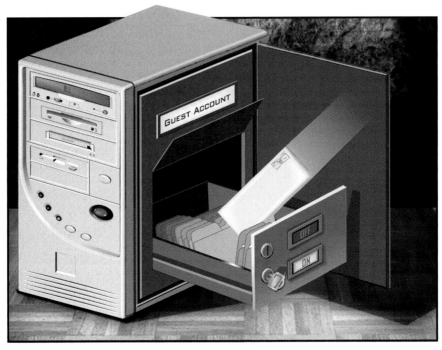

You can turn on the Guest account to allow a person who does not have a user account set up on your computer to use the computer. For example, a visiting friend may want to use the Guest account to check their e-mail.

Windows automatically creates the Guest account on your computer.

You must be logged on to Windows as a computer administrator to turn on the Guest account.

TURN ON THE GUEST ACCOUNT

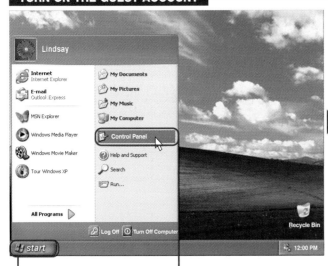

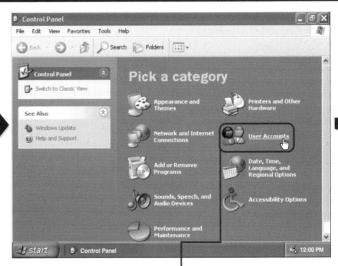

1 Click **start** to display the Start menu.

2 Click **Control Panel** to change your computer's settings.

■ The Control Panel window appears.

3 Click **User Accounts** to work with the user accounts set up on your computer.

What types of tasks can a guest perform on my computer?

For security reasons, a guest can perform only certain tasks on your computer. For example, a guest can run programs already installed on your computer, but cannot install new programs. If your computer uses the NTFS file system, a guest will not be able to view the personal files of any other users set up on your computer. If your computer uses the FAT file system, a guest will be able to view the personal files of other users. For more information about file systems, see page 284.

How do I log on to Windows using the Guest account?

When you turn on your computer, the Welcome screen appears. The Welcome screen displays the user accounts that are set up on your computer and allows you to select the account you want to use. To log on to Windows using the Guest account, click **Guest**.

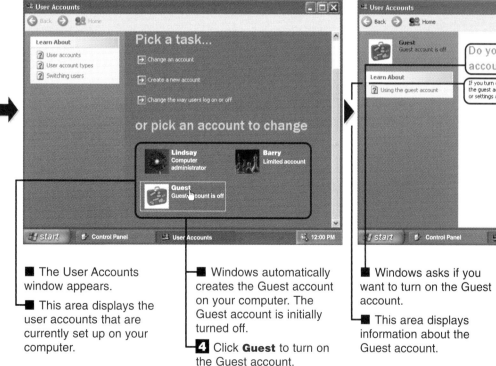

■ The User Accounts window appears.

■ This area displays the user accounts that are currently set up on your computer.

■ Windows automatically creates the Guest account on your computer. The Guest account is initially turned off.

4 Click **Guest** to turn on the Guest account.

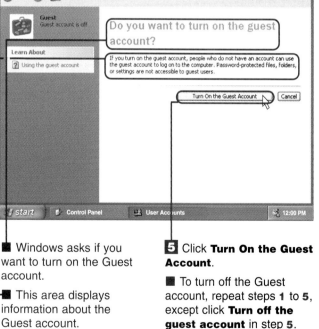

■ Windows asks if you want to turn on the Guest account.

■ This area displays information about the Guest account.

5 Click **Turn On the Guest Account**.

■ To turn off the Guest account, repeat steps **1** to **5**, except click **Turn off the guest account** in step **5**.

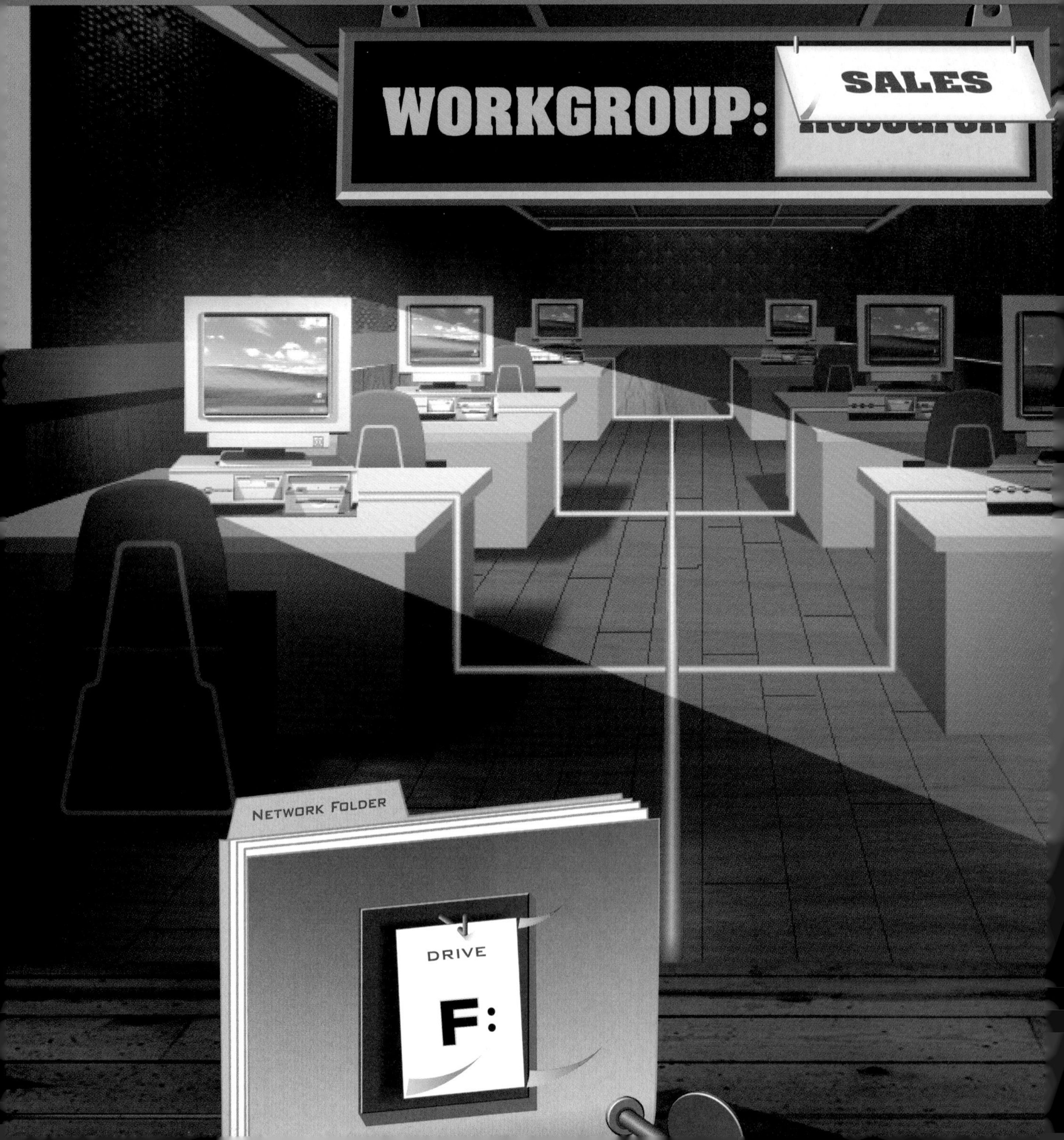
WORKGROUP:
SALES
NETWORK FOLDER
DRIVE
F:

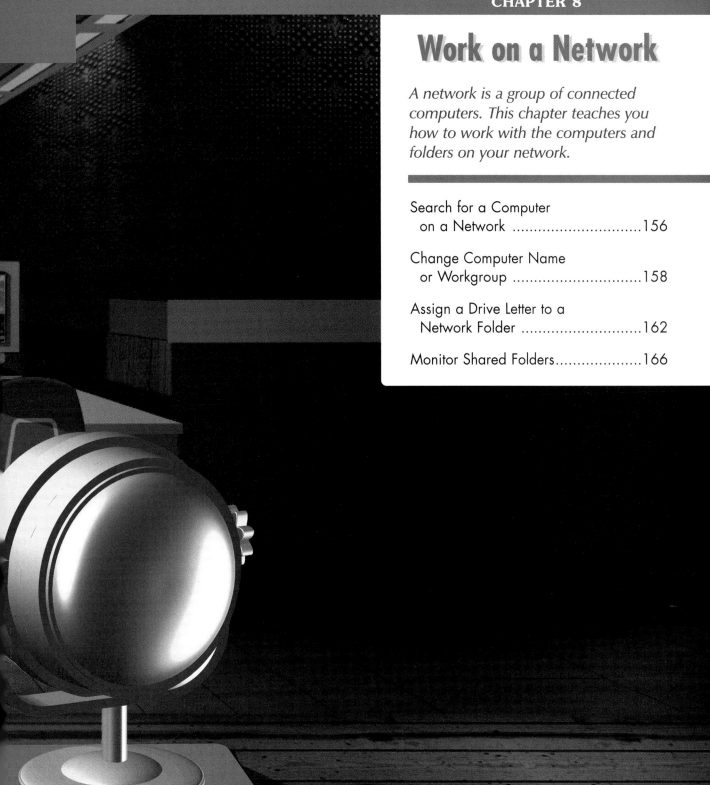

CHAPTER 8

Work on a Network

A network is a group of connected computers. This chapter teaches you how to work with the computers and folders on your network.

SEARCH FOR A COMPUTER ON A NETWORK

You can search for a computer on your network to quickly locate the computer. Searching for a computer is especially useful if your network contains many computers.

When Windows finds a computer on your network, you can work with the information shared on the computer as if the information were stored on your own computer.

SEARCH FOR A COMPUTER ON A NETWORK

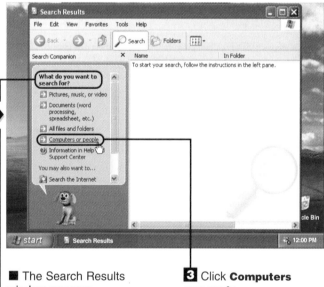

1 Click **start** to display the Start menu.

2 Click **Search** to search for a computer on your network.

■ The Search Results window appears.

■ Windows asks what you want to search for.

3 Click **Computers or people**.

Can I search for a computer if I know only part of the computer's name?

Yes. You can search for a computer even when you know only part of the computer's name. For example, if you search for **ray**, Windows will find computers named **Raymond** and **Murray**. When you specify only part of a computer's name, Windows will find only computers in the workgroup your computer belongs to. A workgroup is a collection of computers on a network that frequently share resources, such as files and printers.

Can I stop a search?

Yes. In the Search Results window, you can click the **Stop** button at any time to end a search. Stopping a search is useful when the search is taking too long.

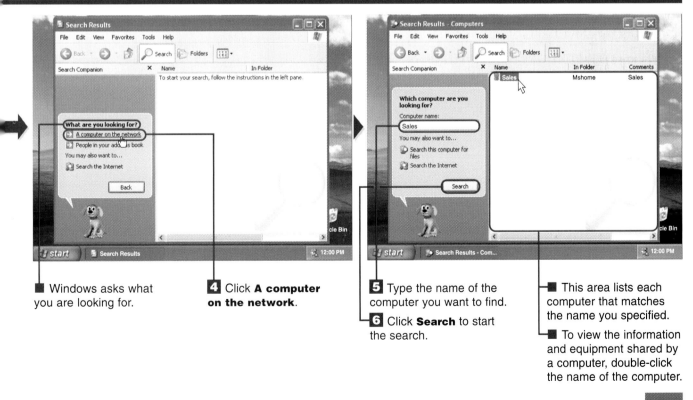

■ Windows asks what you are looking for.

4 Click **A computer on the network**.

5 Type the name of the computer you want to find.

6 Click **Search** to start the search.

■ This area lists each computer that matches the name you specified.

■ To view the information and equipment shared by a computer, double-click the name of the computer.

157

CHANGE COMPUTER NAME OR WORKGROUP

You can change the name of your computer and the workgroup your computer belongs to. Windows uses this information to identify your computer on a network.

When your computer was set up on a network, a computer name and workgroup were specified for the computer.

On a business network, you should consult your network administrator before changing your computer name or workgroup.

CHANGE COMPUTER NAME OR WORKGROUP

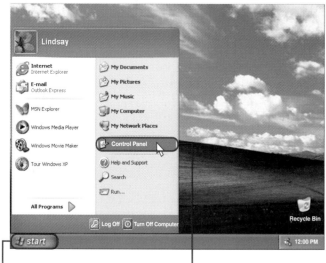

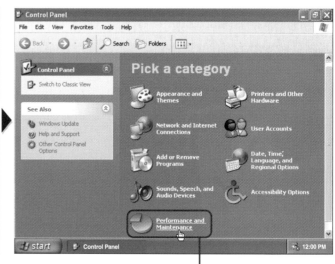

■ Before changing your computer name or workgroup, make sure you close all open programs.

1 Click **start** to display the Start menu.

2 Click **Control Panel** to change your computer's settings.

■ The Control Panel window appears.

3 Click **Performance and Maintenance**.

What is a workgroup?

A workgroup is a group of computers that frequently share resources, such as files and printers, on a network. On a business network, a workgroup often consists of computers located close to each other, such as computers in an accounting or sales department. If you do not know the name of your workgroup, you can ask your network administrator. On a home network, all the computers usually belong to the same workgroup.

When I change my computer name or workgroup, should I notify other people on the network?

Yes. After you change your computer name or workgroup, you should inform the people on the network who access resources on your computer of the change. These people will need to know your new computer name or workgroup in order to access resources on your computer.

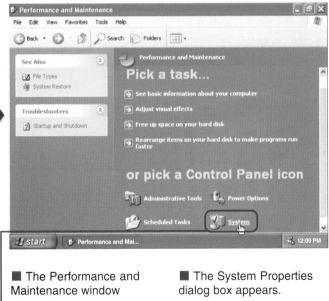

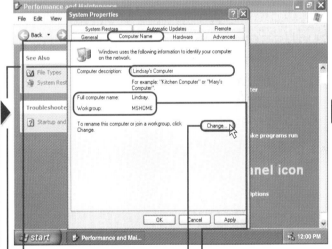

■ The Performance and Maintenance window appears.

4 Click **System** to view information about your computer.

■ The System Properties dialog box appears.

5 Click the **Computer Name** tab.

6 This area displays a description of your computer. To change the description, drag the mouse I over the current text until you highlight the text and then type a new description.

■ This area displays the name of your computer and the workgroup your computer belongs to.

7 Click **Change** to rename the computer or join a different workgroup.

CONTINUED

CHANGE COMPUTER NAME OR WORKGROUP

When changing the name of your computer, you should use a descriptive name that will help other people on the network identify the computer.

For example, a name such as "JohnSmith" will make your computer easier to identify than a name such as "Computer3."

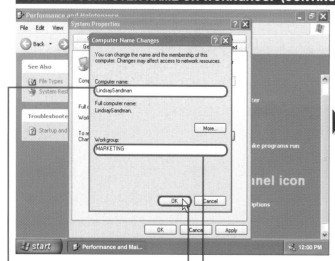

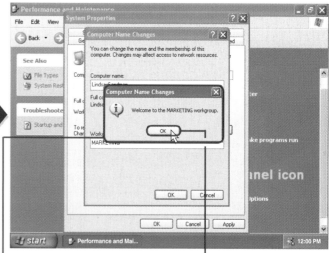

■ The Computer Name Changes dialog box appears.

8 To change your computer's name, drag the mouse I over the current name until you highlight the name and then type a new name.

9 To change the workgroup your computer belongs to, drag the mouse I over the current workgroup name until you highlight the name and then type a new workgroup name.

10 Click **OK** to confirm your changes.

■ If you specified a different workgroup, the Computer Name Changes dialog box appears, welcoming you to the workgroup.

11 Click **OK** to close the dialog box.

What should I consider when changing my computer name or workgroup?

✔ Each computer on your network must have a unique name.

✔ A computer name cannot be the same as the workgroup name.

✔ A computer and workgroup name can contain up to 15 characters.

✔ A computer and workgroup name cannot contain special characters such as the ; : , " < > * + = \ | or ? character.

✔ If your computer has a direct connection to the Internet, such as a computer that uses a cable modem to connect to the Internet, your Internet service provider may require you to use a specific name for the computer. An Internet service provider is a company that gives you access to the Internet.

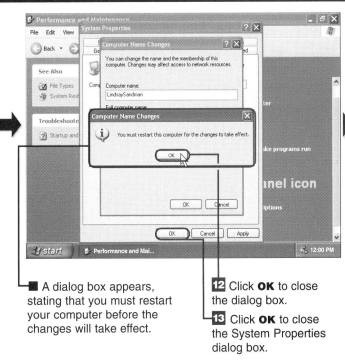

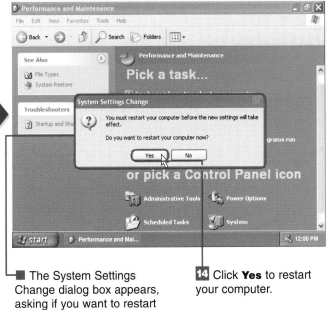

■ A dialog box appears, stating that you must restart your computer before the changes will take effect.

12 Click **OK** to close the dialog box.

13 Click **OK** to close the System Properties dialog box.

■ The System Settings Change dialog box appears, asking if you want to restart your computer now.

14 Click **Yes** to restart your computer.

ASSIGN A DRIVE LETTER TO A NETWORK FOLDER

You can assign a drive letter to a folder on your network to provide a quick way of accessing the folder at any time.

Assigning a drive letter to a network folder is useful when you frequently access information stored on another computer on the network.

A network folder you assign a drive letter to is often referred to as a mapped network drive.

ASSIGN A DRIVE LETTER TO A NETWORK FOLDER

1 Click **start** to display the Start menu.

2 Click **My Computer** to view the contents of your computer.

■ The My Computer window appears.

3 Click **Tools**.

4 Click **Map Network Drive**.

Can assigning a drive letter to a network folder help me use certain programs?

Yes. Some programs, such as MS-DOS or older Windows programs, cannot access folders stored on a network. Assigning a drive letter to a folder on the network allows these programs to access the network folder as if the folder were stored on your computer.

What drive letter should I select for a network folder?

You should choose a drive letter between F and Z. It is a good idea to reserve the letters A through E for your floppy drive, hard drive, CD-ROM drive and any removable drives you use on your computer.

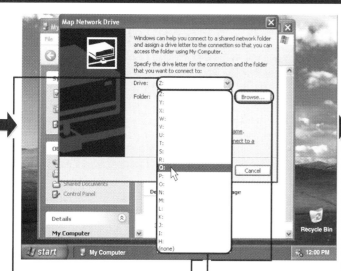

■ The Map Network Drive wizard appears.

5 Click this area to display a list of the available drive letters you can assign to a folder on your network.

6 Click the drive letter you want to assign to a folder.

7 Click **Browse** to locate the folder on your network that you want to assign the drive letter to.

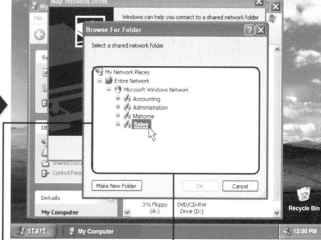

■ The Browse For Folder dialog box appears.

■ This area displays the available workgroups on your network. Windows automatically highlights the name of the workgroup that your computer belongs to.

Note: A workgroup is a group of computers that frequently share information on a network.

8 Click the name of the workgroup that contains the folder you want to assign the drive letter to.

CONTINUED

ASSIGN A DRIVE LETTER TO A NETWORK FOLDER

After you assign a drive letter to a network folder, Windows will automatically connect to the folder each time you log on to Windows.

ASSIGN A DRIVE LETTER TO A NETWORK FOLDER (CONTINUED)

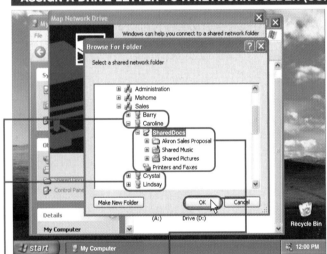

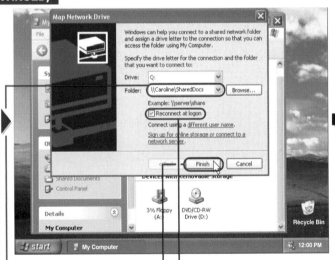

■ The computers in the workgroup you selected appear.

9 Click the name of the computer that contains the folder you want to assign the drive letter to.

■ The shared folders and printers on the computer appear.

10 Click the name of the folder you want to assign the drive letter to.

11 Click **OK** to confirm your selection.

■ This area displays the location and name of the folder you selected.

12 This option instructs Windows to connect to the folder each time you log on to Windows. If a check mark (✔) does not appear beside the option, click the option to turn the option on (☐ changes to ☑).

13 Click **Finish** to complete the wizard.

164

Why does an X appear on the icon for a network folder I assigned a drive letter to?

A network folder displays an X on its icon in the My Computer window if Windows could not connect to the folder when you logged on to Windows. Windows will not be able to connect to a network folder if the folder is no longer shared or if the computer that stores the folder is turned off.

How do I remove the drive letter I assigned to a network folder?

To remove the drive letter you assigned to a network folder, perform steps 1 and 2 on page 162 to display the My Computer window. Right-click the network folder you want to remove the drive letter from and then select **Disconnect** from the menu that appears. Windows will remove the network folder from the My Computer window.

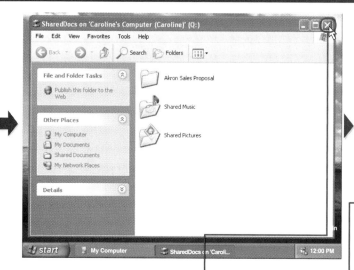

■ A window appears, displaying the contents of the folder you assigned the drive letter to.

14 When you finish viewing the contents of the folder, click ☒ to close the window.

■ The My Computer window reappears.

■ The Network Drives area displays an icon for each folder on the network you have assigned a drive letter to.

DISPLAY THE CONTENTS OF A NETWORK FOLDER

1 In the My Computer window, double-click the network folder whose contents you want to display.

Note: To display the My Computer window at any time, perform steps 1 and 2 on page 162.

165

MONITOR SHARED FOLDERS

Windows allows you to monitor the folders you have shared on your computer and the people on your network who are connected to your shared folders.

MONITOR SHARED FOLDERS

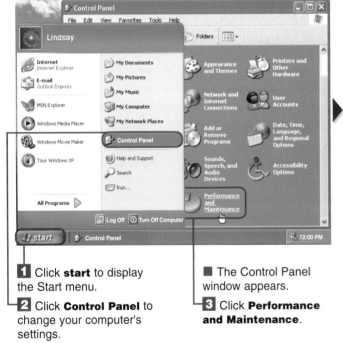

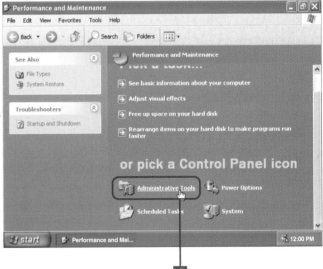

1 Click **start** to display the Start menu.

2 Click **Control Panel** to change your computer's settings.

■ The Control Panel window appears.

3 Click **Performance and Maintenance**.

■ The Performance and Maintenance window appears.

4 Click **Administrative Tools**.

How can I monitor my shared folders?

Windows offers three ways you can view information about the shared folders on your computer.

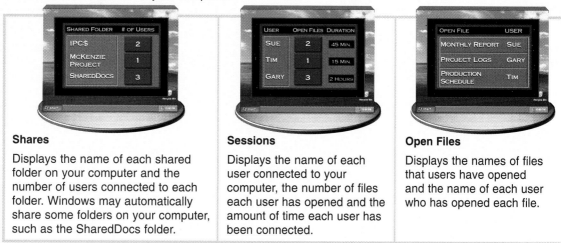

Shares

Displays the name of each shared folder on your computer and the number of users connected to each folder. Windows may automatically share some folders on your computer, such as the SharedDocs folder.

Sessions

Displays the name of each user connected to your computer, the number of files each user has opened and the amount of time each user has been connected.

Open Files

Displays the names of files that users have opened and the name of each user who has opened each file.

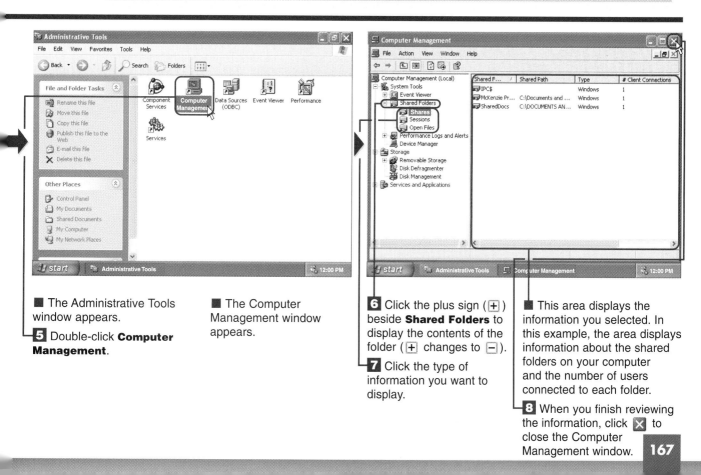

■ The Administrative Tools window appears.

5 Double-click **Computer Management**.

■ The Computer Management window appears.

6 Click the plus sign (⊞) beside **Shared Folders** to display the contents of the folder (⊞ changes to ⊟).

7 Click the type of information you want to display.

■ This area displays the information you selected. In this example, the area displays information about the shared folders on your computer and the number of users connected to each folder.

8 When you finish reviewing the information, click ✖ to close the Computer Management window.

REMOTE COMPUTER

Accessing Remote Computer

Please Wait....

Recycle Bin

start

Lindsay's Computer

CHAPTER 9

Connect Computers

Windows XP offers several ways that you can connect computers to exchange information. In this chapter, you will learn how to exchange information between computers at the office or while traveling.

USING BRIEFCASE

Briefcase allows you to easily transfer files between computers, such as your office computer and your home or portable computer.

When you finish working with the files on another computer, you can return to the original computer and have Windows update all the files you changed.

TRANSFER FILES TO A BRIEFCASE

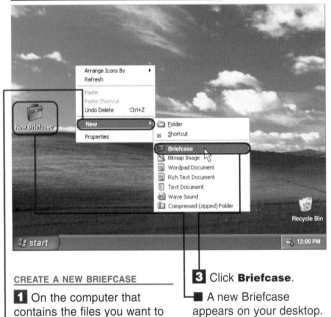

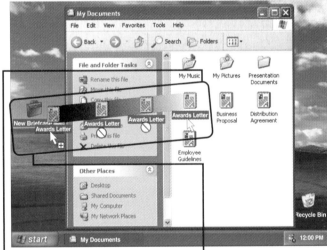

CREATE A NEW BRIEFCASE

1 On the computer that contains the files you want to transfer to another computer, right-click a blank area on your desktop. A menu appears.

2 Click **New**.

3 Click **Briefcase**.

■ A new Briefcase appears on your desktop.

ADD FILES TO A BRIEFCASE

1 Locate a file or folder you want to work with while away from your main computer.

2 Position the mouse over the file or folder.

3 Drag the file or folder to the Briefcase.

■ Windows adds a copy of the file or folder to the Briefcase.

4 To add other files or folders to the Briefcase, repeat steps **1** to **3** for each file or folder.

Can I create more than one Briefcase?

Yes. You can create as many Briefcases as you need. If you create more than one Briefcase, you may want to rename each Briefcase so you can easily distinguish between the Briefcases. To rename a Briefcase, click the Briefcase and then press the [F2] key. Type a new name for the Briefcase and then press the [Enter] key.

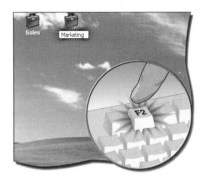

What types of disks can I use to transfer files using a Briefcase?

When using a Briefcase to transfer small amounts of data, you may want to use a floppy disk. A floppy disk can store up to 1.44 MB of data. When transferring large amounts of data, you may want to use a Zip disk. A Zip disk is used with a Zip drive and can store up to 250 MB of data.

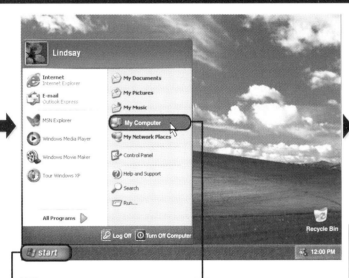

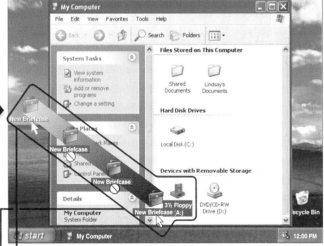

5 Insert a floppy disk or other removable disk into a drive on your computer.

6 Click **start** to display the Start menu.

7 Click **My Computer** to view the contents of your computer.

■ The My Computer window appears.

8 To move the Briefcase to the disk, position the mouse ⬚ over the Briefcase.

9 Drag the Briefcase to the drive that contains the disk.

■ Windows moves the Briefcase to the disk.

10 Remove the disk from the drive so you can work with the files in the Briefcase on another computer.

CONTINUED

USING BRIEFCASE

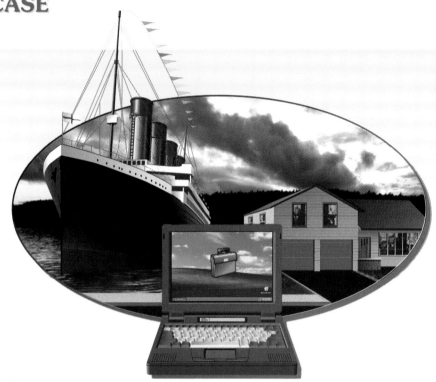

When traveling or at home, you can work with Briefcase files as you would work with any files on a computer.

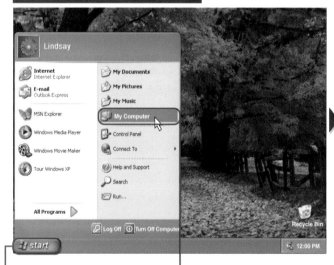

1 On the computer you want to transfer the files to, insert the disk that contains the Briefcase into a drive.

2 Click **start** to display the Start menu.

3 Click **My Computer** to view the contents of your computer.

■ The My Computer window appears.

4 Double-click the drive that contains the disk.

Can I rename the files in a Briefcase?

You should not rename the files in a Briefcase or the original files on your main computer. You should also not move the original files on your main computer. If you rename or move the files, Windows will not be able to update the files.

If I create a new file in a Briefcase, will Windows update the file when I return to my main computer?

If you want Windows to update a new file you create in a Briefcase, you must create the file in an existing folder in the Briefcase. If you do not create the file in an existing folder, Windows will not update the file when you return to your main computer because Windows will not know where to store the file.

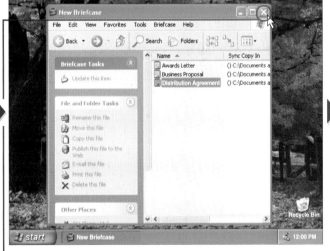

■ The contents of the disk appear.

5 Double-click the Briefcase.

Note: When you open a Briefcase for the first time, a dialog box appears, explaining how you can use Briefcase to keep your documents up to date when using multiple computers. When you finish reviewing the information, click Finish to close the dialog box.

■ The contents of the Briefcase appear. You can open, edit and save the files in the Briefcase as you would any files.

6 When you finish working with the files in the Briefcase, click ✖ to close the Briefcase window.

7 Remove the disk from the drive so you can return the disk to your main computer.

CONTINUED ▶

173

USING BRIEFCASE

When you return to the office, you can update the files you changed while at home or traveling.

Windows compares the files in the Briefcase to the files on your office computer to determine which files need to be updated.

UPDATE BRIEFCASE FILES

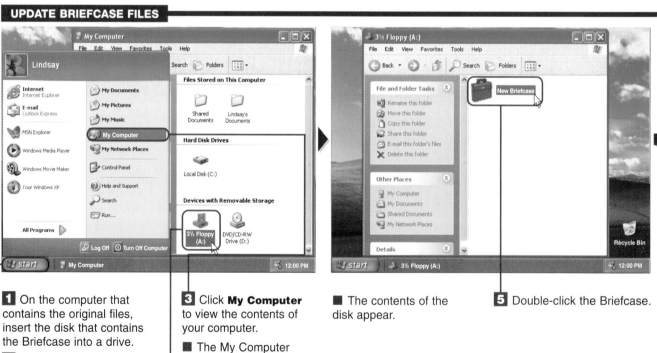

1 On the computer that contains the original files, insert the disk that contains the Briefcase into a drive.

2 Click **start** to display the Start menu.

3 Click **My Computer** to view the contents of your computer.

■ The My Computer window appears.

4 Double-click the drive that contains the disk.

■ The contents of the disk appear.

5 Double-click the Briefcase.

How can I have Windows update a file?

By default, Windows replaces the older version of the file with the newer version of the file, but you can select the way you want Windows to update a file. If both the original and Briefcase files have been changed, Windows will indicate this and not update the file.

⇒ Replace	Replace the original file with the Briefcase file.
⇐ Replace	Replace the Briefcase file with the original file.
↘ Skip	Do not update the file.

Can I delete a Briefcase I no longer need?

Yes. To delete a Briefcase you no longer need, click the Briefcase and then press the `Delete` key. In the confirmation dialog box that appears, click **Yes** to delete the Briefcase. Deleting a Briefcase will not remove the original files from your computer.

■ The contents of the Briefcase appear.

6 Click 🔲 to update all the files.

■ The Update dialog box appears.

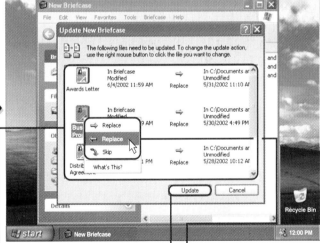

■ This area displays the name of each file that needs to be updated and the way Windows will update each file.

7 To change the way Windows will update a file, right-click the file. A menu appears.

8 Click the way you want Windows to update the file.

Note: For information on the ways Windows can update a file, see the top of this page.

9 Click **Update** to update the files.

USING REMOTE DESKTOP CONNECTION

You can use Remote Desktop Connection to remotely control another computer connected to your network or the Internet.

When you remotely control another computer, you can access information, programs and network resources on the remote computer as if you were working directly at the computer.

USING REMOTE DESKTOP CONNECTION

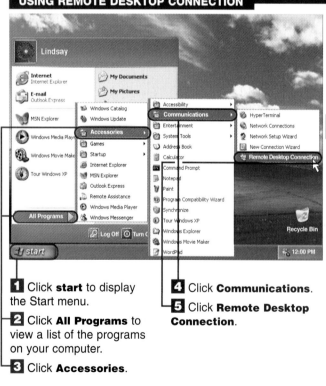

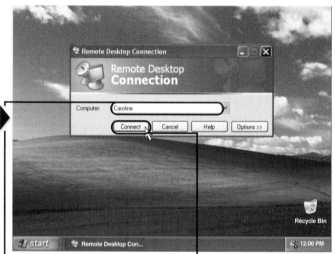

1 Click **start** to display the Start menu.

2 Click **All Programs** to view a list of the programs on your computer.

3 Click **Accessories**.

4 Click **Communications**.

5 Click **Remote Desktop Connection**.

■ The Remote Desktop Connection window appears.

6 Type the name or IP (Internet Protocol) address of the remote computer you want to connect to.

Note: An IP address is a unique number, such as 172.31.255.255, assigned to a computer connected to a network or the Internet.

7 Click **Connect** to connect to the remote computer.

Note: If you are connecting to a remote computer over the Internet, a dialog box may appear, allowing you to connect.

Do I need to set up the remote computer before I can connect?

Yes. The remote computer you want to connect to must be using Windows XP Professional, have a user account that you can use to log on to the computer and be set up to accept remote desktop connections. You can consult your network administrator for more information about setting up a computer for remote desktop connections.

How can I display the remote desktop in a window?

When you first connect to a remote computer, the remote desktop is displayed using the entire screen. To display the remote desktop in a window, click ⬚ on the bar that appears at the top of the screen. Displaying the remote desktop in a window allows you to view the contents of your desktop and the remote desktop at the same time. To once again view the remote desktop using the entire screen, click ⬚ in the remote desktop window.

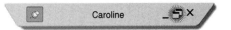

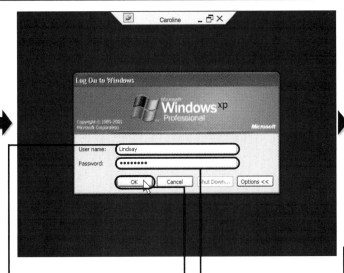

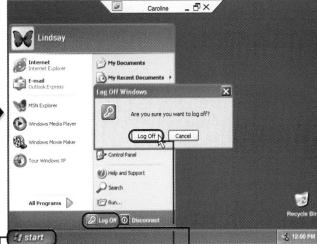

■ The Log On to Windows dialog box appears.

8 Double-click this area and type the user name for the account you can use to log on to the remote computer.

9 Click this area and type the password for the account.

10 Click **OK** to continue.

■ The remote desktop appears on your screen. You can now work on the remote computer as if you were working directly at the computer.

11 When you finish using the remote computer, click **start** to display the Start menu.

12 Click **Log Off**.

■ The Log Off Windows dialog box appears.

13 Click **Log Off** to log off the remote computer and close the connection to the computer.

SET UP AN INCOMING CONNECTION

You can set up an incoming connection on a computer so you can connect to the computer from another location.

Setting up an incoming connection is useful when you are at home or traveling and you want to access information stored on a computer at work. If the computer you connect to is attached to a network, you may also be able to access information on the network.

SET UP AN INCOMING CONNECTION

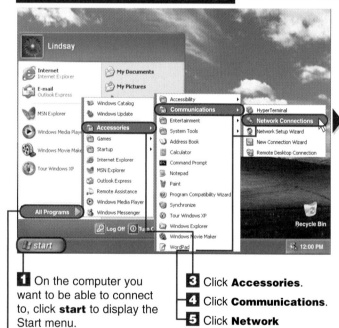

1 On the computer you want to be able to connect to, click **start** to display the Start menu.

2 Click **All Programs** to view a list of the programs on your computer.

3 Click **Accessories**.

4 Click **Communications**.

5 Click **Network Connections**.

■ The Network Connections window appears, displaying any connections currently set up on your computer.

6 Click **Create a new connection**.

What other tasks do I need to perform on a computer I want to connect to from another location?

After setting up an incoming connection on the computer, you should make sure the information and devices, such as a printer, you want to access on the computer are shared. Otherwise, you will not be able to access the information and devices from another location. You should also make sure the computer will be turned on when you want to connect to the computer from another location.

Can I set up more than one incoming connection?

No. Windows allows you to set up only one incoming connection. After you set up an incoming connection on a computer, running the New Connection Wizard again will simply change the incoming connection you have already set up.

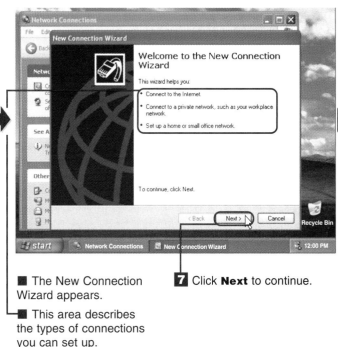

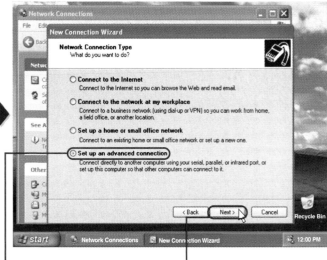

■ The New Connection Wizard appears.

■ This area describes the types of connections you can set up.

7 Click **Next** to continue.

8 Click **Set up an advanced connection** to set up a connection that allows other computers to connect to your computer (○ changes to ◉).

9 Click **Next** to continue.

CONTINUED

SET UP AN INCOMING CONNECTION

When setting up an incoming connection, Windows allows you to select the modem that other computers can use to connect to the computer.

SET UP AN INCOMING CONNECTION (CONTINUED)

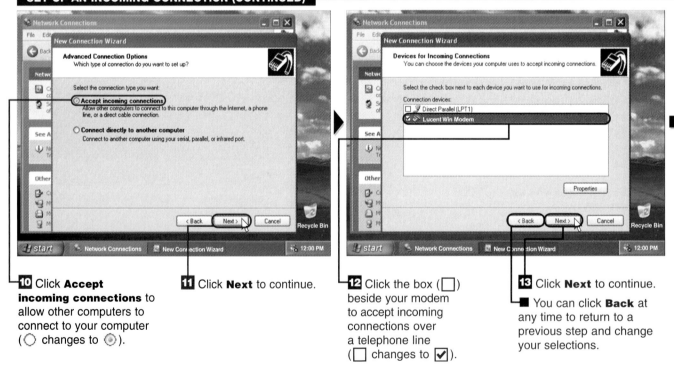

10 Click **Accept incoming connections** to allow other computers to connect to your computer (○ changes to ◉).

11 Click **Next** to continue.

12 Click the box (☐) beside your modem to accept incoming connections over a telephone line (☐ changes to ☑).

13 Click **Next** to continue.

■ You can click **Back** at any time to return to a previous step and change your selections.

What is a virtual private network connection?

A Virtual Private Network (VPN) connection allows one computer to securely connect to another computer over the Internet. A VPN connection helps users save money on long-distance telephone charges by connecting computers over the Internet instead of over a telephone line.

Who can I allow to connect to my computer?

Each person you want to be able to connect to your computer must have a user account set up on the computer. To set up a user account on a computer, see page 144. The users you allow to connect to your computer will have to enter their user name to connect to the computer.

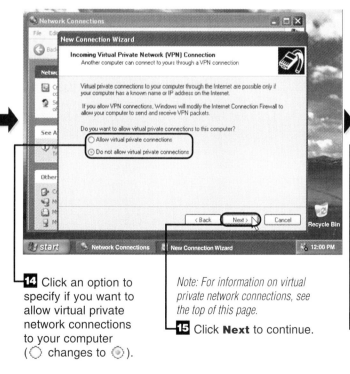

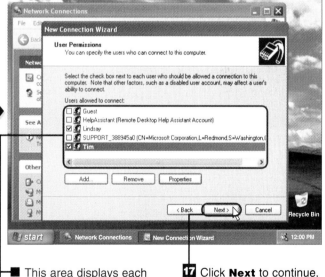

14 Click an option to specify if you want to allow virtual private network connections to your computer (○ changes to ◉).

Note: For information on virtual private network connections, see the top of this page.

15 Click **Next** to continue.

■ This area displays each user account available on your computer.

16 Click the box (☐) beside each user you want to be able to connect to your computer (☐ changes to ☑).

17 Click **Next** to continue.

CONTINUED

SET UP AN INCOMING CONNECTION

Windows allows you to select the types of networking software you want the computer to use for incoming connections.

Networking software, such as Internet Protocol (TCP/IP) and Client for Microsoft Networks, allow a computer to communicate with other computers.

SET UP AN INCOMING CONNECTION (CONTINUED)

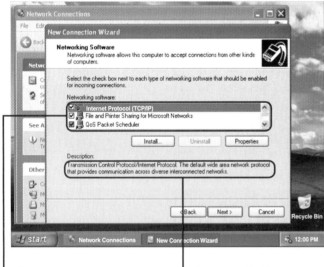

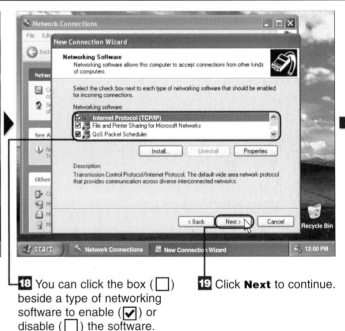

■ This area displays the types of networking software your computer can use to communicate with other computers.

■ This area displays a description of the highlighted type of networking software.

Note: To display a description for another type of networking software, click the software.

18 You can click the box (☐) beside a type of networking software to enable (☑) or disable (☐) the software.

19 Click **Next** to continue.

How do I know when a user is connected to my computer?

When a user is connected to your computer, an icon ( ) appears on the taskbar. To view information about the connection, such as the name of the connected user and the speed of the connection, you can position the mouse over the icon. A yellow box will appear, displaying information about the connection.

How do I delete an incoming connection?

To delete an incoming connection you no longer need, perform steps **1** to **5** on page 178 to display the Network Connections window. Click the incoming connection you want to delete and then press the Delete key. In the confirmation dialog box that appears, click **Yes** to delete the connection.

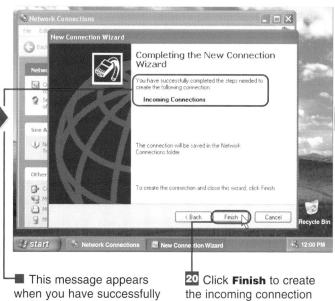

■ This message appears when you have successfully completed the wizard.

20 Click **Finish** to create the incoming connection on your computer and close the wizard.

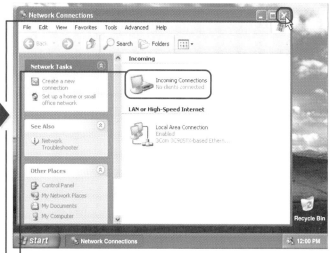

■ An icon for the incoming connection appears in the Network Connections window.

21 Click ✕ to close the Network Connections window.

■ You now need to set up a dial-up connection on the computer you want to use to connect to this computer. For information on setting up a dial-up connection, see page 184.

SET UP A DIAL-UP CONNECTION

You can set up a dial-up connection that will allow you to use a modem to connect to another computer.

Connecting to another computer is useful when you are at home or traveling and you need to access information stored on a computer at work. If the computer you connect to is attached to a network, you may also be able to access information on the network.

SET UP A DIAL-UP CONNECTION

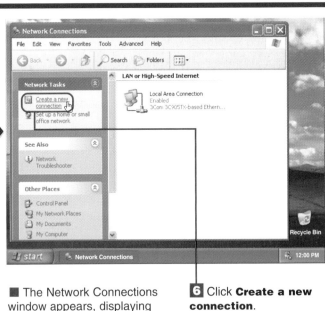

1 On your home or portable computer, click **start** to display the Start menu.

2 Click **All Programs** to view a list of the programs on your computer.

3 Click **Accessories**.

4 Click **Communications**.

5 Click **Network Connections**.

■ The Network Connections window appears, displaying any connections currently set up on your computer.

6 Click **Create a new connection**.

How do I prepare the computer at work so I can connect from home or when traveling?

Before you can connect to a computer at work, the computer must be set up to accept incoming connections. To set up a computer to accept incoming connections, see page 178.

What information can I access on the computer at work?

When your home or portable computer is connected to a computer at work, you will be able to access any shared information on the computer. You will be able to work with the shared files as if the files were stored on your home or portable computer. You will also be able to print files on a shared printer connected to the computer at work.

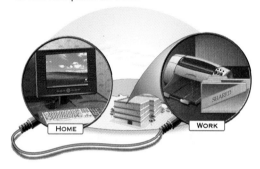

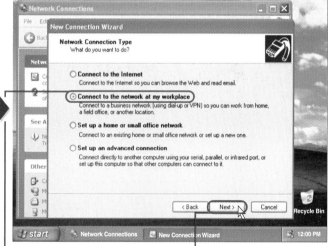

■ The New Connection Wizard appears.

■ This area describes the types of connections you can set up.

7 Click **Next** to continue.

8 Click this option to set up a connection to a computer at work so you can work from home or another location (○ changes to ⊙).

9 Click **Next** to continue.

CONTINUED ▶

SET UP A DIAL-UP CONNECTION

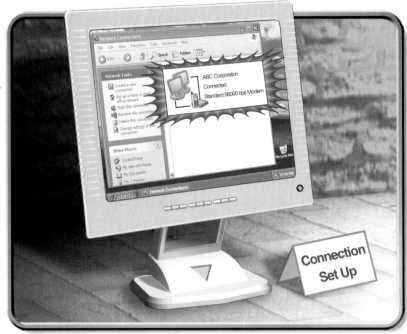

You need to set up a dial-up connection to another computer only once.

After you set up a connection, Windows will display an icon for the connection in the Network Connections window.

SET UP A DIAL-UP CONNECTION (CONTINUED)

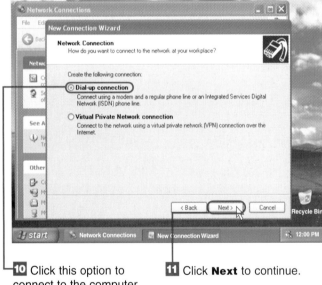

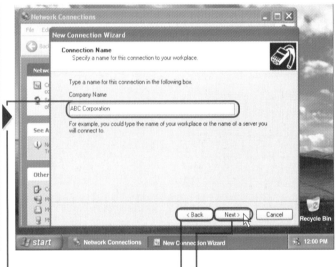

10 Click this option to connect to the computer at work using a modem (○ changes to ◉).

11 Click **Next** to continue.

12 Type the name you want to use for the connection to the computer at work, such as your company name.

13 Click **Next** to continue.

■ You can click **Back** at any time to return to a previous step and change your selections.

—

Why did a Connect dialog box appear after I set up a connection?

Each time you set up a connection to another computer, the Connect dialog box appears, allowing you to immediately use the connection. To connect to another computer using the Connect dialog box, see page 188. If you do not want to immediately connect to another computer, click **Cancel** to close the dialog box.

How do I delete a connection I no longer use?

Perform steps **1** to **5** on page 184 to display the Network Connections window. To delete a connection, click the connection you want to delete and then press the Delete key. In the confirmation dialog box that appears, click **Yes** to delete the connection. If you created a shortcut for the connection on the desktop, you can delete the shortcut the same way you delete a connection.

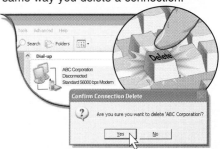

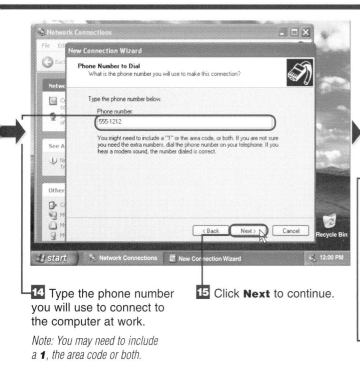

14 Type the phone number you will use to connect to the computer at work.

*Note: You may need to include a **1**, the area code or both.*

15 Click **Next** to continue.

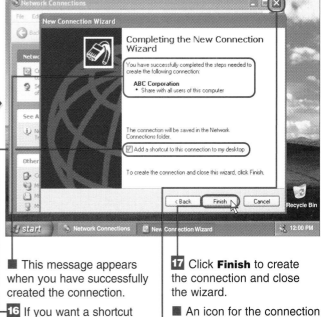

■ This message appears when you have successfully created the connection.

16 If you want a shortcut to appear on your desktop to give you quick access to the connection, click this option (☐ changes to ☑).

17 Click **Finish** to create the connection and close the wizard.

■ An icon for the connection will appear in the Network Connections window.

18 Click ☒ to close the Network Connections window.

CONNECT TO ANOTHER COMPUTER

After you set up a connection to another computer, you can connect to the computer to access information on the computer.

For example, while you are away from the office, you can connect to a computer at work to access files you need. If the computer you connect to is attached to a network, you may also be able to access information on the network.

CONNECT TO ANOTHER COMPUTER

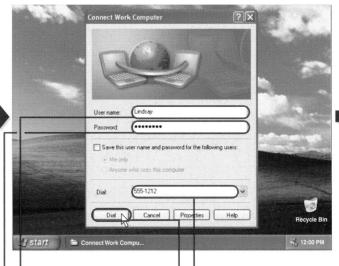

1 Click **start** to display the Start menu.

2 Click **Connect To**.

3 Click the connection for the computer you want to connect to.

Note: To set up a connection to another computer, see page 184.

■ The Connect dialog box appears.

4 Click this area and type the user name that allows you to log on to the other computer.

5 Click this area and type your password.

■ This area displays the phone number Windows will dial. To change the number, you can click the current number and type a new number.

6 Click **Dial** to connect to the computer.

How can I access information on the other computer?

After you connect to the other computer, you can search for the computer to access the shared information on the computer. To search for a computer, see page 156. After you find the computer, you can double-click the icon for the computer to access any information that has been shared on the computer.

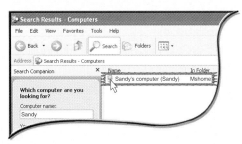

Why did my modem disconnect from the other computer?

If there is interference on the telephone line, your modem may disconnect from the other computer. Try connecting again to get a better telephone line connection. Your modem may also disconnect from the other computer if you do not use your computer for a period of time or if the computer you are connected to is turned off.

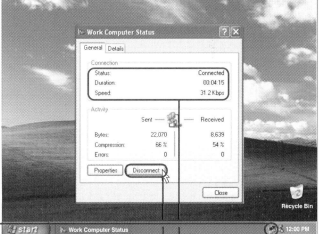

■ When you are connected to the other computer, this message and icon ( ) appear.

■ You can now access information on the other computer.

7 When you want to end the connection with the other computer, click .

■ The Status dialog box appears.

■ This area displays information about the connection, such as the length of time you have been connected to the other computer.

8 Click **Disconnect** to end the connection.

189

CHAPTER 10

Browse the Web

This chapter explains how to use Internet Explorer to view and work with Web pages. Learn how to print a Web page, save a picture displayed on a Web page, add a Web page to your Favorites list and more.

START INTERNET EXPLORER

You can start
Internet Explorer
to browse through
the information
on the Web.

If you do not set up
your connection to
the Internet before
starting Internet
Explorer, the New
Connection Wizard
will appear. Follow
the instructions in
the wizard to set
up your Internet
connection.

START INTERNET EXPLORER

1 Click **start** to display
the Start menu.

2 Click **All Programs** to
view a list of the programs
on your computer.

3 Click **Internet Explorer**.

■ The Microsoft Internet
Explorer window appears,
displaying your home page.

*Note: If you are not currently
connected to the Internet, a dialog
box will appear that allows you to
connect.*

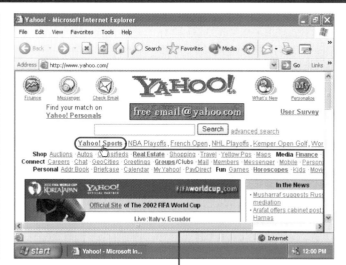

SELECT A LINK

**You can select a link to
display another Web page.
A link connects text or an
image on one Web page
to another Web page.**

1 To select a link, position
the mouse ⍺ over a
highlighted word or image
of interest. The mouse ⍺
changes to a hand ⍭
when over a link.

2 To display the linked
Web page, click the word
or image.

What should I do if a Web page is taking a long time to appear on my screen?

If a Web page is taking a long time to appear on your screen, you can click (⊠) in the Internet Explorer window to stop the transfer of the Web page. You may also want to stop the transfer of a Web page if you realize a page contains information that does not interest you.

How can I redisplay a Web page I previously viewed?

To move backward or forward through the Web pages you have viewed since you last started Internet Explorer, click the Back (⬅ Back) or Forward (➡) button.

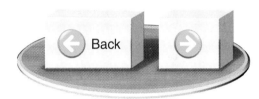

DISPLAY A SPECIFIC WEB PAGE

You can display any page on the Web that you have heard or read about.

■ You need to know the address of a Web page that you want to view. Each page on the Web has a unique address.

1 Click this area to highlight the current Web page address.

2 Type the address of the Web page you want to display and then press the Enter key.

■ This area shows the progress of the transfer.

■ The Web page appears on your screen.

3 When you finish browsing through information on the Web, click ⊠ to close the Microsoft Internet Explorer window.

REFRESH A WEB PAGE

You can refresh a Web page to transfer a fresh copy of the page to your computer.

Refreshing a Web page is useful for updating pages that contain regularly changing information, such as news, stock market data or images from a live camera.

REFRESH A WEB PAGE

1 Click 🖹 to transfer a fresh copy of the displayed Web page to your computer.

■ A fresh copy of the Web page appears on your screen.

You can produce a paper copy of the Web page displayed on your screen.

When you print a Web page, the page number and total number of pages appear at the top of each printed page. The Web page address and current date set in your computer appear at the bottom of each printed page.

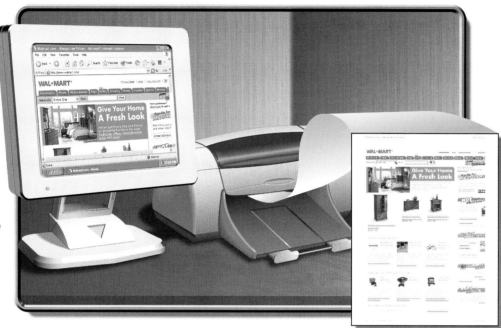

PRINT A WEB PAGE

■ Before printing a Web page, make sure your printer is turned on and contains paper.

1 Click **File**.

2 Click **Print**.

■ The Print dialog box appears.

3 Click the print option you want to use (○ changes to ◉).

All – Prints every page in the Web page.

Pages – Prints the page(s) you specify.

4 If you selected **Pages** in step **3**, type the page(s) you want to print, such as **2** or **3-5**.

5 Click **Print**.

SAVE A PICTURE DISPLAYED ON A WEB PAGE

You can save a picture displayed on a Web page to store the picture on your computer.

After you save a picture displayed on a Web page, you can view and work with the picture as you would view and work with any picture stored on your computer.

SAVE A PICTURE DISPLAYED ON A WEB PAGE

1 Right-click a picture you want to save. A menu appears.

2 Click **Save Picture As**.

■ The Save Picture dialog box appears.

3 Type a name for the picture.

■ This area shows the location where Windows will store the picture. You can click this area to change the location.

Note: By default, Windows stores pictures in the My Pictures folder.

4 Click **Save** to save the picture on your computer.

You can display a Web
page using your entire
screen. This allows you
to view more of the
Web page at once.

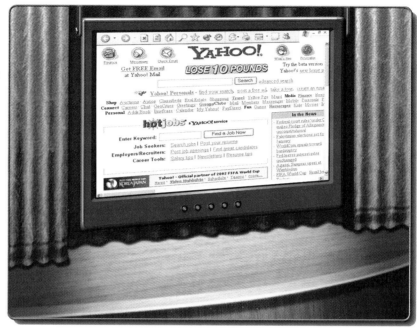

DISPLAY A WEB PAGE USING THE ENTIRE SCREEN

1 Click **View**.

2 Click **Full Screen**.

■ Windows hides the
taskbar and parts of the
Internet Explorer window,
such as toolbars and the
status bar, to display the
Web page in a larger
viewing area.

■ To once again display
the taskbar and hidden
parts of the Internet
Explorer window, click 🗗.

Note: You can also press the
F11 *key to switch between the*
full screen and regular view of
a Web page.

FIND TEXT ON A WEB PAGE

If you are viewing a Web page that contains a lot of text, you can use the Find feature to quickly locate a word or phrase of interest.

By default, Internet Explorer will find text on a Web page even if the text is part of a larger word. For example, if you search for **place**, Internet Explorer will also find **place**s, **place**ment and common**place**.

FIND TEXT ON A WEB PAGE

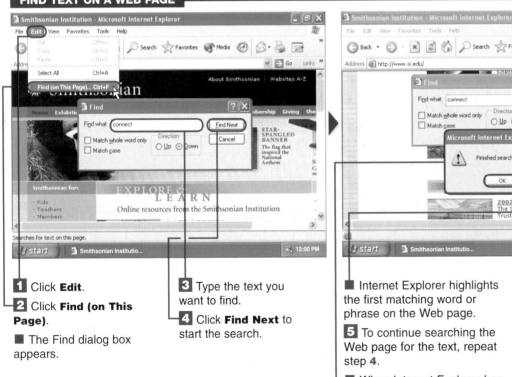

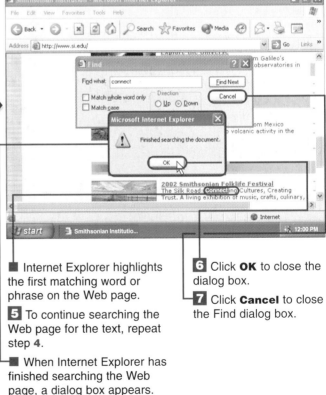

1 Click **Edit**.

2 Click **Find (on This Page)**.

■ The Find dialog box appears.

3 Type the text you want to find.

4 Click **Find Next** to start the search.

■ Internet Explorer highlights the first matching word or phrase on the Web page.

5 To continue searching the Web page for the text, repeat step **4**.

■ When Internet Explorer has finished searching the Web page, a dialog box appears.

6 Click **OK** to close the dialog box.

7 Click **Cancel** to close the Find dialog box.

You can quickly
find Web pages that
contain information
related to the
Web page you are
currently viewing.

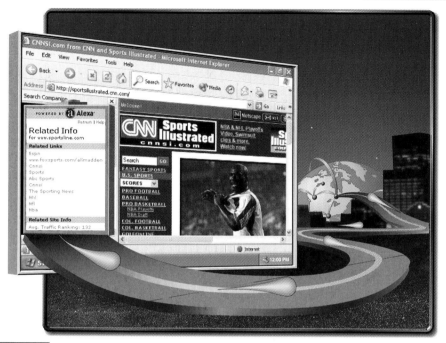

FIND RELATED WEB PAGES

1 To find Web pages that relate to the Web page you are currently viewing, click **Tools**.

2 Click **Show Related Links**.

■ The Search Companion area appears, displaying a list of related Web pages and information about the displayed Web page.

3 To view a related Web page, click the name of the Web page.

■ The Web page you select appears in this area.

4 When you finish viewing the list of related Web pages, click ☒ to hide the Search Companion area.

ADD A WEB PAGE TO FAVORITES

You can use the Favorites feature to create a list of Web pages you frequently visit. The Favorites feature allows you to quickly display a favorite Web page at any time.

Selecting Web pages from your list of favorites saves you from having to remember and constantly retype the same Web page addresses.

ADD A WEB PAGE TO FAVORITES

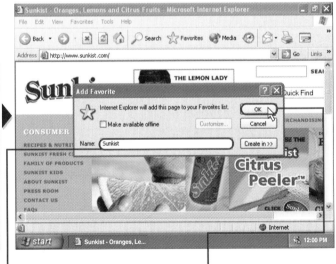

1 Display the Web page you want to add to your list of favorite Web pages.

Note: To display a specific Web page, see page 193.

2 Click **Favorites**.

3 Click **Add to Favorites**.

■ The Add Favorite dialog box appears.

■ The name of the Web page appears in this area. To change the name, you can drag the mouse I over the current name until you highlight the name and then type a new name.

4 Click **OK** to add the Web page to your list of favorites.

200

**Does Internet Explorer automatically add Web
pages to my list of favorites?**

Yes. Internet Explorer automatically adds the Links
folder and two Web pages to your list of favorites.

Links folder

Contains several useful Web
pages, such as the Free
Hotmail page, which is a Web
page that allows you to set up
and use a free e-mail account.

MSN.com

A Web site provided by
Microsoft that offers a great
starting point for exploring
the Web.

Radio Station Guide

A Web site you can use to listen
to radio stations from around
the world that broadcast on the
Internet.

VIEW A FAVORITE WEB PAGE

1 Click **Favorites**.

■ A list of your favorite
Web pages appears.

*Note: If the entire list does not
appear, click ▼ at the bottom
of the menu to browse through
the entire list.*

2 Click the favorite Web
page you want to view.

*Note: To display the favorite
Web pages in a folder, click the
folder (🗀) before performing
step 2.*

■ The favorite Web page
you selected appears.

■ You can repeat steps **1**
and **2** to view another
favorite Web page.

ORGANIZE FAVORITE WEB PAGES

You can organize the Web pages in your Favorites list to help make the list easier to use.

Create Folders

You can create folders to organize Web pages in your Favorites list by topic, such as Hobbies, News and Shopping.

Move Web Pages

You can rearrange the Web pages in your Favorites list to place Web pages you frequently use at the top of the list or move Web pages to folders you have created.

ORGANIZE FAVORITE WEB PAGES

1 Click **Favorites**.

2 Click **Organize Favorites**.

■ The Organize Favorites dialog box appears.

CREATE A NEW FOLDER

3 To create a new folder, click **Create Folder**.

Note: To create a new folder within another folder that contains Web pages, click the folder ( ) before performing step 3.

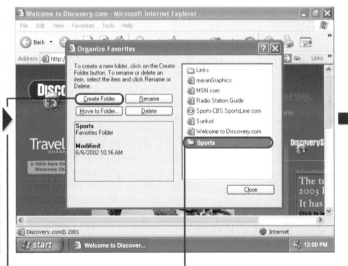

■ The new folder appears, displaying a temporary name.

4 Type a name for the new folder and then press the `Enter` key.

How do I delete a Web page or folder from my Favorites list?

You can delete Web pages and folders you no longer use from your Favorites list to help prevent the list from becoming cluttered. To delete an item from your Favorites list, perform steps **1** and **2** below to display the Organize Favorites dialog box. Click the Web page or folder you want to delete and then press the Delete key. In the confirmation dialog box that appears, click **Yes** to delete the item from your Favorites list. When you delete a folder, all the Web pages stored in the folder will also be deleted.

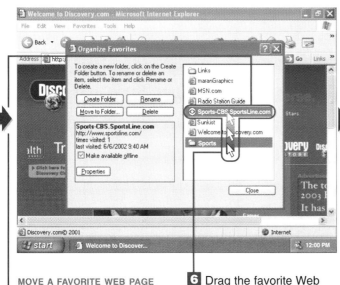

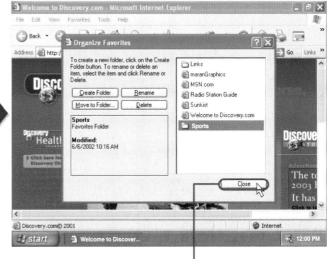

MOVE A FAVORITE WEB PAGE

5 Position the mouse ⌖ over the favorite Web page you want to move.

Note: To display the favorite Web pages in a folder, click the folder ( ).

6 Drag the favorite Web page to a new location in your list of favorites or to a folder.

Note: If you move the Web page to a new location, a solid line indicates where the Web page will appear. If you move the Web page to a folder, Windows will highlight the folder.

■ The favorite Web page appears in the new location.

7 When you finish organizing your favorite Web pages, click **Close** to close the Organize Favorites dialog box.

USING THE MEDIA BAR

You can use the Media bar to play media files, such as music and video files, in Internet Explorer.

You can also use the Media bar to listen to radio stations that broadcast on the Internet.

USING THE MEDIA BAR

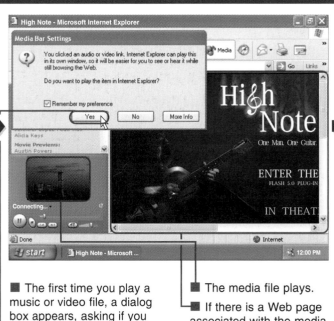

1 Click **Media** to display the Media bar.

■ The Media bar appears, displaying links to media files from the WindowsMedia.com Web page. You can use the scroll bar to browse through the available links.

2 Click the link for the media file you want to play.

■ The first time you play a music or video file, a dialog box appears, asking if you want to play the media file in Internet Explorer.

3 Click **Yes** to play the media file in Internet Explorer.

■ The media file plays.

■ If there is a Web page associated with the media file, this area displays the Web page.

How is information organized in the Media bar?

The Media bar organizes media links into categories, including Today, Music, Movies, Radio and MSN Music. The Media bar displays the media links in only one category at a time. To view the media links in another category, you can click the name of the category.

Can I display the viewing area of the Media bar as a separate window?

Yes. To display the viewing area of the Media bar as a separate window, click ☒ . Displaying the viewing area as a separate window increases the size of the area that plays media files. To return the viewing area to the Media bar, click ☒ in the Media window.

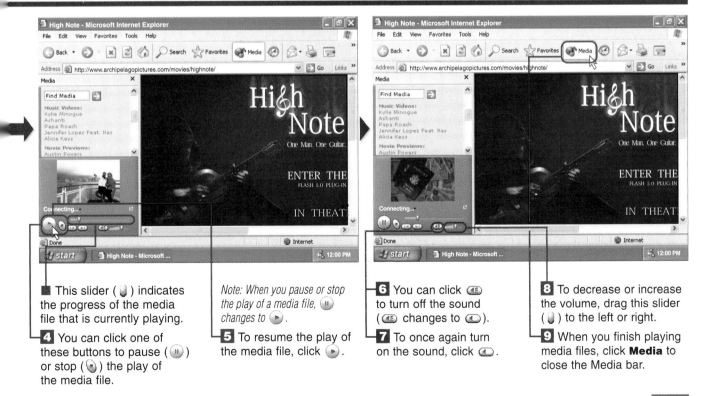

■ This slider ( ) indicates the progress of the media file that is currently playing.

4 You can click one of these buttons to pause ( ) or stop ( ) the play of the media file.

Note: When you pause or stop the play of a media file, changes to .

5 To resume the play of the media file, click .

6 You can click to turn off the sound (changes to).

7 To once again turn on the sound, click .

8 To decrease or increase the volume, drag this slider ( ) to the left or right.

9 When you finish playing media files, click **Media** to close the Media bar.

CHAPTER 11

Exchange E-mail Messages

Outlook Express allows you to exchange e-mail messages with people around the world. In this chapter, you will learn how to read, send and work with e-mail messages.

READ AND SEND MESSAGES

You can use Outlook Express to exchange e-mail messages with people around the world.

The first time you start Outlook Express, a wizard will appear if you have not yet set up your Internet connection or e-mail account. Follow the instructions in the wizard to set up your Internet connection and/or e-mail account.

READ MESSAGES

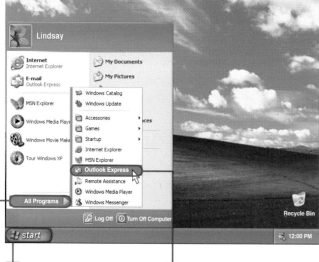

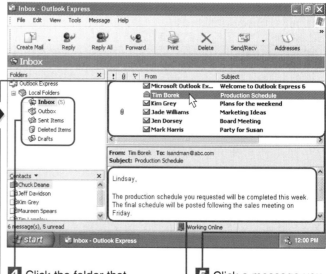

1 Click **start** to display the Start menu.

2 Click **All Programs** to view a list of the programs on your computer.

3 Click **Outlook Express**.

■ The Outlook Express window appears.

Note: If you are not currently connected to the Internet, a dialog box will appear that allows you to connect.

4 Click the folder that contains the messages you want to read. The folder is highlighted.

■ This area displays the messages in the folder you selected. Unread messages display a closed envelope (✉) and appear in **bold**.

5 Click a message you want to read.

■ This area displays the contents of the message you selected.

What folders does Outlook Express use to store my messages?

📭 Inbox	Stores messages sent to you.
📤 Outbox	Temporarily stores messages that have not yet been sent.
📬 Sent Items	Stores copies of messages you have sent.
🗑 Deleted Items	Stores messages you have deleted.
📝 Drafts	Stores messages you have not yet completed.

How can I check for new messages?

When you are connected to the Internet, Outlook Express automatically checks for new messages every 30 minutes. To check for new messages at any time, click the **Send/Recv** button. When you have new messages, a new e-mail icon (🖂) appears on the right side of your taskbar.

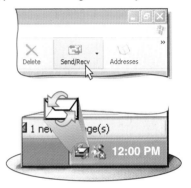

SEND A MESSAGE

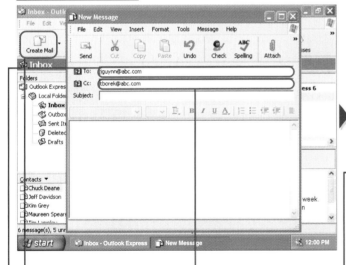

1 Click **Create Mail** to send a new message.

■ The New Message window appears.

2 Type the e-mail address of the person you want to receive the message.

3 To send a copy of the message to a person who is not directly involved but would be interested in the message, click this area and then type the person's e-mail address.

4 Click this area and then type a subject for the message.

5 Click this area and then type the message.

6 Click **Send** to send the message.

■ Outlook Express sends the message and stores a copy of the message in the Sent Items folder.

FORMAT TEXT IN A MESSAGE

You can format the text in a message you are creating to enhance the appearance of the message.

You can change the font, size and color of text in a message to make the text easier to read or draw attention to important information.

FORMAT TEXT IN A MESSAGE

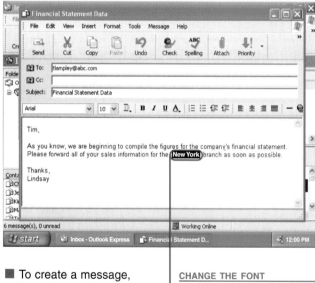

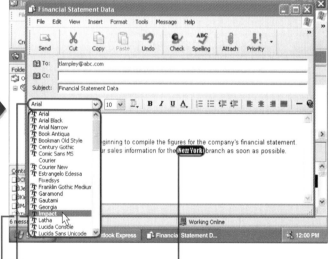

■ To create a message, perform steps **1** to **5** on page 209.

CHANGE THE FONT

1 To select the text you want to change to a different font, drag the mouse I over the text until the text is highlighted.

2 Click ⌄ in this area to display a list of the available fonts.

3 Click the font you want to use.

■ The text changes to the new font.

■ To deselect text, click outside the selected area.

How can I bold, italicize or underline text in a message?

To select the text you want to bold, italicize or underline, drag the mouse I over the text until the text is highlighted. Then click the bold (**B**), italic (*I*) or underline (U) button. To remove a bold, italic or underline style from text, repeat these steps.

Why does Outlook Express underline and change the color of e-mail and Web page addresses I type in a message?

When you type an e-mail or Web page address in a message, Outlook Express automatically converts the address to a link. The person who receives your message will be able to click the link to quickly send a message to the e-mail address or open the Web page you specified.

jsmith@abc.com

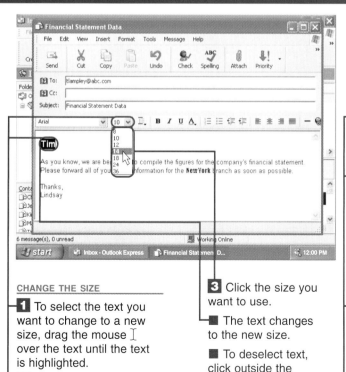

CHANGE THE SIZE

1 To select the text you want to change to a new size, drag the mouse I over the text until the text is highlighted.

2 Click this area to display a list of the available sizes.

3 Click the size you want to use.

■ The text changes to the new size.

■ To deselect text, click outside the selected area.

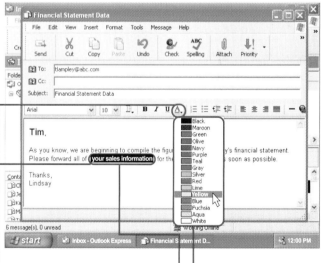

CHANGE THE COLOR

1 To select the text you want to display in a different color, drag the mouse I over the text until the text is highlighted.

2 Click A to display a list of the available colors.

3 Click the color you want to use.

■ The text appears in the color you selected.

■ To deselect text, click outside the selected area.

SEND A MESSAGE DISPLAYING A DESIGN

You can send a message that displays an attractive design. Outlook Express includes several designs that you can choose from.

If you send a message with a design to a person who does not use Outlook Express, the design of the message may not be shown or may be shown in a different way.

SEND A MESSAGE DISPLAYING A DESIGN

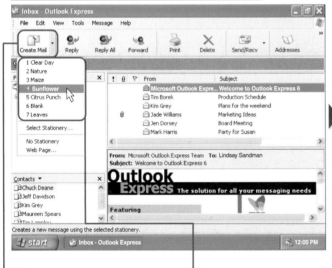

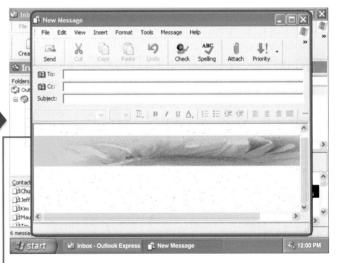

1 To send a message that displays a design, click ⁀ in this area to display a list of the available designs.

2 Click the design you want to use.

■ The New Message window appears, displaying the design you selected.

■ To complete and send the message, perform steps **2** to **6** on page 209.

212

When sending a message, you can change the priority of the message to indicate its importance.

You can choose a high, normal or low priority for a message. When a person receives the message, a symbol will appear beside a high (!) or low (↓) priority message. A normal priority message will not display a symbol.

If you send a message to a person who does not use Outlook Express, the priority of the message may not be shown or may be shown in a different way.

CHANGE MESSAGE PRIORITY

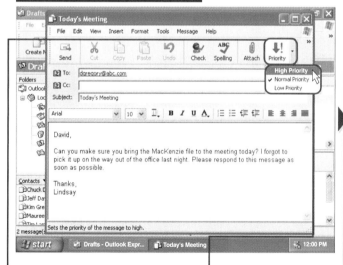

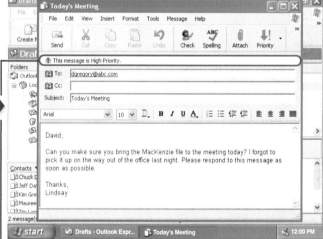

■ To create a message, perform steps **1** to **5** on page 209.

1 To change the priority of the message, click ▾ in this area to display a list of the available priority options.

2 Click the priority option you want to use.

■ If you selected **High Priority** or **Low Priority**, Windows indicates the priority in this area.

■ If you want to return the message to a normal priority, repeat steps **1** and **2**, selecting **Normal Priority** in step **2**.

MARK A MESSAGE AS UNREAD

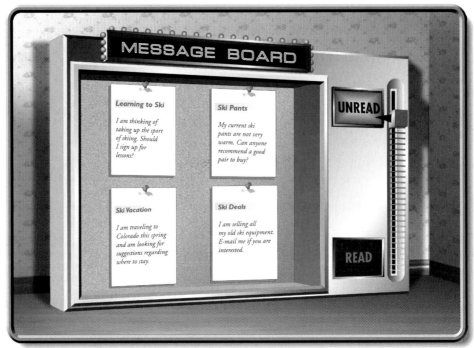

You can make a message appear as if you have not read the message. Marking a message as unread can help remind you to review the message again at a later time.

MARK A MESSAGE AS UNREAD

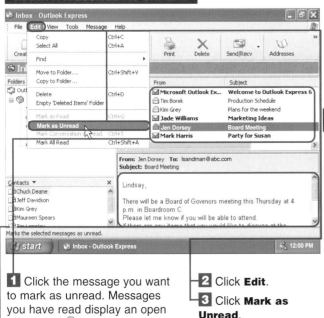

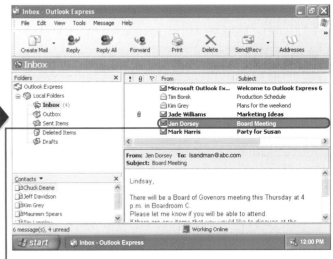

1 Click the message you want to mark as unread. Messages you have read display an open envelope (📂) and appear in regular type.

■ This area displays the contents of the message.

2 Click **Edit**.

3 Click **Mark as Unread**.

■ The message appears unread. Unread messages display a closed envelope (📧) and appear in **bold** type.

■ To once again display a message as read, repeat steps **1** to **3**, except select **Mark as Read** in step **3**.

You can have Outlook Express display a flag beside an important message to make the message stand out. Flagging a message can help you quickly find the message at a later time.

A staff meeting will be held in Conference Room A at 4:10 p.m. on each of the following days:
June 17th, 2002
July 7th, 2002
August 23rd, 2002
September 15th, 2002
All staff members must attend these meetings!

David Walker
President

FLAG A MESSAGE

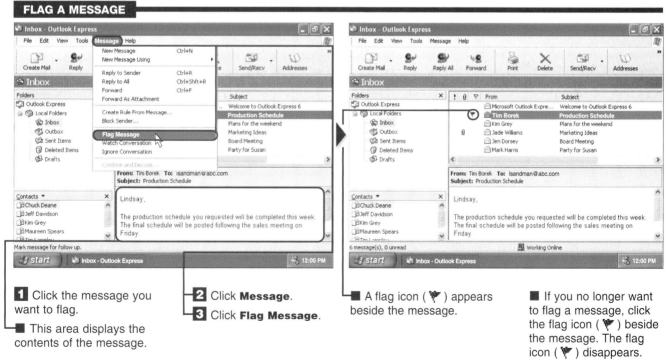

1 Click the message you want to flag.

■ This area displays the contents of the message.

2 Click **Message**.

3 Click **Flag Message**.

■ A flag icon (🚩) appears beside the message.

■ If you no longer want to flag a message, click the flag icon (🚩) beside the message. The flag icon (🚩) disappears.

CHANGE HOW OFTEN OUTLOOK EXPRESS CHECKS FOR MESSAGES

You can change how often Outlook Express automatically checks for new messages.

Outlook Express automatically checks for new messages every 30 minutes.

By default, if you are not connected to the Internet when Outlook Express checks for new messages, Outlook Express will not connect. You can choose to have Outlook Express connect to the Internet to check for new messages only when you are not working offline or always connect when checking for new messages.

Check for messages every:

4 minutes

CHANGE HOW OFTEN OUTLOOK EXPRESS CHECKS FOR MESSAGES

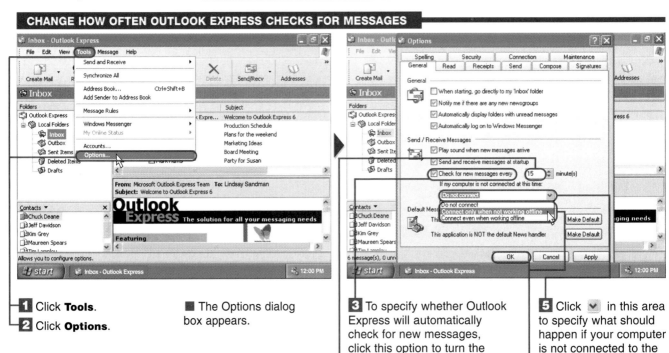

1 Click **Tools**.

2 Click **Options**.

■ The Options dialog box appears.

3 To specify whether Outlook Express will automatically check for new messages, click this option to turn the option on (☑) or off (☐).

4 Double-click this area and type how often you want Outlook Express to check for new messages.

5 Click ☑ in this area to specify what should happen if your computer is not connected to the Internet when checking for new messages.

6 Click the option you want to use.

7 Click **OK**.

216

EMPTY THE DELETED ITEMS FOLDER

You can delete all the messages in your Deleted Items folder. Outlook Express will permanently remove the messages from your computer.

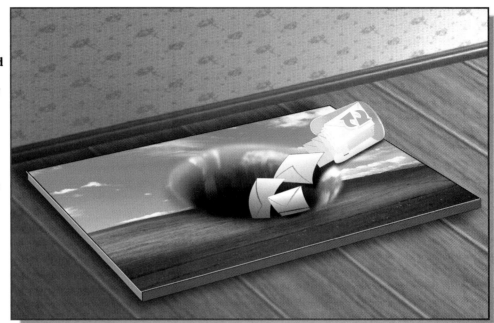

The Deleted Items folder stores all the messages you have deleted. You should regularly empty the Deleted Items folder to save space on your computer.

Before emptying your Deleted Items folder, make sure the folder does not contain any messages you want to keep.

EMPTY THE DELETED ITEMS FOLDER

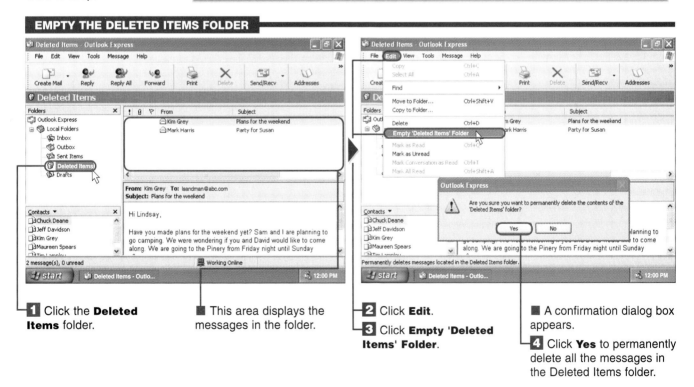

1 Click the **Deleted Items** folder.

■ This area displays the messages in the folder.

2 Click **Edit**.

3 Click **Empty 'Deleted Items' Folder**.

■ A confirmation dialog box appears.

4 Click **Yes** to permanently delete all the messages in the Deleted Items folder.

CREATE A NEW FOLDER

You can create a folder in Outlook Express to help you organize your messages.

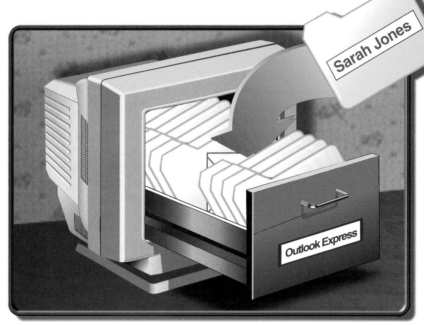

Creating folders can help you keep related messages together so you can easily find messages of interest. For example, you can create a folder to store all the messages for a specific client or project.

CREATE A NEW FOLDER

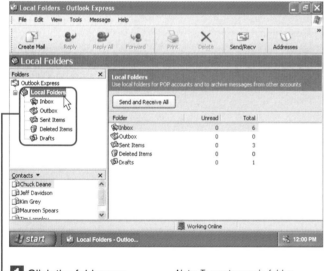

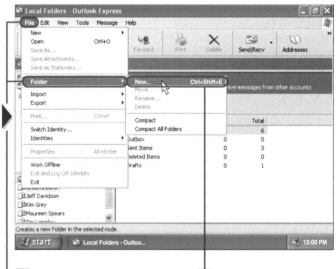

1 Click the folder you want to contain the new folder.

*Note: To create a main folder, click **Local Folders**. To create a new folder within another folder, click the folder, such as Inbox.*

2 Click **File**.

3 Click **Folder**.

4 Click **New**.

How do I rename a folder?

Click the folder you want to rename and then press the F2 key. In the dialog box that appears, type a new name for the folder and then press the Enter key. You can rename only folders that you created.

How do I delete a folder I created?

Click the folder you want to delete and then press the Delete key. In the confirmation dialog box that appears, click **Yes** to delete the folder. If the folder contains messages, the messages will also be deleted. Outlook Express places a deleted folder in the Deleted Items folder. To remove the folder from your computer, you can delete the folder from the Deleted Items folder.

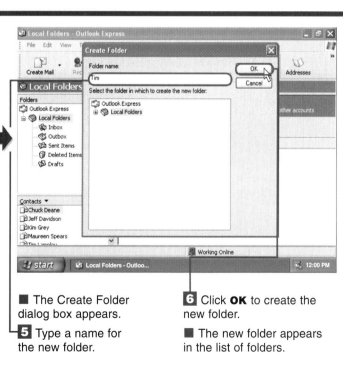

■ The Create Folder dialog box appears.

5 Type a name for the new folder.

6 Click **OK** to create the new folder.

■ The new folder appears in the list of folders.

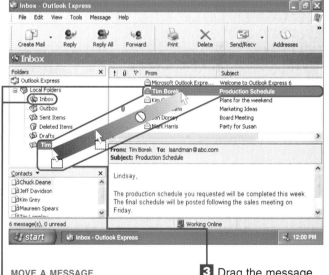

**MOVE A MESSAGE
TO ANOTHER FOLDER**

1 Click the folder that contains the message you want to move to another folder.

2 Position the mouse ⟋ over the message you want to move.

3 Drag the message to the folder you want to store the message.

■ Outlook Express moves the message to the folder.

FIND MESSAGES

If you cannot find a message you want to review, you can have Outlook Express search for the message.

For example, you can search for a message you received from a specific person or a message that contains specific text.

FIND MESSAGES

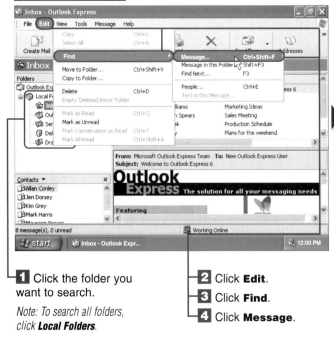

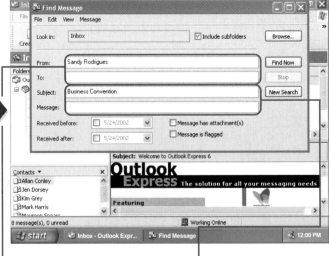

1 Click the folder you want to search.

*Note: To search all folders, click **Local Folders**.*

2 Click **Edit**.

3 Click **Find**.

4 Click **Message**.

■ The Find Message window appears.

5 To find messages you received from or sent to a specific person, click the appropriate area and then type the name of the person.

6 To find messages that have a specific subject or contain specific text, click the appropriate area and then type the subject or text.

Is there another way I can find a message of interest?

You can sort your messages to find a message you want to review. You can sort messages by name, subject or date.

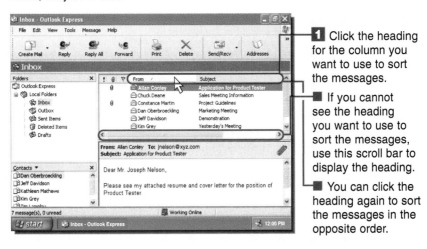

1 Click the heading for the column you want to use to sort the messages.

■ If you cannot see the heading you want to use to sort the messages, use this scroll bar to display the heading.

■ You can click the heading again to sort the messages in the opposite order.

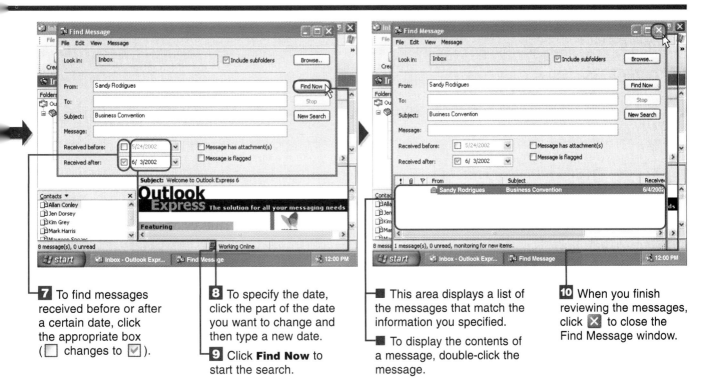

7 To find messages received before or after a certain date, click the appropriate box (☐ changes to ☑).

8 To specify the date, click the part of the date you want to change and then type a new date.

9 Click **Find Now** to start the search.

■ This area displays a list of the messages that match the information you specified.

■ To display the contents of a message, double-click the message.

10 When you finish reviewing the messages, click ☒ to close the Find Message window.

SORT INCOMING MESSAGES

You can have Outlook Express sort the messages you receive. Sorting incoming messages allows Outlook Express to organize incoming messages before you read them. You must create a rule that explains how you want Outlook Express to sort incoming messages. For example, you can create a rule that moves messages you receive from certain people to a specific folder.

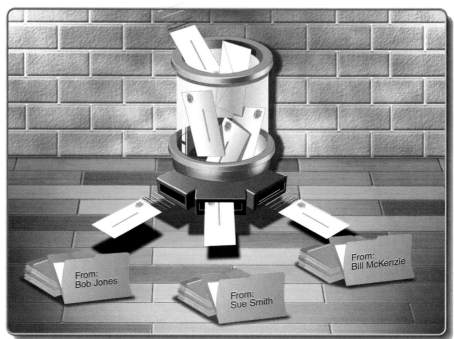

SORT INCOMING MESSAGES

1 Click **Tools**.

2 Click **Message Rules**.

3 Click **Mail**.

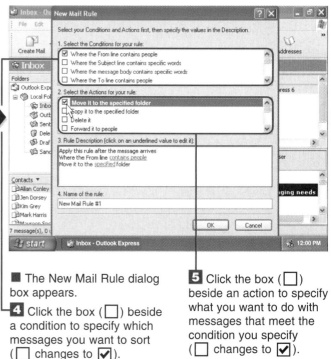

■ The New Mail Rule dialog box appears.

4 Click the box (☐) beside a condition to specify which messages you want to sort (☐ changes to ☑).

5 Click the box (☐) beside an action to specify what you want to do with messages that meet the condition you specify (☐ changes to ☑).

222

Why does the Message Rules dialog box appear instead of the New Mail Rule dialog box?

If you have already created a rule to sort incoming messages, the Message Rules dialog box will appear after you perform steps **1** to **3** below. To display the New Mail Rule dialog box so you can create a new rule, click the New button in the Message Rules dialog box.

Can I sort incoming messages using more than one condition?

Yes. You can sort incoming messages using as many conditions as you need. For example, you can sort messages from certain people that contain specific words. When creating a rule, click the check box (☐) beside each condition you want to use to sort messages (☐ changes to ☑). Outlook Express will sort only incoming messages that meet all the conditions you specify.

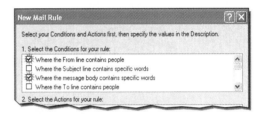

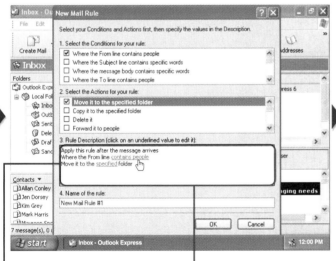

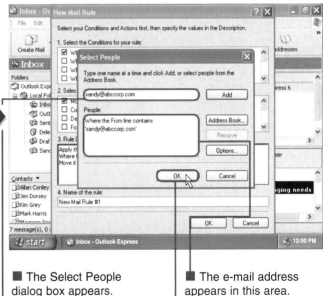

■ This area displays the condition and action you selected. You need to specify additional information for text that appears underlined and blue in color.

Note: In this example, Outlook Express will move messages you receive from certain people to a specific folder.

6 Click the first instance of text that appears underlined and blue in color to specify the required information.

■ The Select People dialog box appears.

Note: The dialog box that appears depends on the text you selected in step 6.

7 Type an e-mail address you want to apply the rule to and then press the Enter key.

■ The e-mail address appears in this area.

8 To specify additional e-mail addresses, repeat step 7 for each address.

9 Click **OK**.

CONTINUED

223

SORT INCOMING MESSAGES

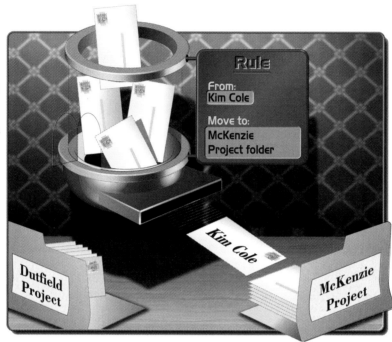

When creating a rule, you must specify information for the action you want Outlook Express to perform on messages that meet a certain condition.

For example, if you are creating a rule to move messages from certain people to a specific folder, you must specify which folder you want to move the messages to.

A rule you create will only affect new messages you receive.

SORT INCOMING MESSAGES (CONTINUED)

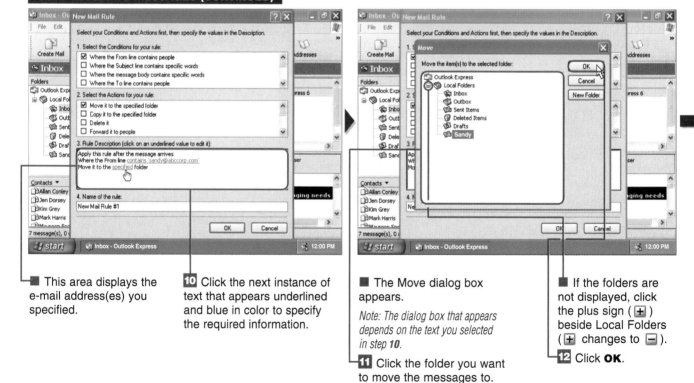

■ This area displays the e-mail address(es) you specified.

10 Click the next instance of text that appears underlined and blue in color to specify the required information.

■ The Move dialog box appears.

Note: The dialog box that appears depends on the text you selected in step 10.

11 Click the folder you want to move the messages to.

■ If the folders are not displayed, click the plus sign (⊞) beside Local Folders (⊞ changes to ⊟).

12 Click **OK**.

How do I remove a rule I no longer need?

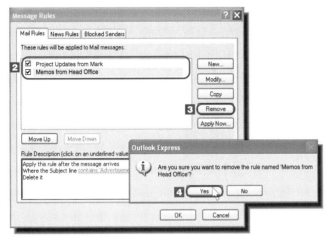

2 Click the name of the rule you want to remove.

3 Click **Remove**.

■ A confirmation dialog box appears.

4 Click **Yes** to remove the rule.

1 To remove a rule you no longer want to apply to incoming messages, perform steps **1** to **3** on page 222.

■ The Message Rules dialog box appears.

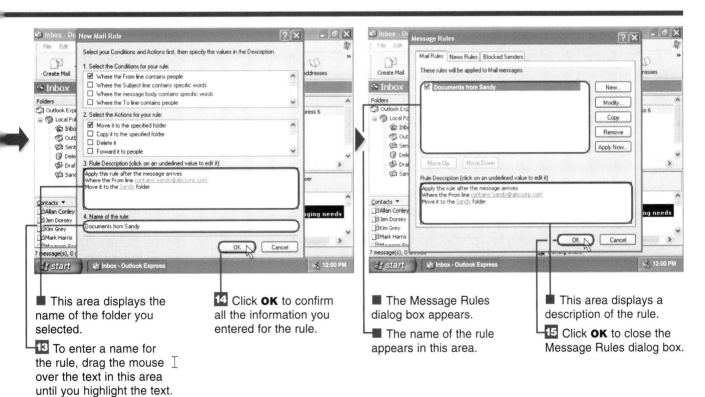

■ This area displays the name of the folder you selected.

13 To enter a name for the rule, drag the mouse over the text in this area until you highlight the text. Then type a name.

14 Click **OK** to confirm all the information you entered for the rule.

■ The Message Rules dialog box appears.

■ The name of the rule appears in this area.

■ This area displays a description of the rule.

15 Click **OK** to close the Message Rules dialog box.

Contact List

  Bob
  Sandy
  Dylan
  Richard
  Maxine
  Ann
  John
  Dave

Messenger Service

Contact List

  James
  Ruth
  Dana

Messenger Service

Windows Messenger

PASSPORT

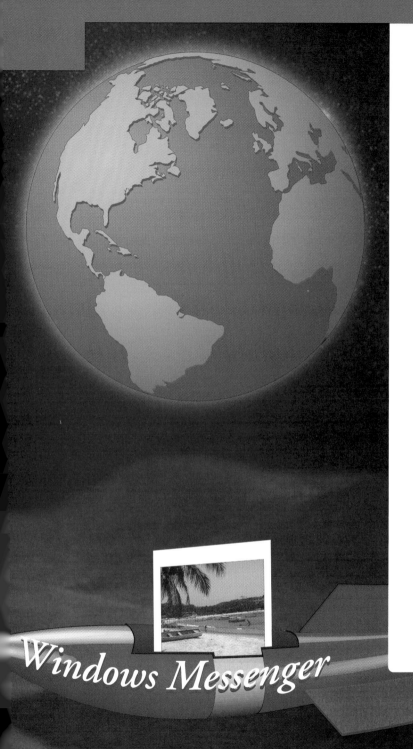

CHAPTER 12

Exchange Instant Messages

You can use Windows Messenger to communicate and work with other people on the Internet. This chapter shows you how to send an instant message, share a program and call a computer to have a voice conversation with another person.

Windows Messenger

START WINDOWS MESSENGER

You can use Windows Messenger to see when your friends are online and exchange instant messages with them.

START WINDOWS MESSENGER

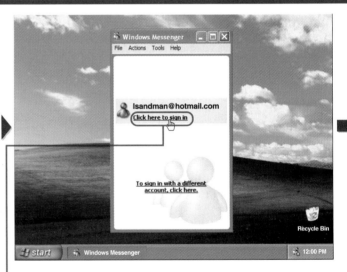

■ The Windows Messenger icon indicates if you are signed in (👤) or signed out (👥) of Windows Messenger.

Note: If the Windows Messenger icon is hidden, you can click ◀ on the taskbar to display the icon.

1 Double-click 👤 or 👥 to start Windows Messenger.

■ The Windows Messenger window appears.

2 Click this link to sign in to Windows Messenger.

■ If you are not currently connected to the Internet, a dialog box may appear, allowing you to connect.

Note: If you are already signed in to Windows Messenger, you do not need to perform step 2.

Why does a wizard appear when I start Windows Messenger?

The first time you start Windows Messenger, a wizard appears to help you add a Passport to your user account. You must add a Passport to your user account to use Windows Messenger. Follow the instructions in the wizard to add a Passport to your user account.

Why does my Windows Messenger window look different than the Window shown below?

You may be using an older version of Windows Messenger. When you sign in to Windows Messenger, a link may appear at the top of the window that you can click to obtain the latest version of Windows Messenger. You can also visit the messenger.microsoft.com Web site to obtain the latest version of Windows Messenger.

■ If you have added people to your contact list, this area displays the contacts that are currently online and not online.

Note: To add people to your contact list, see page 230.

SIGN OUT OF WINDOWS MESSENGER

When you finish using Windows Messenger, you can sign out of the service.

1 In the Windows Messenger window, click **File**.

2 Click **Sign Out**.

3 Click ✕ to close the Windows Messenger window.

ADD A CONTACT

You can add people to your contact list to see when they are online and available to exchange instant messages.

Windows Messenger allows you to add up to 150 people to your contact list.

■ This area displays each person you have added to your contact list. You can see the contacts that are currently **online** and **not online**.

*Note: If you cannot see the contacts that are currently online or not online, click (⊗) beside **Online** or **Not Online** (⊗ changes to ⊗).*

1 Click **Add a Contact** to add a person to your contact list.

■ The Add a Contact wizard appears.

2 Click this option to add a contact by specifying the person's e-mail address (○ changes to ◉).

3 Click **Next** to continue.

Who can I add to my contact list?

Each person you want to add to your contact list requires a Passport. A Passport can be obtained when Windows Messenger is set up on a computer. If a person you want to add to your contact list uses a program other than Windows Messenger to send instant messages, the person can obtain a Passport at the passport.com Web site.

How do I remove a person from my contact list?

In the Windows Messenger window, click the name of the person you want to remove from your contact list and then press the Delete key. In the confirmation dialog box that appears, click **Yes** to remove the person from your contact list. People you remove from your contact list will still be able to contact you unless you block them. To block a person from contacting you, see page 246.

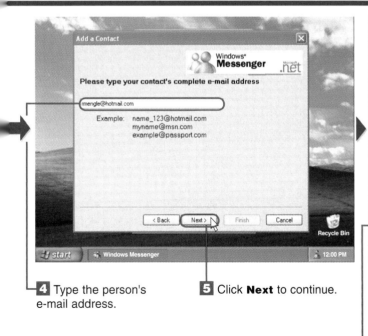

4 Type the person's e-mail address.

5 Click **Next** to continue.

■ This message appears if the wizard successfully added the person to your contact list.

6 Click **Finish** to close the wizard.

■ The person appears in your contact list.

Note: Windows Messenger will notify the person that you added them to your contact list.

SEND AN INSTANT MESSAGE

You can send an instant message to a person in your contact list. The person must be currently signed in to Windows Messenger.

For information on adding a person to your contact list, see page 230.

When sending instant messages, never give out your password or credit card information.

SEND AN INSTANT MESSAGE

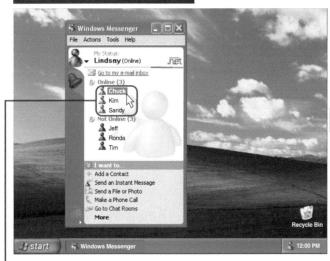

1 Double-click the name of the person you want to send an instant message to.

Note: The person must be currently online.

■ The Conversation window appears.

2 Click this area and type your message.

Note: A message can be up to 400 characters long.

3 To send the message, click **Send** or press the Enter key.

Note: To start a new paragraph while typing a message, press and hold down the Shift key as you press the Enter key.

How can I express emotions in my instant messages?

You can use emoticons in your instant messages to express emotions, such as happiness ( ) or sadness ( ). To add an emoticon to a message, click in the Conversation window and then click the emoticon you want to add.

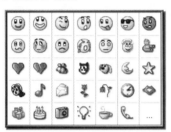

What happens when I receive an instant message?

When you receive an instant message that is not part of an ongoing conversation, your computer makes a sound and briefly displays a box containing the first part of the message. The Conversation button also flashes on the taskbar. To display the message, you can click inside the box or click the Conversation button on the taskbar.

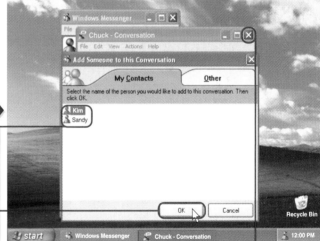

■ This area displays the message you sent and the ongoing conversation.

■ This area displays the date and time you last received a message from the other person. If the other person is typing a message, this area indicates that the person is typing.

ADD A PERSON TO A CONVERSATION

1 To add a person to your conversation, click **Invite Someone to this Conversation**.

Note: You can exchange instant messages with up to four other people at once.

■ The Add Someone to this Conversation dialog box appears.

2 Click the name of the person you want to add to the conversation.

3 Click **OK** to add the person.

■ The person you added will receive the next message in the conversation.

4 When you finish exchanging messages, click to close the Conversation window.

*Note: A dialog box may appear, stating that you will not receive future instant messages from this conversation. Click **OK** to close the dialog box.*

233

FORMAT TEXT IN INSTANT MESSAGES

You can change the
format of text in all
the instant messages
you send.

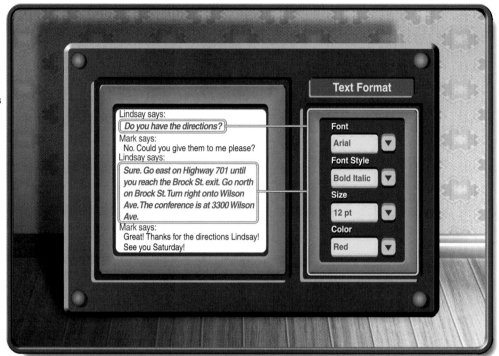

You cannot change
the format of text for
only part of an instant
message.

FORMAT TEXT IN INSTANT MESSAGES

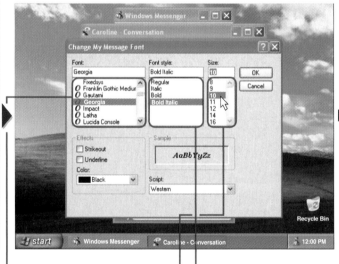

1 While exchanging instant
messages with another
person, click **A Font** to change
the format of all the text you
type in your instant messages.

*Note: To exchange instant
messages with another person,
see page 232.*

■ The Change My
Message Font dialog
box appears.

2 To change the font,
click the font you want
to use.

3 To change the font
style, click the font style
you want to use.

4 To change the text
size, click the size you
want to use.

How can I return to the text format Windows Messenger originally used?

Windows Messenger initially uses the Microsoft Sans Serif font, Regular font style, a text size of 10 and the color black to format the text in your instant messages. To return to these settings at any time, perform steps **1** to **7** below.

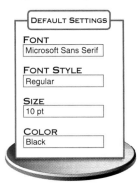

DEFAULT SETTINGS

FONT
Microsoft Sans Serif

FONT STYLE
Regular

SIZE
10 pt

COLOR
Black

Will other people see the new format I selected for the text in my instant messages?

After you change the format of text, people who receive your instant messages will see the new font, style and color you selected. If you selected a new text size, the new size will affect the appearance of text in your Conversation window only. Other people will not see the new text size.

LINDSAY

MARK

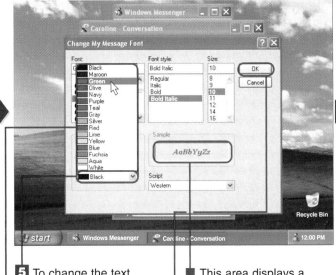

5 To change the text color, click this area to display a list of the available colors.

6 Click the color you want to use.

■ This area displays a sample of the way the text will appear.

7 Click **OK** to confirm your changes.

■ Windows Messenger uses the new format for all the text you type in the current instant message and all your future instant messages.

Note: If you selected a new text size, the new size will affect all the text displayed in the Conversation window.

You can save an instant message conversation as a file on your computer so you can later review the contents of the conversation.

If you do not save an instant message conversation, you will lose the contents of the conversation when you close the Conversation window.

SAVE AN INSTANT MESSAGE CONVERSATION

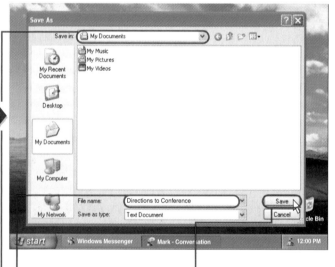

1 While exchanging instant messages with another person, click **File** to save the text for the conversation.

Note: To exchange instant messages with another person, see page 232.

2 Click **Save**.

3 Type a name for the file that will store the text for the conversation.

■ This area shows the location where Windows Messenger will store the file. You can click this area to change the location.

4 Click **Save** to save the file on your computer.

■ To later open the file, locate the file on your computer and then double-click the file.

You can change your online status to let other people know that you are currently not available.

When you change your online status, people can still send you instant messages, unless you select the Appear Offline status.

When you do not use your computer for more than 10 minutes, Windows Messenger automatically changes your online status to Away. When you resume using your computer, your status will automatically return to Online.

CHANGE YOUR ONLINE STATUS

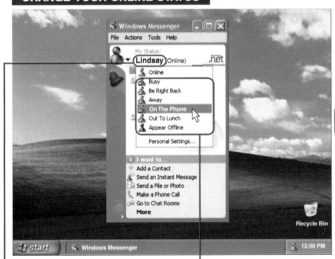

1 Click your name at the top of the Windows Messenger window.

2 Click the option that best describes your online status.

■ Windows Messenger changes your online status. The icon and text on either side of your name indicate your current online status.

■ If you appear in another person's contact list, your new online status will appear beside your name in the person's Windows Messenger window.

■ To once again set your status to Online, repeat steps **1** and **2**, selecting **Online** in step **2**.

ORGANIZE CONTACTS INTO GROUPS

You can organize your contacts into groups, such as Coworkers, Family, Friends and Other Contacts. Organizing your contacts into groups can help you quickly find the contacts you want to communicate with.

By default, Windows Messenger organizes your contacts by their current status, which indicates whether they are online or not online.

ORGANIZE CONTACTS INTO GROUPS

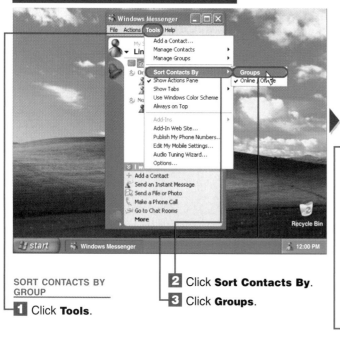

SORT CONTACTS BY GROUP

1 Click **Tools**.

2 Click **Sort Contacts By**.

3 Click **Groups**.

■ Windows Messenger sorts your contacts into groups.

■ The color of the icon beside each contact indicates if the contact is currently online (👤) or not online (👤).

■ To hide or display the contacts in a group, click ⊗ or ⊗ beside the name of the group.

■ To once again sort contacts by online status, repeat steps **1** to **3**, selecting **Online / Offline** in step **3**.

Can I rename a group?

Yes. Right-click the name of the group you want to rename and then click **Rename Group** on the menu that appears. Type a new name for the group and then press the Enter key. You cannot rename the Other Contacts group.

How do I create a new group?

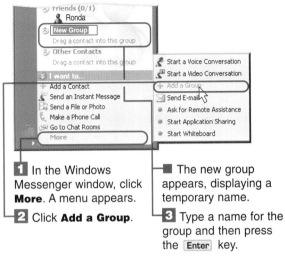

1 In the Windows Messenger window, click **More**. A menu appears.

2 Click **Add a Group**.

■ The new group appears, displaying a temporary name.

3 Type a name for the group and then press the Enter key.

Note: You can move contacts to the new group.

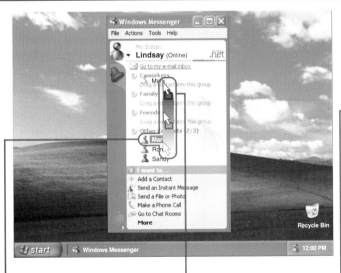

MOVE A CONTACT TO A DIFFERENT GROUP

1 Click the contact you want to move to a different group. The contact is highlighted.

2 Position the mouse ⟍ over the contact.

3 Drag the contact to the group you want to add the contact to.

Note: Windows Messenger adds an orange highlight to the group the contact will move to.

DELETE A GROUP

1 Click the group you want to delete.

2 Press the Delete key to delete the group.

Note: You can delete only a group that does not contain contacts. If a group you want to delete contains contacts, you must first move the contacts to another group. You cannot delete the Other Contacts group.

USING THE WHITEBOARD

When using Windows Messenger, you can work on a Whiteboard with another person. You can both draw images on the Whiteboard that will instantly appear on both computer screens.

You can use the Whiteboard to help describe, create and edit a project with another person.

You can use the Whiteboard only with a person who is using a computer with Windows XP installed.

USING THE WHITEBOARD

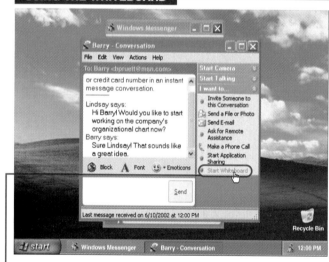

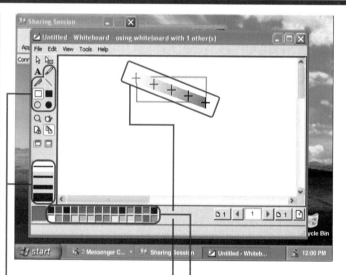

1 While exchanging instant messages with another person, click **Start Whiteboard**.

Note: To exchange instant messages with another person, see page 232.

■ Windows Messenger sends the other person an invitation to use the Whiteboard. When the other person accepts the invitation, the Whiteboard window and the Sharing Session window appear.

DRAW A LINE OR SHAPE

1 Click the tool for the type of object you want to draw.

2 Click a width for the object.

Note: The width options are not available for some tools.

3 Click a color for the object.

4 Position the mouse ⬚ over the area where you want to begin drawing the object (⬚ changes to ✎, + or ✎). Then drag the mouse until the object appears the way you want.

What tools can I use to draw lines and shapes on the Whiteboard?

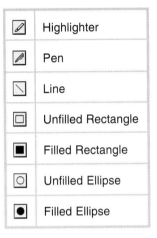 Highlighter	
	Pen
	Line
	Unfilled Rectangle
	Filled Rectangle
	Unfilled Ellipse
	Filled Ellipse

How do I point out or delete an object on the Whiteboard?

Point Out an Object

To point out an object on the Whiteboard, click ☞ to display a hand (☞) on the Whiteboard. Position the mouse ⬉ over the hand and then drag the hand to the area you want to point out. To remove the hand, click ☞ again.

Delete an Object

To delete an object or text on the Whiteboard, click and then click the object or text you want to delete.

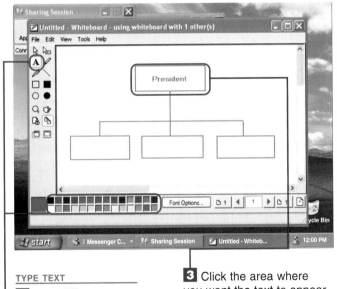

TYPE TEXT

1 Click **A** to add text to the Whiteboard.

2 Click a color for the text.

3 Click the area where you want the text to appear. Then type the text.

4 Click outside the text area when you finish typing the text.

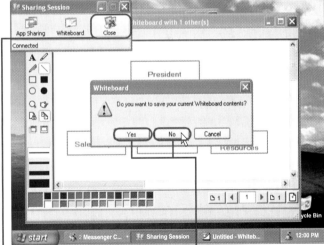

CLOSE THE WHITEBOARD

1 When you finish using the Whiteboard, click **Close** in the Sharing Session window to close the connection with the other person's computer.

■ A dialog box appears, asking if you want to save the contents of the Whiteboard.

2 Click **Yes** or **No** to specify if you want to save the Whiteboard contents.

*Note: If you select **Yes**, a dialog box will appear. Type a name for the file that will store the Whiteboard contents and then press the **Enter** key.*

SHARE A PROGRAM

When using Windows Messenger, you can share a program with another person. Sharing a program allows you and the other person to work together on the same document.

When sharing a program, the other person's computer does not need to have the shared program installed, but the computer must use Windows XP.

When sharing a program, only one person can control and make changes in the program at a time. When a person makes changes in a program, the changes will appear on both computer screens.

SHARE A PROGRAM

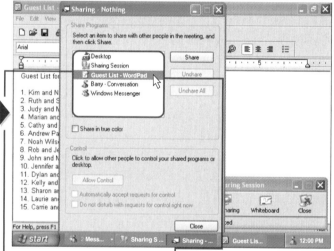

1 While exchanging instant messages with another person, click **Start Application Sharing**.

Note: To exchange instant messages with another person, see page 232.

■ Windows Messenger sends the other person an invitation to start sharing programs. When the other person accepts the invitation, the Sharing Session window and the Sharing window appear.

2 Start the program you want to share. In this example, the WordPad program was started.

■ The Sharing window lists the programs running on your computer that you can share.

Note: If you cannot clearly see the Sharing window, click its button on the taskbar.

3 Double-click the program you want to share.

How can I ensure the other person can clearly view a program I am sharing?

When sharing a program, make sure the shared program appears in front of all other windows on your screen. If another window appears in front of the shared program, a pattern of colored squares will cover the shared program on the other person's screen. To place the shared program in front of all other windows, click anywhere inside the program.

How can the other person ask for control of a program I am sharing?

In the window for the shared program, the other person can click the **Control** menu and then select **Request Control** to ask for control of the program you are sharing. The Request Control option is available only if you chose to allow the other person to work with the program in step **4** below.

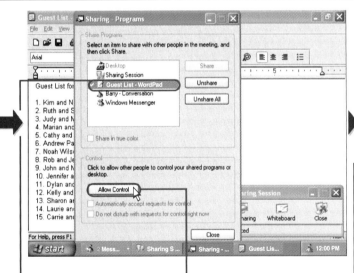

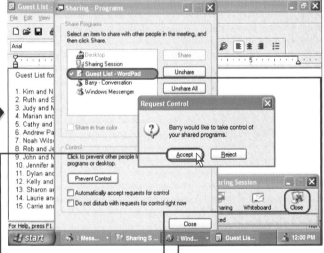

■ A check mark (✔) appears beside the program you selected to share.

■ When you work in the shared program, the other person will be able to see the changes you make.

4 If you want the other person to be able to work with the program, click **Allow Control** in the Sharing window.

*Note: When you click **Allow Control**, the button changes to **Prevent Control**. You can click **Prevent Control** at any time to stop allowing the other person to work with the program.*

■ A dialog box appears when the other person wants to control the program.

5 Click **Accept** to allow the person to take control of the program and make changes.

Note: To regain control of the program so you can make changes, click your mouse.

■ To stop sharing a program, double-click the program in the Sharing window. The check mark (✔) beside the program disappears.

6 When you finish sharing programs, click **Close** in the Sharing Session window.

CALL A COMPUTER

You can call a computer to talk to another person over the Internet. You can also call a computer to view live video of the other person during a voice conversation.

Did you win your baseball game this afternoon?

When you call a computer to talk to another person, you avoid long-distance telephone charges.

If your computer is connected to a network with a firewall, you may not be able to call a computer outside the network.

CALL A COMPUTER USING VOICE

1 While exchanging instant messages with another person, click **Start Talking**.

Note: To exchange instant messages with another person, see page 232.

■ Windows Messenger sends the other person an invitation to start a voice conversation.

■ This message appears when the other person accepts the invitation.

2 Use your microphone to talk to the other person.

3 To decrease or increase the volume of your speakers, drag this slider ( ) to the left or right.

4 To decrease or increase the volume of your microphone, drag this slider ( ) to the left or right.

5 When you want to end the voice conversation, click **Stop Talking**.

244

What hardware and software do I need to call a computer?

To call a computer and have a voice conversation, your computer and the computer you call must both have sound capabilities and a microphone. To send video of yourself to the other person during a voice conversation, you must have a Web camera connected to your computer. To view video of the other person, the other person's computer must also have a Web camera connected. Your computer and the other person's computer must both use Windows XP to have a video and voice conversation.

Why does the Audio and Video Tuning Wizard appear when I call a computer?

The first time you call a computer, the Audio and Video Tuning Wizard appears on your screen to help you verify that your speakers, microphone and Web camera are working properly. Follow the instructions on your screen to complete the wizard.

CALL A COMPUTER USING VIDEO AND VOICE

1 While exchanging instant messages with another person, click **Start Camera**.

Note: To exchange instant messages with another person, see page 232.

■ Windows Messenger sends the other person an invitation to start a video and voice conversation.

■ This message appears when the other person accepts the invitation.

2 Use your microphone to talk to the other person.

■ This area displays the video sent by the other person's camera and a smaller image of the video sent by your camera.

3 When you want to end the video and voice conversation, click **Stop Camera**.

BLOCK PEOPLE

You can block
a person to
prevent the
person from
viewing your
online status
and sending
you instant
messages.

When you block a
person, the person will
not know that you have
blocked them. You will
always appear to be
offline to the person.

BLOCK PEOPLE

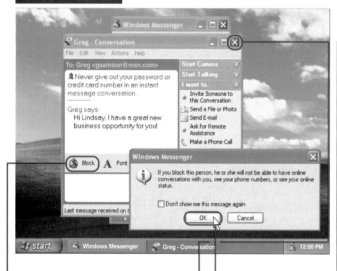

1 When you receive an instant
message from a person you do
not want to receive messages
from, click [Block].

■ A dialog box appears, stating
that if you block the person, the
person will not be able to send
you instant messages or view
your online status.

2 Click **OK** to block
the person.

3 Click ✕ to close
the Conversation
window.

VIEW YOUR BLOCK LIST

1 In the Windows
Messenger window,
click **Tools**.

2 Click **Options**.

■ The Options dialog
box appears.

246

Can a person who does not appear in the My Allow List contact me?

Yes. Anyone who knows the e-mail address you use with Windows Messenger can contact you, as long as you have not blocked the person. If you want only the people in your My Allow List to be able to contact you, perform steps **1** to **5** starting on page 246 to move **All other users** from the My Allow List to the My Block List. Then click **OK**.

How will Windows Messenger alert me when a person adds me to their contact list?

When a person adds you to their contact list, a dialog box appears on your screen. You can click an option to specify if you want to allow the person to contact you or if you want to block the person (○ changes to ◉). To confirm your choice, press the `Enter` key. A person you allow to contact you will be added to your contact list and My Allow List. A person you block will be added to your My Block List.

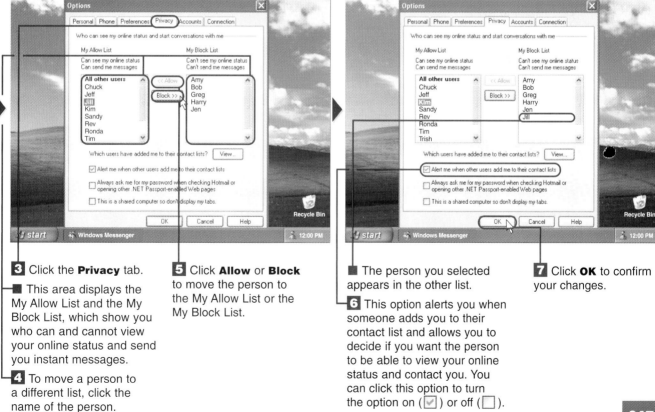

3 Click the **Privacy** tab.

■ This area displays the My Allow List and the My Block List, which show you who can and cannot view your online status and send you instant messages.

4 To move a person to a different list, click the name of the person.

5 Click **Allow** or **Block** to move the person to the My Allow List or the My Block List.

■ The person you selected appears in the other list.

6 This option alerts you when someone adds you to their contact list and allows you to decide if you want the person to be able to view your online status and contact you. You can click this option to turn the option on (☑) or off (☐).

7 Click **OK** to confirm your changes.

CHAPTER 13

Work With Newsgroups

Newsgroups are discussion groups on the Internet that allow people with common interests to communicate. This chapter shows you how to subscribe to newsgroups and read and post newsgroup messages.

rec.autos

SET UP A NEWS ACCOUNT

You must set up a news account before you can use Outlook Express to read or post messages in newsgroups.

Newsgroups are discussion groups on the Internet that allow people with common interests to communicate with each other.

SET UP A NEWS ACCOUNT

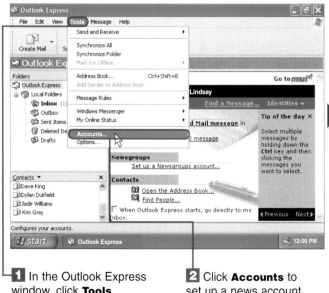

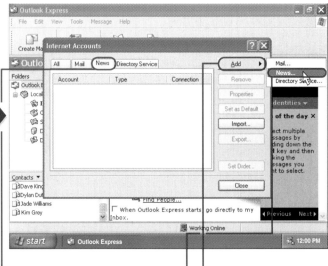

1 In the Outlook Express window, click **Tools**.

Note: To display the Outlook Express window, see page 208.

2 Click **Accounts** to set up a news account.

■ The Internet Accounts dialog box appears.

3 Click the **News** tab to display a list of the news accounts set up on your computer.

4 Click **Add** to set up a news account.

5 Click **News**.

When setting up a news account, do I have to use my real name and e-mail address?

No. You do not have to use your real name and e-mail address. Specifying a false e-mail address will help you avoid receiving junk e-mail messages. If you specify a false e-mail address, remember to include your real e-mail address in the body of each message you post to newsgroups if you want other readers to be able to contact you.

Can I set up more than one news account?

Yes. You can set up multiple news accounts in Outlook Express. Setting up multiple news accounts allows you to access newsgroups from different sources. For example, you could set up one news account to access newsgroups offered by your Internet service provider and another news account to access newsgroups offered by a company to provide product support.

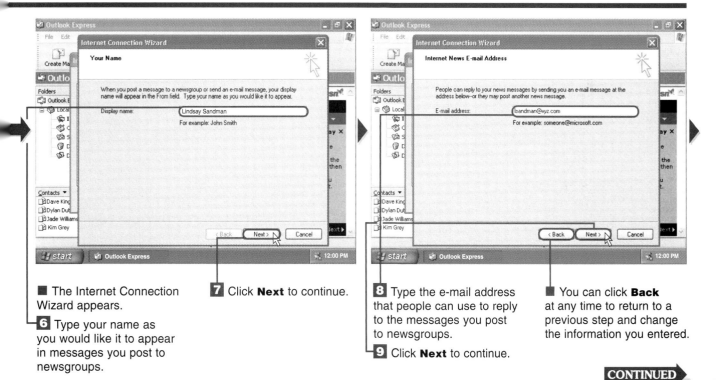

■ The Internet Connection Wizard appears.

6 Type your name as you would like it to appear in messages you post to newsgroups.

7 Click **Next** to continue.

8 Type the e-mail address that people can use to reply to the messages you post to newsgroups.

9 Click **Next** to continue.

■ You can click **Back** at any time to return to a previous step and change the information you entered.

CONTINUED ▶

SET UP A NEWS ACCOUNT

When setting up a news account, you must specify the name of the news server you want to connect to.

News servers are computers that store newsgroups. News servers are usually run and maintained by Internet service providers, which are companies that provide access to the Internet. If you do not know the name of your news server, contact your Internet service provider.

SET UP A NEWS ACCOUNT (CONTINUED)

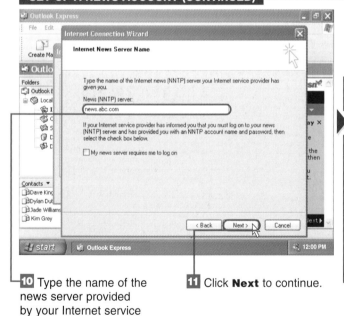

10 Type the name of the news server provided by your Internet service provider.

11 Click **Next** to continue.

■ The wizard indicates that you have successfully entered all the information required to set up your news account.

12 Click **Finish** to set up the news account.

Does Microsoft offer newsgroups that can help me with Windows XP?

Yes. Microsoft provides the **msnews.microsoft.com** news server, which contains hundreds of newsgroups that discuss various Microsoft products, including Windows XP. The messages in these newsgroups may provide information that can help you use Windows XP.

How do I delete a news account I no longer use?

To delete a news account, perform steps **1** to **3** on page 250 to display the list of news accounts set up on your computer. Click the news account you want to delete and then click the **Remove** button. In the confirmation dialog box that appears, click **Yes** to delete the news account.

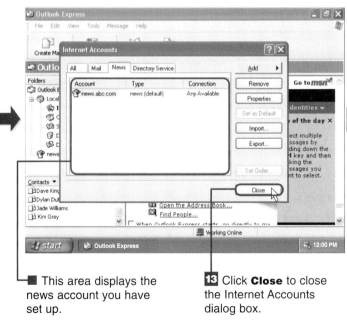

■ This area displays the news account you have set up.

13 Click **Close** to close the Internet Accounts dialog box.

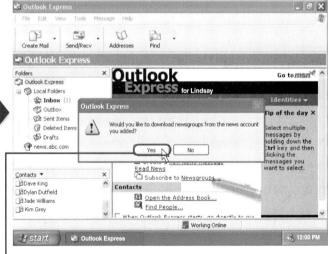

■ A dialog box appears, asking if you want to download a list of newsgroups for the news account.

14 Click **Yes** to download the list of newsgroups.

Note: You need to download the list only once.

■ A dialog box will appear, indicating the download progress.

Note: When the download is complete, you can subscribe to newsgroups of interest. To subscribe to newsgroups, see page 254.

253

SUBSCRIBE TO NEWSGROUPS

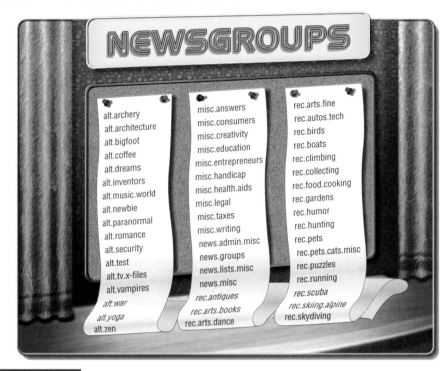

You can subscribe to newsgroups to give you quick access to information you want to read on a regular basis.

Outlook Express provides a list of all the available newsgroups to help you find newsgroups of interest. Each newsgroup discusses a particular topic, such as cars, music or job opportunities.

SUBSCRIBE TO NEWSGROUPS

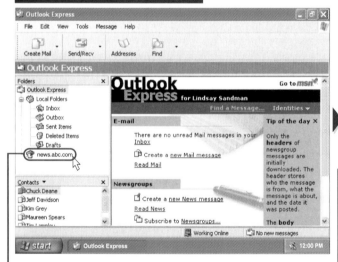

1 In the Outlook Express window, click the news server that offers the newsgroups you want to subscribe to.

Note: To display the Outlook Express window, see page 208.

■ A dialog box appears if you are not subscribed to any newsgroups on the news server.

2 Click **Yes** to display a list of the available newsgroups on the news server.

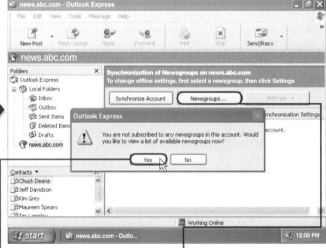

■ If the dialog box does not appear, click **Newsgroups** to display a list of the available newsgroups.

How are newsgroups named?

The name of a newsgroup describes the type of information discussed in the newsgroup. A newsgroup name consists of two or more words, separated by dots (.). The first word describes the main topic of the newsgroup. Each of the following words narrows the topic. For example, the **rec.music.folk** newsgroup contains messages from folk music enthusiasts.

What are the main newsgroup topics?

The main newsgroup topics include alt (alternative), biz (business), comp (computers), k12 (kindergarten to grade 12 or education related), misc (miscellaneous), news, rec (recreation), sci (science), soc (social) and talk.

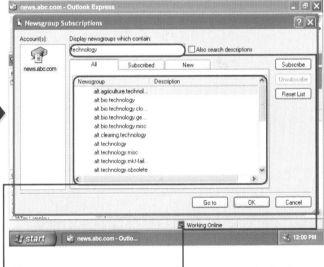

■ The Newsgroup Subscriptions dialog box appears.

■ This area displays an alphabetical list of the available newsgroups. You can use the scroll bar to browse through the list.

3 To find newsgroup names that contain a word of interest, click this area and then type the word of interest.

Note: For best results, type only lowercase letters when searching for a newsgroup name.

■ This area displays the newsgroup names that contain the word you typed.

■ To once again display all the newsgroup names, double-click the word you typed in this area and then press the `Delete` key.

CONTINUED

SUBSCRIBE TO NEWSGROUPS

You can find newsgroups on almost every subject imaginable. You can find newsgroups that discuss subjects such as football, politics and stamp collecting.

SUBSCRIBE TO NEWSGROUPS (CONTINUED)

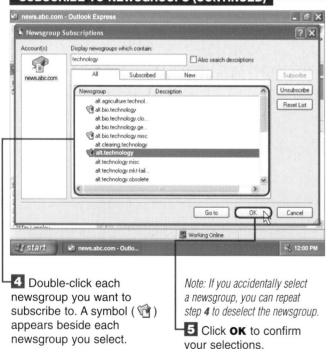

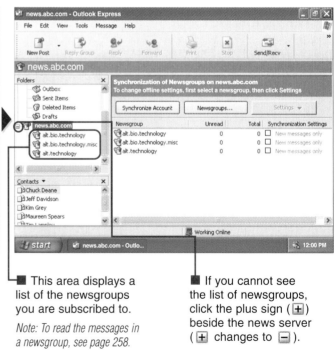

4 Double-click each newsgroup you want to subscribe to. A symbol ( ) appears beside each newsgroup you select.

Note: If you accidentally select a newsgroup, you can repeat step 4 to deselect the newsgroup.

5 Click **OK** to confirm your selections.

■ This area displays a list of the newsgroups you are subscribed to.

Note: To read the messages in a newsgroup, see page 258.

■ If you cannot see the list of newsgroups, click the plus sign ( ) beside the news server (changes to).

Why is my newsgroup list different from the list shown below?

The newsgroups available to you depend on your news server. News servers are computers that store newsgroups and are usually run and maintained by Internet service providers. Different Internet service providers may offer different newsgroups on their news servers.

Are there any newsgroups designed for beginners?

Yes. The **news.newusers.questions** newsgroup provides useful information for beginners and allows you to ask questions about newsgroups.

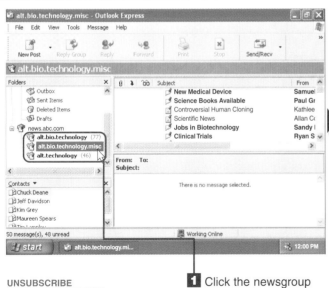

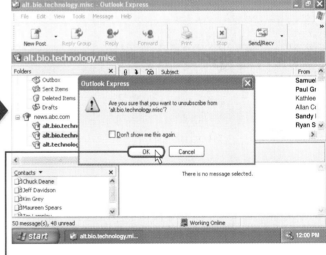

**UNSUBSCRIBE
FROM A NEWSGROUP**

You can unsubscribe from a newsgroup at any time if the information discussed in the newsgroup no longer interests you.

1 Click the newsgroup you want to unsubscribe from. The newsgroup is highlighted.

2 Press the Delete key.

■ A confirmation dialog box appears.

3 Click **OK** to unsubscribe from the newsgroup.

■ Windows removes the newsgroup from the Outlook Express window.

READ NEWSGROUP MESSAGES

You can read the messages in a newsgroup to learn the opinions and ideas of thousands of people around the world.

READ NEWSGROUP MESSAGES

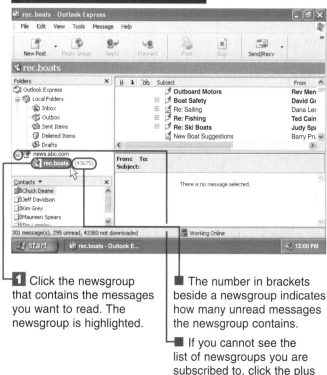

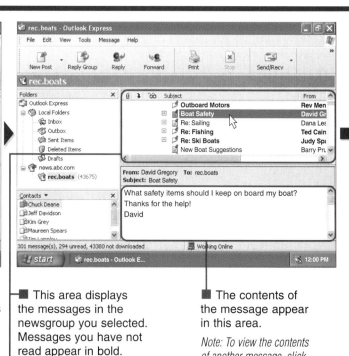

1 Click the newsgroup that contains the messages you want to read. The newsgroup is highlighted.

■ The number in brackets beside a newsgroup indicates how many unread messages the newsgroup contains.

■ If you cannot see the list of newsgroups you are subscribed to, click the plus sign (⊞) beside the news server (⊞ changes to ⊟).

■ This area displays the messages in the newsgroup you selected. Messages you have not read appear in bold.

2 Click a message you want to read.

■ The contents of the message appear in this area.

Note: To view the contents of another message, click the message.

Where can I find a list of questions that are commonly asked in a newsgroup?

Some newsgroups include a message called a FAQ (Frequently Asked Questions). A FAQ contains a list of questions and answers that regularly appear in the newsgroup. A FAQ helps prevent new readers from posting questions that have already been answered. You can also find FAQs for a wide variety of newsgroups at the **news.answers** newsgroup.

Why can't I find a message I previously read in a newsgroup?

After a few days or weeks, newsgroup messages are removed from the news server that stores the messages to make room for new messages. Newsgroup messages you read today may not be available at a later time.

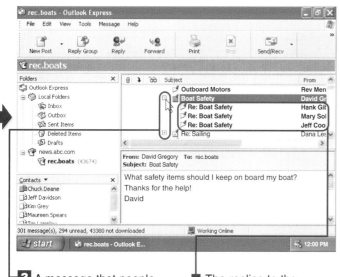

3 A message that people have replied to displays a plus sign (⊞). To display the replies to a message, click the plus sign beside the message (⊞ changes to ⊟).

■ The replies to the message appear.

Note: You can click the minus sign (⊟) beside a message to once again hide the replies to the message (⊟ changes to ⊞).

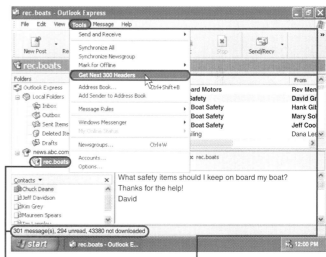

DOWNLOAD MORE MESSAGES

1 Click the newsgroup that contains additional messages you want to download.

■ This area shows the number of displayed messages, unread messages and messages you have not yet downloaded for the newsgroup.

2 Click **Tools**.

3 Click **Get Next 300 Headers** to download more messages.

REPLY TO A NEWSGROUP MESSAGE

You can reply to a message in a newsgroup to answer a question, express an opinion or supply information. You can send a reply to the entire newsgroup or to only the author of the message.

Original Message

The baked potatoes that I serve to my guests are not very appetizing. How can I make them more appealing?

Reply

Try adding sour cream and paprika, and then sprinkle chili powder on top. Bon appetit!

You should reply to a newsgroup message only when you have something important to say. A reply such as "Me too" or "I agree" is not very informative.

Send a reply to the entire newsgroup when you think everyone in the newsgroup would be interested in your response. Send a reply to only the author of the message when you want to send a private response.

REPLY TO A NEWSGROUP MESSAGE

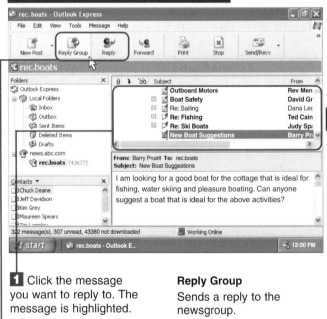

1 Click the message you want to reply to. The message is highlighted.

2 Click the reply option you want to use.

Reply Group

Sends a reply to the newsgroup.

Reply

Sends a reply to only the author of the message.

■ A window appears for you to compose your reply.

■ Outlook Express fills in the newsgroup name or the e-mail address of the author for you.

■ Outlook Express also fills in the subject, starting the subject with **Re:**.

What should I consider when replying to a newsgroup message?

A MESSAGE WRITTEN IN CAPITAL LETTERS IS ANNOYING AND DIFFICULT TO READ. THIS IS CALLED SHOUTING. Always use uppercase and lowercase letters when replying to or posting new messages in newsgroups.

What is a flame?

When other readers do not like your message, they may reply to your message in a negative or hostile manner. These rude messages are called flames. You should ignore flames.

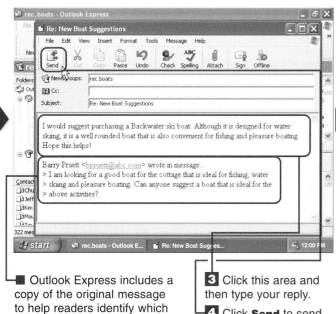

■ Outlook Express includes a copy of the original message to help readers identify which message you are replying to. This is called quoting. A symbol (>) appears beside each line of quoted text.

3 Click this area and then type your reply.

4 Click **Send** to send the reply.

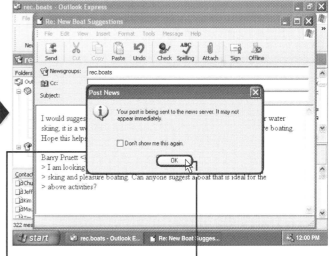

■ If you sent your reply to the newsgroup, a dialog box appears, stating that your message is being sent to the news server and may not appear immediately in the newsgroup.

5 Click **OK** to close the dialog box.

■ Outlook Express sends the message and stores a copy of the message in the Sent Items folder.

POST A MESSAGE TO A NEWSGROUP

You can post, or send, a new message to a newsgroup to ask a question or express an opinion.

I am starting Yoga next week and I was wondering what I should wear to class. Also, is there anything that I should bring?

Thanks,
Katie Johnson

When posting a message to a newsgroup, keep in mind that thousands of people around the world may read the message.

To practice posting a message, post a message to the misc.test or alt.test newsgroup. Do not send practice messages to other newsgroups since you may receive unwanted replies.

POST A MESSAGE TO A NEWSGROUP

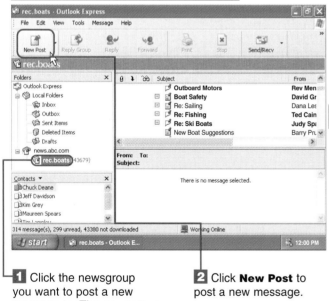

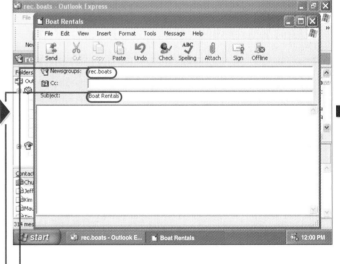

1 Click the newsgroup you want to post a new message to. The newsgroup is highlighted.

2 Click **New Post** to post a new message.

■ The New Message window appears.

■ Outlook Express fills in the name of the newsgroup for you.

3 Click this area and then type a subject for the message.

Note: Make sure your subject clearly identifies the contents of the message. For example, the subject "Top 10 Movies of All Time" is more informative than "Read this now."

Should I read the messages in a newsgroup before posting a message?

Yes. Before posting a message to a newsgroup, read the messages in the newsgroup for at least one week. Reading the messages in a newsgroup can help you avoid sending information that others have already read and is a great way to learn how people in the newsgroup communicate.

Why didn't my message appear in a newsgroup?

Some newsgroups are moderated. In moderated newsgroups, a person or moderation program reviews each message sent to the newsgroup to determine if the message is suitable for posting. If the message is not suitable, the message will not be posted for everyone to read. Moderated newsgroups may include the word "moderated" at the end of the newsgroup name, such as **misc.taxes.moderated**.

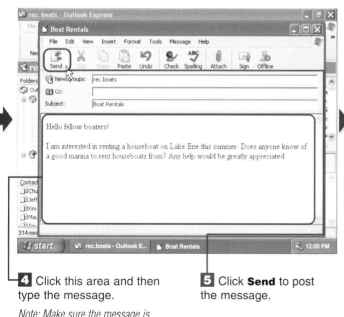

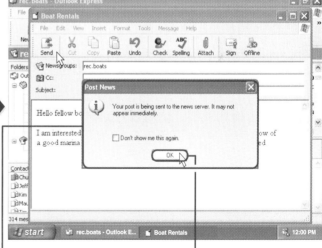

4 Click this area and then type the message.

Note: Make sure the message is clear, concise and does not contain any spelling or grammar errors.

5 Click **Send** to post the message.

■ A dialog box appears, stating that your message is being sent to the news server and may not appear immediately in the newsgroup.

6 Click **OK** to close the dialog box.

■ Outlook Express sends the message and stores a copy of the message in the Sent Items folder.

CHAPTER 14

Manage & Troubleshoot Your Computer

This chapter teaches you how to use Windows XP to enhance your computer's performance and troubleshoot problems.

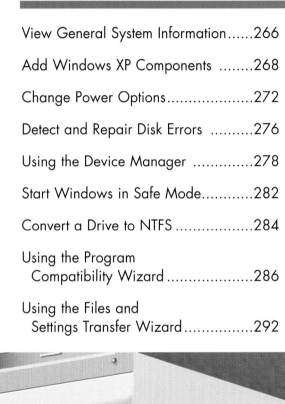

VIEW GENERAL SYSTEM INFORMATION

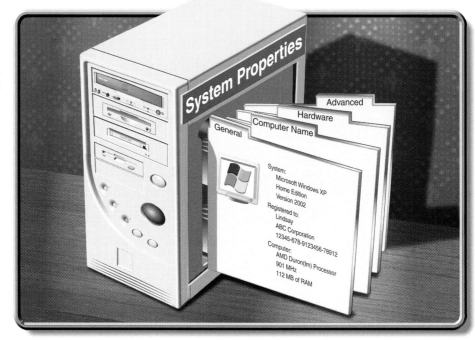

You can view general information about Windows and your computer.

For example, you can view the edition of Windows you are using and the amount of memory in your computer.

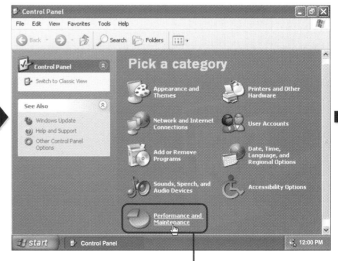

1 Click **start** to display the Start menu.

2 Click **Control Panel** to change your computer's settings.

■ The Control Panel window appears.

3 Click **Performance and Maintenance**.

What editions of Windows are available?

Windows XP is available in two editions—Windows XP Home Edition and Windows XP Professional. The Professional edition has all the features of the Home edition plus additional features, such as greater networking capabilities and file encryption, which are not available in the Home edition.

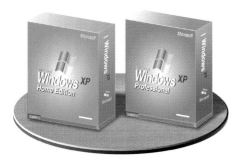

Can the system information change?

Yes. The system information is automatically updated when you make changes to Windows or your computer. For example, if you install Windows updates or add more memory to your computer, the new information will automatically be displayed in the System Properties dialog box.

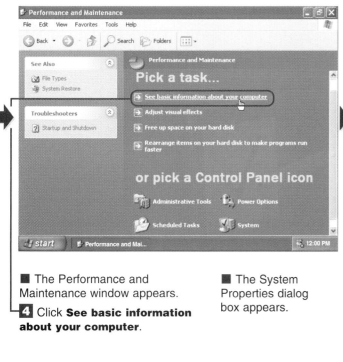

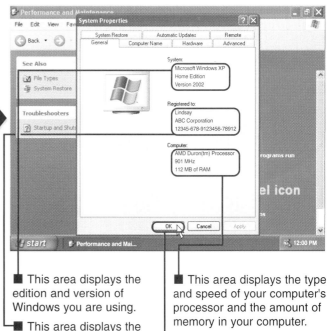

■ The Performance and Maintenance window appears.

4 Click **See basic information about your computer**.

■ The System Properties dialog box appears.

■ This area displays the edition and version of Windows you are using.

■ This area displays the name of the person who is registered to use this copy of Windows and the registration number.

■ This area displays the type and speed of your computer's processor and the amount of memory in your computer.

5 When you finish reviewing the information, click **OK** to close the System Properties dialog box.

You can add Windows
components to add
capabilities and
enhancements to your
computer.

You may need
the Windows XP
CD-ROM disc
that came with
Windows to
add Windows
components to
your computer.

ADD WINDOWS XP COMPONENTS

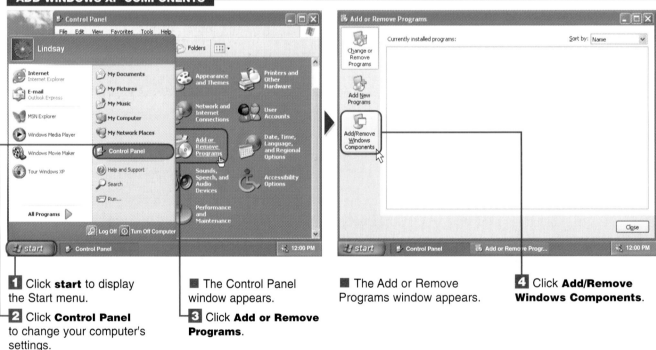

1 Click **start** to display
the Start menu.

2 Click **Control Panel**
to change your computer's
settings.

■ The Control Panel
window appears.

3 Click **Add or Remove
Programs**.

■ The Add or Remove
Programs window appears.

4 Click **Add/Remove
Windows Components**.

Why are all Windows components not automatically installed on my computer?

When you install Windows, the installation program does not add all the components included with Windows to your computer. This prevents less commonly used components from taking up storage space on your computer.

What Windows components can I add to my computer?

Windows offers many useful components that you can add to your computer. For example, the Fax Services component allows you to send and receive faxes using your computer. The Management and Monitoring Tools component provides tools to help you monitor and enhance the performance of your network.

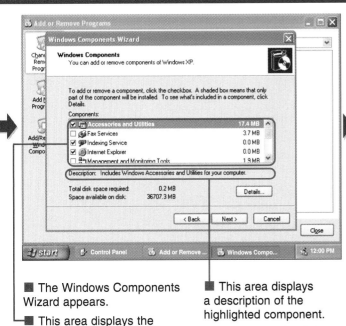

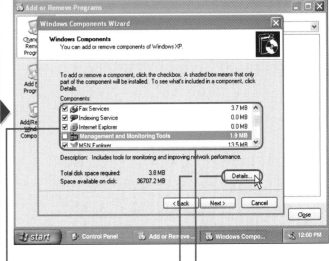

■ The Windows Components Wizard appears.

■ This area displays the components you can add to your computer and the amount of hard disk space each component requires.

■ This area displays a description of the highlighted component.

Note: To display a description of another component, click the component.

■ The box beside each component indicates if all (☑), some (☑) or none (☐) of the subcomponents of the component are installed on your computer.

5 Click the box (☐) beside each component you want to add to your computer (☐ changes to ☑).

6 To display the subcomponents of a component, click the component.

7 Click **Details**.

Note: If the Details button is dimmed, the component does not contain any subcomponents.

CONTINUED

ADD WINDOWS XP COMPONENTS

When adding Windows components to your computer, you can view the total amount of hard disk space required to add the components and the total amount of free hard disk space on your computer.

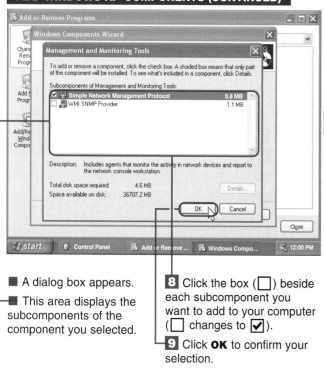

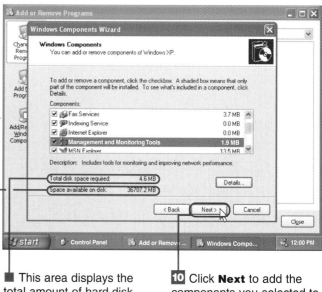

■ A dialog box appears.

■ This area displays the subcomponents of the component you selected.

8 Click the box (☐) beside each subcomponent you want to add to your computer (☐ changes to ☑).

9 Click **OK** to confirm your selection.

■ This area displays the total amount of hard disk space required to add the components you selected.

■ This area displays the total amount of free hard disk space on your computer.

10 Click **Next** to add the components you selected to your computer.

■ Windows begins installing the components.

How do I remove a component I do not use?

To remove a component you do not use, perform steps **1** to **14** starting on page 268. When you click a box beside a component you want to remove in step **5** or **8**, ☑ changes to ☐. For example, if you do not use the games included with Windows, you can remove the Games subcomponent of the Accessories and Utilities component. Removing components you do not use frees up storage space on your computer.

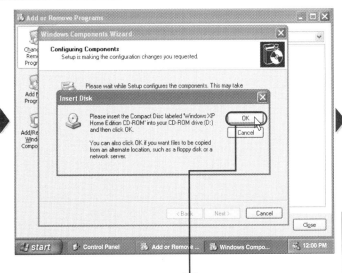

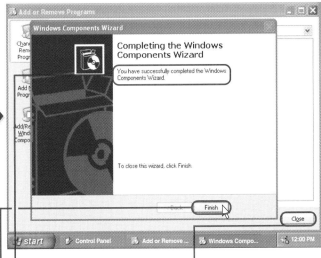

■ The Insert Disk dialog box may appear, asking you to insert the Windows XP CD-ROM disc.

11 Insert the CD-ROM disc into your CD-ROM drive.

12 Click **OK** to continue.

*Note: If the Welcome to Microsoft Windows XP screen appears, click **Exit** in the bottom left corner of the screen to remove the screen.*

■ This message appears when you have successfully completed the wizard. The components you selected are now installed.

13 Click **Finish** to close the wizard.

14 Click **Close** to close the Add or Remove Programs window.

■ You can now use the components you added to your computer.

CHANGE POWER OPTIONS

You can change the power options on your computer to manage the amount of power the computer uses.

Power management is useful for reducing the amount of power your desktop computer uses or increasing the battery life of a portable computer.

Windows can conserve power by turning off your monitor or hard disk or putting your computer on standby or into hibernation when the computer has been idle for a period of time.

CHANGE POWER OPTIONS

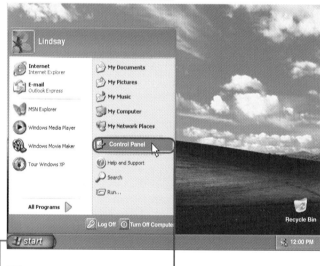

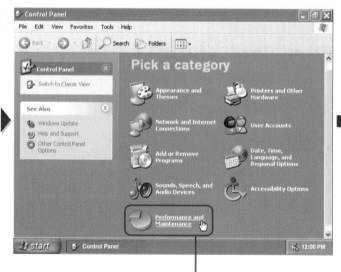

1 Click **start** to display the Start menu.

2 Click **Control Panel** to change your computer's settings.

■ The Control Panel window appears.

3 Click **Performance and Maintenance**.

What is the difference between standby and hibernation?

Standby

When your computer is on standby, Windows turns off devices on your computer to conserve power. You should save your documents before your computer goes on standby. If a power outage occurs while your computer is on standby, you will lose any unsaved information. When you resume using your computer, any open documents and programs will appear as you left them.

Hibernation

When your computer is in hibernation, Windows automatically saves all information on your computer and turns off devices to conserve power. When you resume using your computer, any open documents and programs will appear as you left them. Bringing your computer out of hibernation takes longer than bringing your computer out of standby.

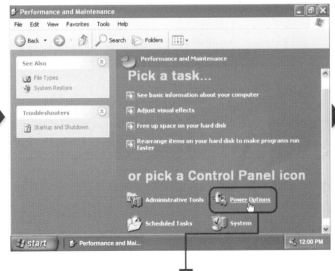

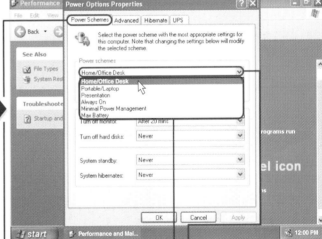

■ The Performance and Maintenance window appears.

4 Click **Power Options** to change the energy-saving settings for your computer.

■ The Power Options Properties dialog box appears.

5 Click the **Power Schemes** tab.

6 Click this area to display a list of the available power schemes.

7 Click the power scheme that best describes the way you use your computer.

CONTINUED

CHANGE POWER OPTIONS

You can change the
amount of time your
computer must be
inactive before your
monitor or hard disk
automatically turns off.
You can also change
the amount of time
your computer must
be inactive before
going on standby
or into hibernation.

The power options
available on a
computer depend
on the computer's
hardware.

CHANGE POWER OPTIONS (CONTINUED)

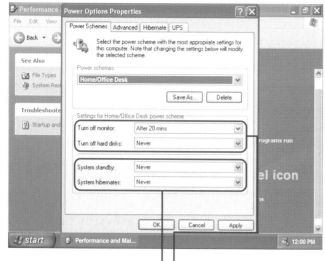

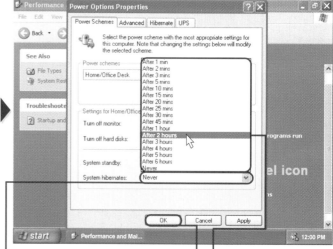

■ Windows displays the
settings for the power
scheme you selected.

■ These areas display the
amount of time your computer
must be inactive before
your monitor and hard disk
automatically turn off.

■ These areas display the
amount of time your computer
must be inactive before going
on standby or into hibernation.

8 To change the amount of
time your computer must be
inactive before your monitor
or hard disk turn off or your
computer goes on standby
or into hibernation, click the
appropriate area.

9 Click the amount of
time you want to set.

10 Click **OK** to confirm
all your changes.

Which power conservation mode should I use?

You may want your monitor and hard disk to turn off after your computer has been inactive for a short period of time, such as 20 minutes. If you plan to be away from your computer for more than 45 minutes, you may want the computer to go on standby. If you plan to be away from your computer for more than 2 hours, you may want the computer to go into hibernation.

How do I resume using my computer when it is in a power conservation mode?

If your monitor or hard disk is turned off or if your computer is on standby or in hibernation, you may be able to move the mouse on your desk or press a key on your keyboard to resume using your computer. On some computers, you may have to press the computer's power button to bring the computer out of standby or hibernation.

INSTANTLY PUT COMPUTER ON STANDBY OR INTO HIBERNATION

1 Click **start** to display the Start menu.

2 Click **Turn Off Computer**.

■ The Turn off computer dialog box appears.

3 To put your computer on standby, click **Stand By**.

■ To put your computer into hibernation, press and hold down the **Shift** key. When the Stand By option changes to **Hibernate**, click **Hibernate**.

■ Your computer enters a power conservation mode.

DETECT AND REPAIR DISK ERRORS

Windows provides an error-checking tool that you can use to detect and repair errors on your hard disk.

You should check your hard disk for errors about once a month. If you experience any problems with your hard disk, such as an inability to open or save a file, you should check for errors immediately.

Detecting and repairing errors on a hard disk can take a long time if the disk contains a large number of files.

DETECT AND REPAIR DISK ERRORS

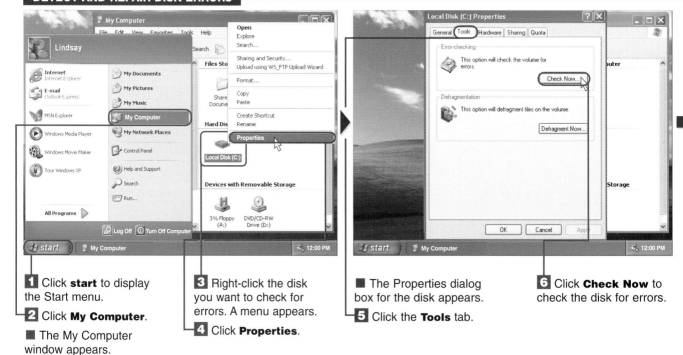

1 Click **start** to display the Start menu.

2 Click **My Computer**.

■ The My Computer window appears.

3 Right-click the disk you want to check for errors. A menu appears.

4 Click **Properties**.

■ The Properties dialog box for the disk appears.

5 Click the **Tools** tab.

6 Click **Check Now** to check the disk for errors.

How does Windows check for errors on my hard disk?

Windows checks for errors on your hard disk by searching for file system errors and bad sectors on the disk. A file system error is an error that occurs in the organization of the files and folders stored on a hard disk. A bad sector is a physically damaged area that can no longer store information on a hard disk.

Why did a dialog box appear, stating that the disk check could not be performed?

A dialog box appears if Windows cannot access certain files on your hard drive. Click **Yes** or **No** in the dialog box to specify if you want Windows to check the disk the next time you start your computer.

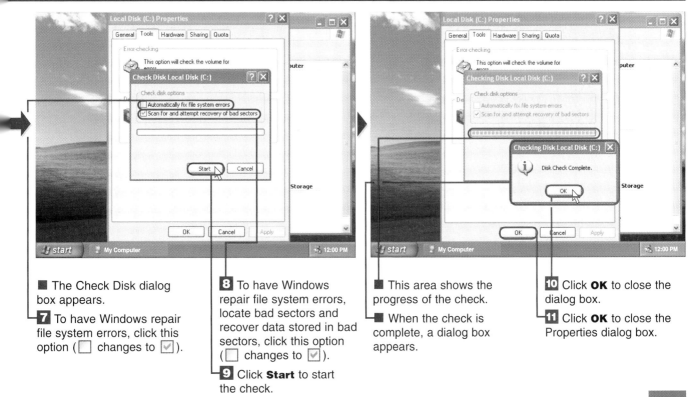

■ The Check Disk dialog box appears.

7 To have Windows repair file system errors, click this option (□ changes to ☑).

8 To have Windows repair file system errors, locate bad sectors and recover data stored in bad sectors, click this option (□ changes to ☑).

9 Click **Start** to start the check.

■ This area shows the progress of the check.

■ When the check is complete, a dialog box appears.

10 Click **OK** to close the dialog box.

11 Click **OK** to close the Properties dialog box.

USING THE DEVICE MANAGER

DEVICE MANAGER

HARDWARE

DISK DRIVES
IOMEGA JAZ-1GB
SYQUEST-SYJET

MONITOR
VIEWSONIC-PT813

SCANNER
UMAX-1200P

You can use the Device Manager to view a list of all the hardware devices installed on your computer.

If you are having trouble with a hardware device installed on your computer, the Device Manager can help you identify the problem.

USING THE DEVICE MANAGER

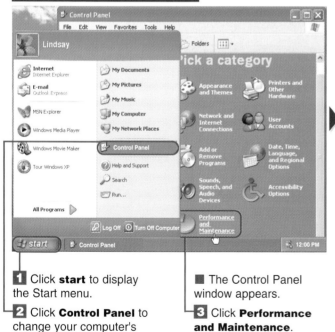

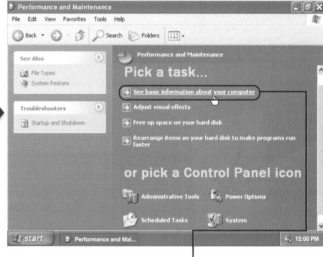

1 Click **start** to display the Start menu.

2 Click **Control Panel** to change your computer's settings.

■ The Control Panel window appears.

3 Click **Performance and Maintenance**.

■ The Performance and Maintenance window appears.

4 Click **See basic information about your computer**.

**How will the Device Manager indicate
that a device is not working properly?**

If there is a problem with a device,
the Device Manager will display an
exclamation mark (**!**) over the icon
for the device. For example, a hardware
device that was not installed properly
may display an exclamation mark.

A hardware device with a red X
through its icon indicates the device
has been disabled. A disabled device
is temporarily unavailable for use.

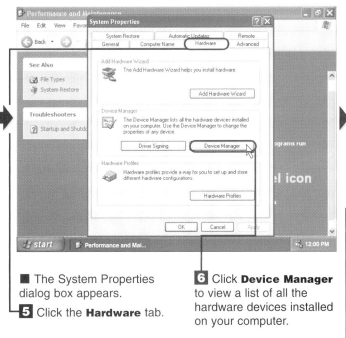

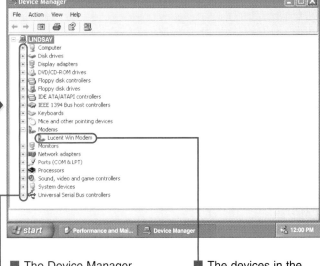

■ The System Properties
dialog box appears.

5 Click the **Hardware** tab.

6 Click **Device Manager**
to view a list of all the
hardware devices installed
on your computer.

■ The Device Manager
window appears, displaying
the types of hardware devices
installed on your computer.

7 Click the plus sign (⊞)
beside a type of hardware
device to see the devices
in the category (⊞ changes
to ⊟).

■ The devices in the
category appear.

*Note: You can click the minus
sign (⊟) beside a type of
hardware device to once again
hide the devices in the category.*

CONTINUED

USING THE DEVICE MANAGER

You can use the Device Manager to display information about a device installed on your computer, such as the manufacturer of the device and whether the device is working properly.

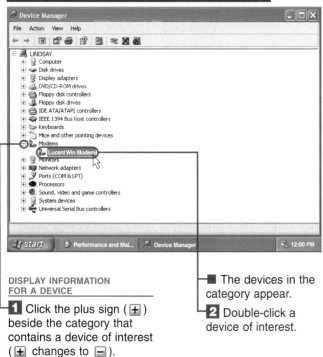

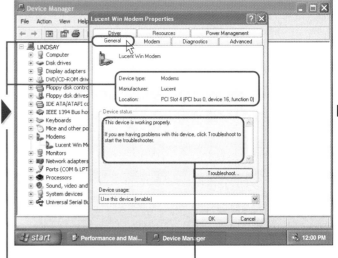

DISPLAY INFORMATION FOR A DEVICE

1 Click the plus sign (⊞) beside the category that contains a device of interest (⊞ changes to ⊟).

■ The devices in the category appear.

2 Double-click a device of interest.

■ A Properties dialog box for the device appears.

3 Click the **General** tab.

■ This area displays general information about the device, such as the device's manufacturer.

■ This area indicates if the device is working properly. If there is a problem with the device, Windows will indicate the type of problem and a suggested solution. Windows may also display a problem code.

Windows displays a problem code for a device that is not working properly. How do I use this information?

When viewing the information for a device, a problem code, such as **Code 10**, may appear for a device that is not working properly. If you plan to call a support line to get help with the device, this problem code can help a support technician identify the problem.

How can I resolve a problem with a device?

When viewing the information for a device, click the **Troubleshoot** button. The Help and Support Center window will appear, displaying a troubleshooter for the device. Follow the instructions in the troubleshooter to try to resolve the problem.

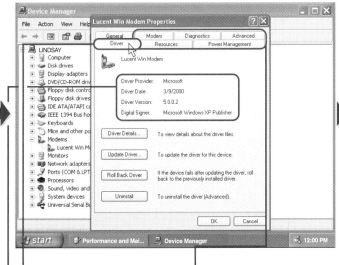

4 Click the **Driver** tab.

■ This area displays information about the driver the computer uses to communicate with the device.

Note: The Driver tab may not appear for some devices.

■ Windows may display additional tabs to provide more information about the device. To display the information on a tab, click the name of the tab.

5 When you finish reviewing information about the device, click **OK** to close the Properties dialog box.

6 Click **X** to close the Device Manager window.

7 Click **OK** to close the System Properties dialog box.

START WINDOWS IN SAFE MODE

If Windows will not start properly, you may be able to start Windows in safe mode to try to correct the problem.

For example, if Windows will not start properly after you install a program or change certain Windows settings, you can try uninstalling the program or restoring the previous settings in safe mode.

Some hardware devices, such as printers, sound cards, modems and some types of mice, are unavailable in safe mode.

START WINDOWS IN SAFE MODE

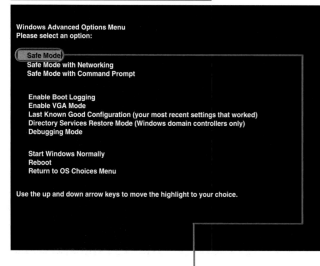

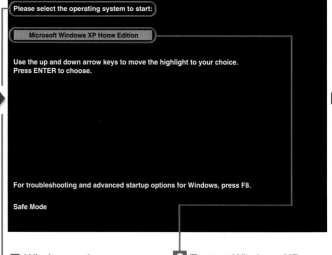

1 After you turn on your computer and monitor, press and hold down the **F8** key.

■ The Windows Advanced Options Menu appears, displaying a list of options for starting Windows.

2 To start Windows in safe mode, press the **↑** or **↓** key until you highlight **Safe Mode**. Then press the **Enter** key.

■ Windows asks you to select the operating system you want to start.

3 To start Windows XP, press the **↑** or **↓** key until you highlight **Microsoft Windows XP Home Edition**. Then press the **Enter** key.

I am not sure how to fix the problem that prevented Windows from starting normally. What can I do?

You can start your computer using the Last Known Good Configuration option. This option allows you to restore the settings Windows used the last time your computer started successfully. To use the Last Known Good Configuration option to start your computer, perform steps **1** to **3** below, except select **Last Known Good Configuration** in step **2**.

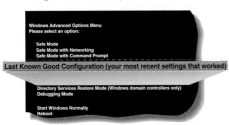

After I fix the problem that prevented Windows from starting normally, how do I exit safe mode?

You can restart your computer to exit safe mode and start Windows normally. To restart your computer, click the **Start** button to display the Start menu and then click **Turn Off Computer**. In the dialog box that appears, click **Restart** to restart your computer.

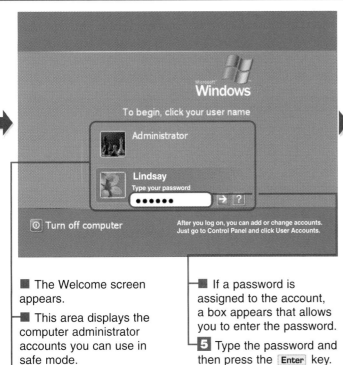

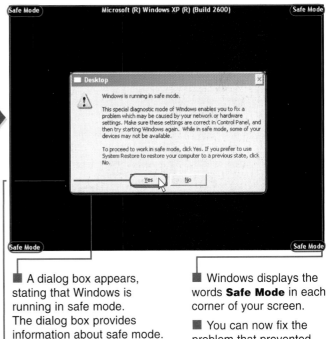

■ The Welcome screen appears.

■ This area displays the computer administrator accounts you can use in safe mode.

4 Click the account you want to use in safe mode.

■ If a password is assigned to the account, a box appears that allows you to enter the password.

5 Type the password and then press the Enter key.

■ A dialog box appears, stating that Windows is running in safe mode. The dialog box provides information about safe mode.

6 Click **Yes** to continue.

■ Windows displays the words **Safe Mode** in each corner of your screen.

■ You can now fix the problem that prevented Windows from starting normally.

CONVERT A DRIVE TO NTFS

You can optimize your computer by converting your hard drive from the FAT or FAT32 file system to the NTFS file system. A file system determines the way information is stored and organized on a hard drive.

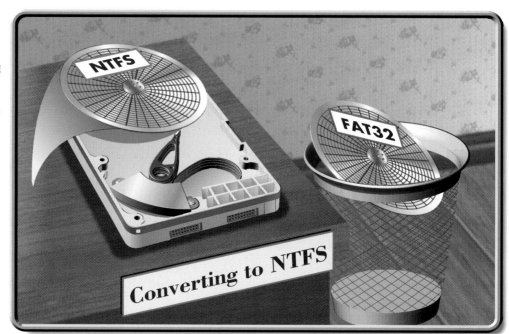

Converting to NTFS

After you convert your hard drive to NTFS, you cannot convert the drive back to a FAT file system.

The file system initially used by a computer is usually selected when Windows is installed.

CONVERT A DRIVE TO NTFS

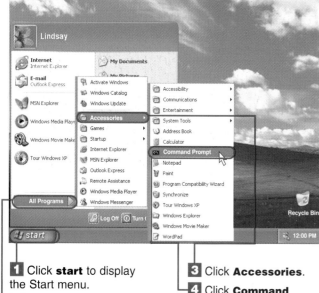

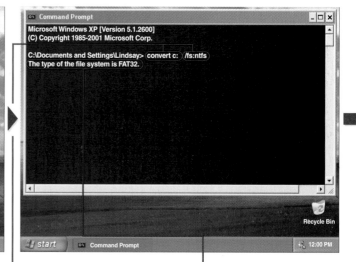

1 Click **start** to display the Start menu.

2 Click **All Programs** to view a list of the programs on your computer.

3 Click **Accessories**.

4 Click **Command Prompt**.

■ The Command Prompt window appears.

5 To convert your hard drive to NTFS, type **convert c:** and then press the **Spacebar**.

6 Type **/fs:ntfs** and then press the Enter key.

■ Windows indicates the file system your hard drive currently uses.

Note: If your hard drive currently uses the NTFS file system, the **Drive C: is already NTFS** message appears. To close the Command Prompt window, skip to step **9**.

284

What file systems does Windows support?

Windows XP supports three file systems.

FAT	FAT32	NTFS
FAT is a file system used by MS-DOS and older Windows operating systems.	FAT32 is an upgrade from FAT and improves the organization of data to reduce wasted space on hard drives larger than 512 MB.	The NTFS file system is recommended for Windows XP and offers many advantages over the FAT file systems. NTFS offers improved file security and performance, disk compression and support for larger hard drives.

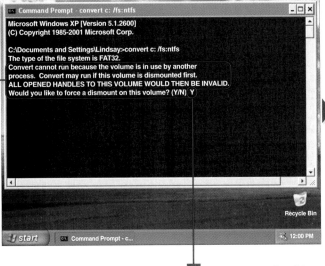

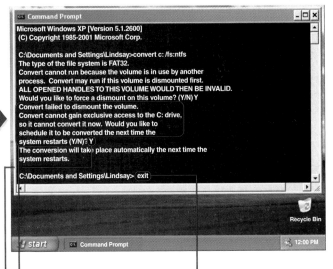

■ Windows states that it cannot convert your hard drive because the drive is currently in use. You must dismount the drive before you can convert the drive.

7 To dismount the drive, type **Y** (for **Yes**) and then press the Enter key.

■ If Windows cannot dismount your hard drive now, Windows states that the drive can be converted the next time you start your computer.

8 To convert the drive the next time you start your computer, type **Y** (for **Yes**) and then press the Enter key.

9 To close the Command Prompt window, type **exit** and then press the Enter key.

■ When you restart your computer, Windows will convert the drive to NTFS.

USING THE PROGRAM COMPATIBILITY WIZARD

If you are having trouble running a program that was designed for a previous version of Windows, you can use the Program Compatibility Wizard to help solve the problem.

USING THE PROGRAM COMPATIBILITY WIZARD

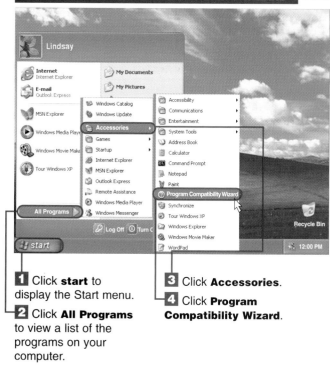

1 Click **start** to display the Start menu.

2 Click **All Programs** to view a list of the programs on your computer.

3 Click **Accessories**.

4 Click **Program Compatibility Wizard**.

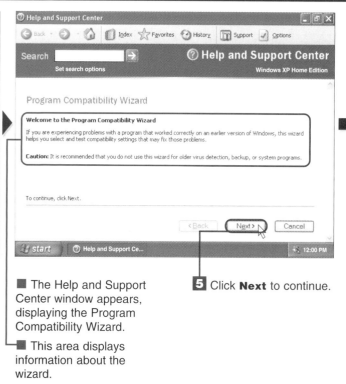

■ The Help and Support Center window appears, displaying the Program Compatibility Wizard.

■ This area displays information about the wizard.

5 Click **Next** to continue.

Can I use the Program Compatibility Wizard with older anti-virus or backup programs?

You should not use the Program Compatibility Wizard with older anti-virus or backup programs. These types of programs are often designed to be used only with a specific version of Windows. If you are having trouble using an older anti-virus or backup program with Windows XP, you should contact the program's manufacturer to try to obtain a more recent version of the program. If a more recent version of the program is not available, consider obtaining a similar program designed for Windows XP.

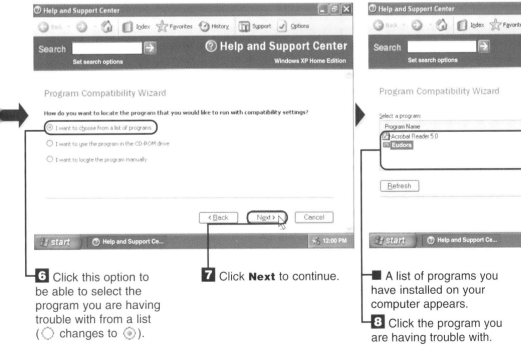

6 Click this option to be able to select the program you are having trouble with from a list (◯ changes to ◉).

7 Click **Next** to continue.

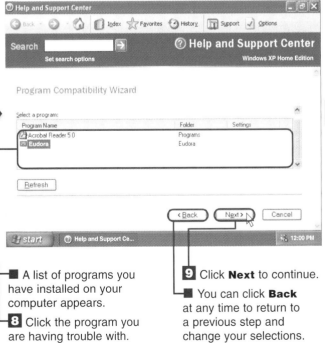

■ A list of programs you have installed on your computer appears.

8 Click the program you are having trouble with.

9 Click **Next** to continue.

■ You can click **Back** at any time to return to a previous step and change your selections.

CONTINUED

USING THE PROGRAM COMPATIBILITY WIZARD

If your program does not run in Windows XP, you can select the version of Windows that can run the program successfully.

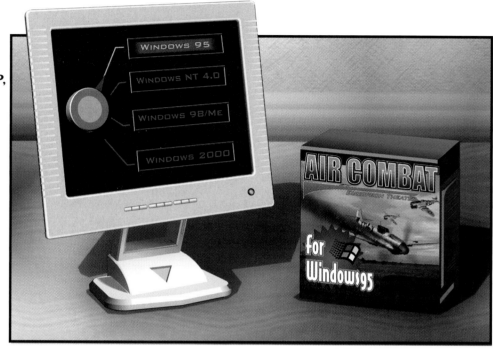

USING THE PROGRAM COMPATIBILITY WIZARD (CONTINUED)

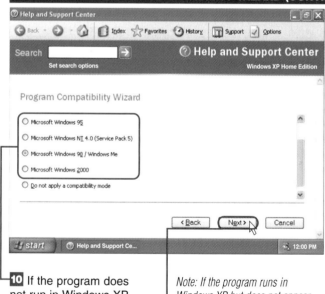

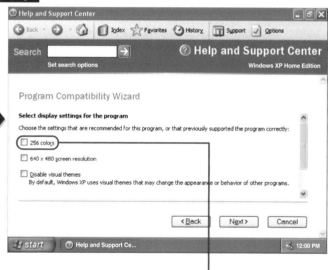

10 If the program does not run in Windows XP, click the version of Windows that can run the program successfully (○ changes to ◉).

*Note: If the program runs in Windows XP but does not appear correctly on your screen, select the **Do not apply a compatibility mode** option.*

11 Click **Next** to continue.

■ The wizard allows you to select the display settings recommended for the program.

Note: The display settings apply most often to games and educational programs. If your program is not a game or educational program, you will most likely not need to select any display settings.

12 If the program requires that the color setting be set to 256 colors, click this option (☐ changes to ☑).

Will using compatibility settings affect the performance of a program?

When you run a program using compatibility settings, the program may operate more slowly than normal.

Will using compatibility settings for a program affect the appearance of my screen?

If you selected display settings for a program, such as a color setting of 256 colors or a screen resolution of 640 x 480, Windows will adjust the display settings your screen uses each time you start the program. If you have other programs open at the same time, these programs will also use the same display settings you selected. Once you close the program that uses compatibility settings, the appearance of your screen will return to normal.

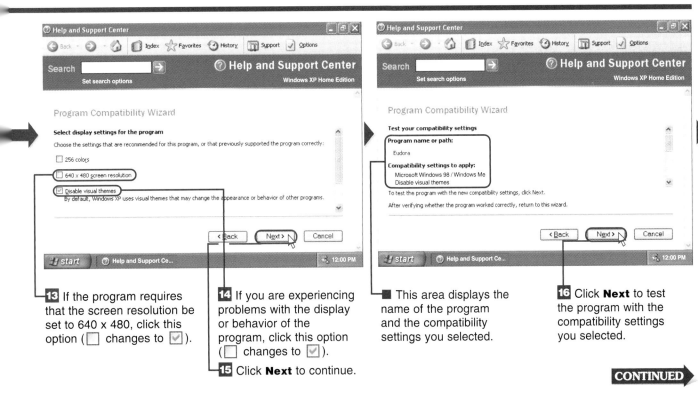

13 If the program requires that the screen resolution be set to 640 x 480, click this option (☐ changes to ☑).

14 If you are experiencing problems with the display or behavior of the program, click this option (☐ changes to ☑).

15 Click **Next** to continue.

■ This area displays the name of the program and the compatibility settings you selected.

16 Click **Next** to test the program with the compatibility settings you selected.

CONTINUED ▶

USING THE PROGRAM COMPATIBILITY WIZARD

The Program Compatibility Wizard allows you to test a program with the settings you selected to determine if the problems with the program were fixed.

USING THE PROGRAM COMPATIBILITY WIZARD (CONTINUED)

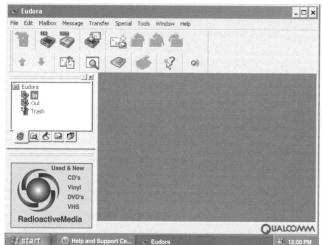

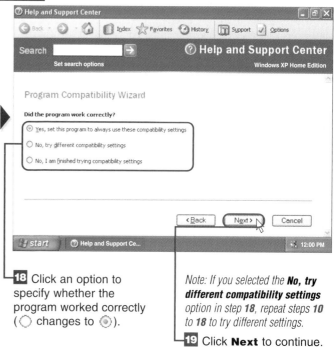

■ The program opens using the compatibility settings you selected.

17 When you finish verifying whether the program works correctly, close the program to return to the wizard.

Note: Depending on the program, you may be able to click ⊠ *at the top right corner of the window to close the program.*

18 Click an option to specify whether the program worked correctly (○ changes to ◉).

*Note: If you selected the **No, try different compatibility settings** option in step **18**, repeat steps **10** to **18** to try different settings.*

19 Click **Next** to continue.

My program is still not working. What can I do?

Some older programs will not work properly with Windows XP, regardless of the compatibility settings you select. You can contact the program's manufacturer to determine if there is an updated version of the program available that is compatible with Windows XP. You can also check the Windows Update Web site (www.windowsupdate.com) to determine if there is an update available that could help you use the program.

Can I later change or remove the compatibility settings for a program?

Yes. You can run the Program Compatibility Wizard again to change or remove the compatibility settings you selected for a program.

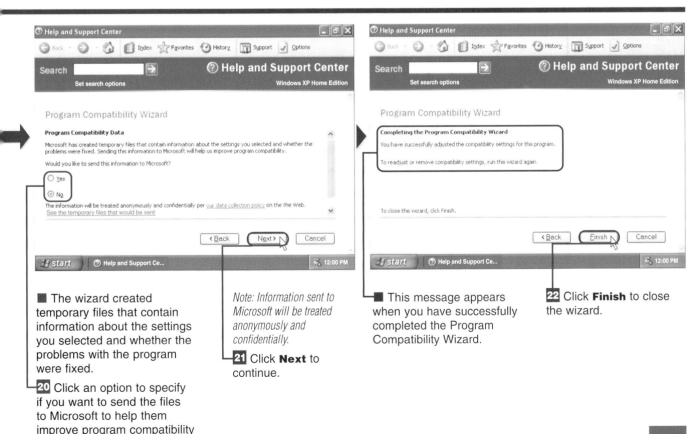

■ The wizard created temporary files that contain information about the settings you selected and whether the problems with the program were fixed.

20 Click an option to specify if you want to send the files to Microsoft to help them improve program compatibility (○ changes to ◉).

Note: Information sent to Microsoft will be treated anonymously and confidentially.

21 Click **Next** to continue.

■ This message appears when you have successfully completed the Program Compatibility Wizard.

22 Click **Finish** to close the wizard.

USING THE FILES AND SETTINGS TRANSFER WIZARD

You can use the Files and Settings Transfer Wizard to transfer your personal files and settings from one computer to another computer.

For example, you may want to transfer files and settings from an office computer to a computer at home or to a new computer.

You can transfer files and settings from a computer that uses Windows 95, Windows 98, Windows Me, Windows NT 4.0, Windows 2000 or Windows XP. The computer you transfer the files and settings to must use Windows XP.

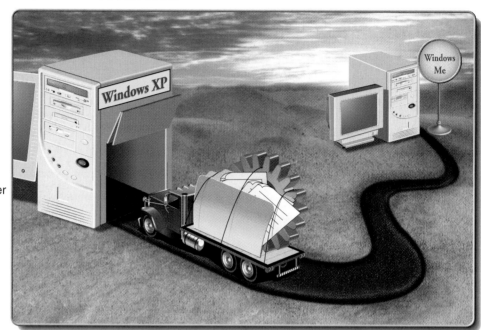

USING THE FILES AND SETTINGS TRANSFER WIZARD

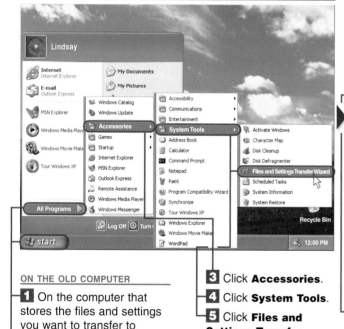

ON THE OLD COMPUTER

1 On the computer that stores the files and settings you want to transfer to another computer, click **start** to display the Start menu.

2 Click **All Programs**.

3 Click **Accessories**.

4 Click **System Tools**.

5 Click **Files and Settings Transfer Wizard**.

■ The Files and Settings Transfer Wizard appears.

■ This area describes the wizard.

■ Before you continue, you should close any open programs on the computer.

6 Click **Next** to continue.

How do I start the Files and Settings Transfer Wizard on a computer running an older version of Windows?

You can use the Windows XP CD-ROM disc to start the Files and Settings Transfer Wizard on a computer running an older version of Windows. Insert the Windows XP CD-ROM disc into a drive on the computer. In the screen that appears, click **Perform additional tasks** and then select **Transfer files and settings** to start the wizard. To complete the wizard, click **Next** and then perform steps **9** to **15** starting below.

What methods can I use to transfer files and settings from one computer to another?

You can use a direct cable connection, your home or small office network, a floppy drive or other removable media device, such as a Zip drive, or you can specify another location, such as a removable drive. Using a direct cable connection or network is the most efficient way to transfer files and settings.

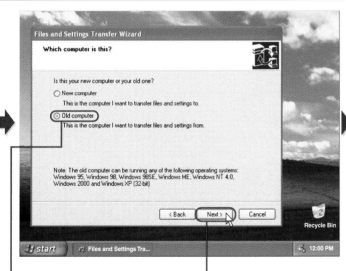

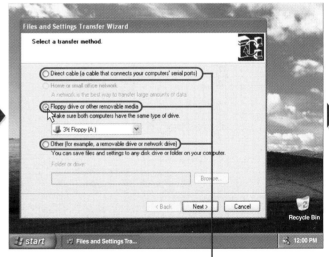

7 Click **Old computer** to specify that this computer has the files and settings you want to transfer to another computer (○ changes to ◉).

8 Click **Next** to continue.

■ The wizard needs you to select the way you want to transfer the files and settings to another computer.

9 Click the way you want to transfer the files and settings (○ changes to ◉).

CONTINUED

USING THE FILES AND SETTINGS TRANSFER WIZARD

You can choose the type of information you want to transfer to the other computer. You can transfer only settings, only files or both files and settings.

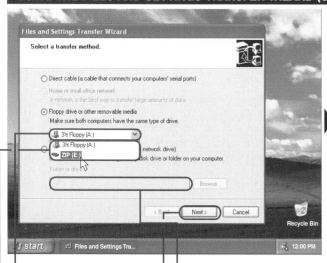

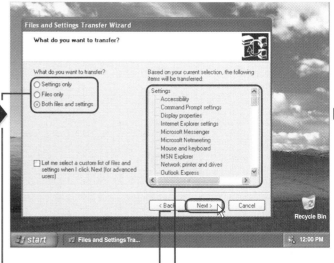

10 If you selected **Floppy drive or other removable media** in step **9**, click this area to display a list of the available drives.

11 Click the drive you want to use to transfer the files and settings to the other computer.

■ If you selected **Other** in step **9**, click this area and type the location you want to use to transfer the files and settings to the other computer.

12 Click **Next** to continue.

13 Click an option to specify the type of information you want to transfer (○ changes to ◉).

■ This area lists the items the wizard will transfer, based on the option you selected in step **13**.

14 Click **Next** to continue.

What files and settings can Windows transfer to another computer?

Files
Windows can transfer folders such as the My Documents, My Pictures and Shared Documents folders. Windows can also transfer common types of files, such as documents, pictures, sounds and videos.

Settings
Windows can transfer settings such as your Web browser, e-mail, network, taskbar, mouse, keyboard and display settings.

Why does the wizard state that I should install a program on the other computer?

The Files and Settings Transfer Wizard displays a message if you need to install a program on the other computer before transferring the program's settings to the computer. You will need to install all the programs you want to use on the other computer since the wizard will not transfer the programs for you. Click **Next** to continue using the wizard.

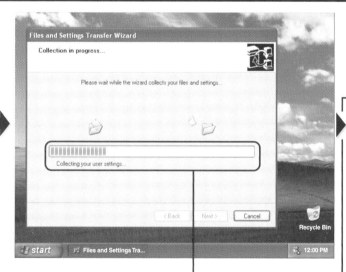

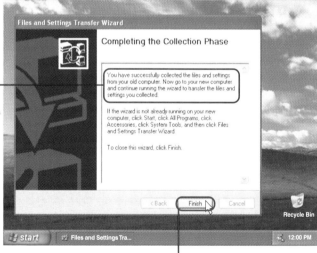

■ The wizard collects the files and settings you selected to transfer.

■ This area shows the progress of the collection.

■ This message appears when the wizard has successfully collected the files and settings on the computer.

15 Click **Finish** to close the wizard.

■ You can now transfer the files and settings to the other computer.

CONTINUED

USING THE FILES AND SETTINGS TRANSFER WIZARD

You need to specify how you will transfer the files and settings the wizard collected from the old computer to the new computer.

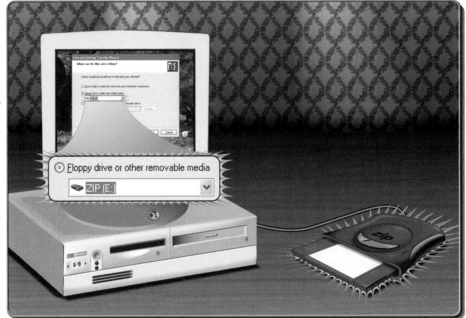

You should select the same transfer method you used when you ran the Files and Settings Transfer Wizard on the old computer.

USING THE FILES AND SETTINGS TRANSFER WIZARD (CONTINUED)

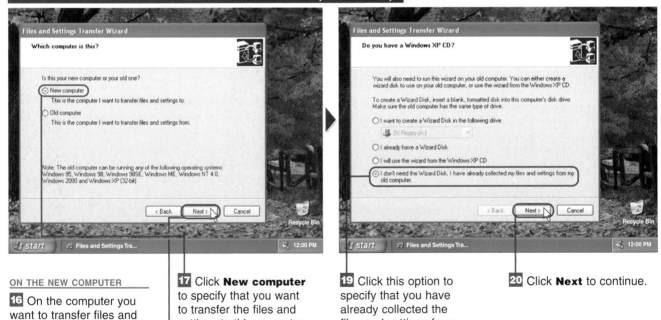

ON THE NEW COMPUTER

16 On the computer you want to transfer files and settings to, perform steps **1** to **6** on page 292 to display the Files and Settings Transfer Wizard.

17 Click **New computer** to specify that you want to transfer the files and settings to this computer (○ changes to ◉).

18 Click **Next** to continue.

19 Click this option to specify that you have already collected the files and settings from the other computer (○ changes to ◉).

20 Click **Next** to continue.

Can I restore the settings the wizard changed on the new computer?

After you use the Files and Settings Transfer Wizard to transfer settings from one computer to another, the settings transferred from the old computer will replace the settings on the new computer. For example, the new computer will now display the same desktop background and use the same screen saver as the old computer. You cannot restore the settings previously used on the new computer, but you can change the settings as you would change the settings on any computer.

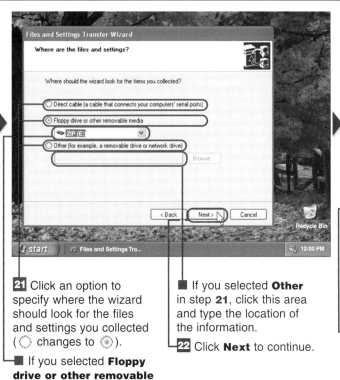

21 Click an option to specify where the wizard should look for the files and settings you collected (○ changes to ◉).

■ If you selected **Floppy drive or other removable media** in step **21**, click this area to select the drive that contains the information.

■ If you selected **Other** in step **21**, click this area and type the location of the information.

22 Click **Next** to continue.

■ This screen appears when the transfer is complete.

23 Click **Finish** to close the wizard.

■ A dialog box will appear, stating that you need to log off Windows before the changes can take effect. Click **Yes** to log off Windows.

Note: When you log off Windows, the Welcome screen will appear, allowing you to select the account you want to use to log on to Windows again.

INDEX

view information for, 71
views in Fonts window, change, 71
format
    of currency, change, 66-67
    of dates, change, 66-67
    of numbers, change, 66-67
    text
        in e-mail messages, 210-211
        in instant messages, 234-235
    of times, change, 66-67

G

group
    contacts, in Windows Messenger, 238-239
    taskbar buttons, 91
groups, in Windows Messenger
    create, 239
    delete, 239
    move contacts to, 239
    rename, 239
Guest account, turn on or off, 152-153

H

hard disk
    convert to NTFS, 284-285
    detect and repair errors, 276-277
hardware, troubleshoot using Device Manager, 278-281
hearing, customize Windows for
    using accessibility options, 114-117
    using Accessibility Wizard, 110-113
hibernation, power option for computer, 273
    instantly put computer into, 275
Hidden attribute, for files, 23
hide
    extensions for known file types, 25
    notification icons on taskbar, 91
    shortcut, on Start menu
        to e-mail program, 100
        to Web browser, 100
    status bar in windows, 18
    taskbar, 90
High Contrast color schemes, use, 117
hyperlinks. See links

I

icons
    add to desktop, 50-51
    change size on Start menu, 99
    for folders, change pictures for, 60-61
    large, display on desktop and Start menu, 48-49
    for monitors, identify when using multiple, 83
    overview, 5
    titles, underline, 63
identify monitors when using multiple, 83
image editing programs, open pictures in, 7
Inbox folder, in Outlook Express, 209

incoming connections
    delete, 183
    set up, 178-183
install, Windows XP components, 268-271
instant messages
    conversations, save, 236
    emoticons, 233
    send, 232-233
    text
        bold, 234
        color, change, 235
        font, change, 234
        italicize, 234
        size, change, 234
Internet Explorer. See also Web, pages
    overview, 51
    start, 192
IP (Internet Protocol) addresses, 176
italicize, text
    in e-mail messages, 211
    in instant messages, 234

K

keyboards
    keys
        control mouse when using MouseKeys, 117
        control Narrator, using, 109
    for On-Screen Keyboard, use, 106-107
    settings, change, 80-81
    shortcuts, turn on accessibility options using, 115
keystroke combination, use to insert special characters, 35

L

Landscape orientation, 77
Language bar, 67
Limited accounts, 151
lines, draw on Whiteboard, 240
links
    in e-mail messages, change text to, 211
    to related Web pages, find, 199
    select, 192
Links folder, 201
Links toolbar, 89
lock taskbar, 86, 90
log on to Windows, 145, 153

M

Magnifier
    open, using Accessibility Wizard, 111
    start or stop, using Utility Manager, 118-119
    use, 104-105
    window
        change size, 105
        invert colors, 105
magnify pictures, in Windows Picture and Fax viewer, 6
Management and Monitoring Tools component, 269
mapped network drives, create, 162-165
Media bar, use, 204-205
Menu bar, 5

INDEX

Read Less – Learn More™

Visual

Simplified®

Simply the Easiest Way to Learn

For visual learners who are brand-new to a topic and want to be shown, not told, how to solve a problem in a friendly, approachable way.

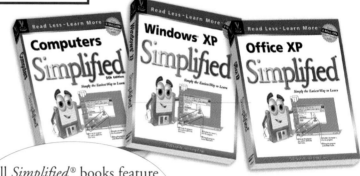

All *Simplified*® books feature friendly Disk characters who demonstrate and explain the purpose of each task.

Title	ISBN	U.S. Price
America Online Simplified, 2nd Ed. (Version 5.0)	0-7645-3433-5	$27.99
America Online Simplified, 3rd Ed. (Version 7.0)	0-7645-3673-7	$24.99
Computers Simplified, 5th Ed.	0-7645-3524-2	$27.99
Creating Web Pages with HTML Simplified, 2nd Ed.	0-7645-6067-0	$27.99
Excel 97 Simplified	0-7645-6022-0	$27.99
Excel 2002 Simplified	0-7645-3589-7	$27.99
FrontPage 2000 Simplified	0-7645-3450-5	$27.99
FrontPage 2002 Simplified	0-7645-3612-5	$27.99
Internet and World Wide Web Simplified, 3rd Ed.	0-7645-3409-2	$27.99
Microsoft Access 2000 Simplified	0-7645-6058-1	$27.99
Microsoft Excel 2000 Simplified	0-7645-6053-0	$27.99
Microsoft Office 2000 Simplified	0-7645-6052-2	$29.99
Microsoft Word 2000 Simplified	0-7645-6054-9	$27.99
More Windows 95 Simplified	1-56884-689-4	$27.99
More Windows 98 Simplified	0-7645-6037-9	$27.99
Office 97 Simplified	0-7645-6009-3	$29.99
Office XP Simplified	0-7645-0850-4	$29.99
PC Upgrade and Repair Simplified, 2nd Ed.	0-7645-3560-9	$27.99
Windows 95 Simplified	1-56884-662-2	$27.99
Windows 98 Simplified	0-7645-6030-1	$27.99
Windows 2000 Professional Simplified	0-7645-3422-X	$27.99
Windows Me Millennium Edition Simplified	0-7645-3494-7	$27.99
Windows XP Simplified	0-7645-3618-4	$27.99
Word 97 Simplified	0-7645-6011-5	$27.99
Word 2002 Simplified	0-7645-3588-9	$27.99

Over 10 million *Visual* books in print!

with these full-color Visual™ guides

The Fast and Easy Way to Learn

Teach Yourself VISUALLY™

Title	ISBN	U.S. Price
Teach Yourself Access 97 VISUALLY	0-7645-6026-3	$29.99
Teach Yourself FrontPage 2000 VISUALLY	0-7645-3451-3	$29.99
Teach Yourself HTML VISUALLY	0-7645-3423-8	$29.99
Teach Yourself the Internet and World Wide Web VISUALLY, 2nd Ed.	0-7645-3410-6	$29.99
Teach Yourself Microsoft Access 2000 VISUALLY	0-7645-6059-X	$29.99
Teach Yourself Microsoft Excel 97 VISUALLY	0-7645-6063-8	$29.99
Teach Yourself Microsoft Excel 2000 VISUALLY	0-7645-6056-5	$29.99
Teach Yourself Microsoft Office 2000 VISUALLY	0-7645-6051-4	$29.99
Teach Yourself Microsoft PowerPoint 97 VISUALLY	0-7645-6062-X	$29.99
Teach Yourself Microsoft PowerPoint 2000 VISUALLY	0-7645-6060-3	$29.99
Teach Yourself Microsoft Word 2000 VISUALLY	0-7645-6055-7	$29.99
Teach Yourself More Windows 98 VISUALLY	0-7645-6044-1	$29.99
Teach Yourself Office 97 VISUALLY	0-7645-6018-2	$29.99
Teach Yourself Red Hat Linux VISUALLY	0-7645-3430-0	$29.99
Teach Yourself VISUALLY Access 2002	0-7645-3591-9	$29.99
Teach Yourself VISUALLY Adobe Acrobat 5 PDF	0-7645-3667-2	$29.99
Teach Yourself VISUALLY Adobe Photoshop Elements	0-7645-3678-8	$29.99
Teach Yourself VISUALLY Adobe Premiere 6	0-7645-3664-8	$29.99
Teach Yourself VISUALLY Computers, 3rd Ed.	0-7645-3525-0	$29.99
Teach Yourself VISUALLY Digital Photography	0-7645-3565-X	$29.99
Teach Yourself VISUALLY Dreamweaver 3	0-7645-3470-X	$29.99
Teach Yourself VISUALLY Dreamweaver 4	0-7645-0851-2	$29.99
Teach Yourself VISUALLY E-commerce with FrontPage	0-7645-3579-X	$29.99
Teach Yourself VISUALLY Excel 2002	0-7645-3594-3	$29.99
Teach Yourself VISUALLY Fireworks 4	0-7645-3566-8	$29.99
Teach Yourself VISUALLY Flash 5	0-7645-3540-4	$29.99
Teach Yourself VISUALLY Flash MX	0-7645-3661-3	$29.99
Teach Yourself VISUALLY FrontPage 2002	0-7645-3590-0	$29.99
Teach Yourself VISUALLY Illustrator 10	0-7645-3654-0	$29.99
Teach Yourself VISUALLY iMac	0-7645-3453-X	$29.99
Teach Yourself VISUALLY Investing Online	0-7645-3459-9	$29.99
Teach Yourself VISUALLY Macromedia Web Collection	0-7645-3648-6	$29.99
Teach Yourself VISUALLY Networking, 2nd Ed.	0-7645-3534-X	$29.99
Teach Yourself VISUALLY Office XP	0-7645-0854-7	$29.99
Teach Yourself VISUALLY Photoshop 6	0-7645-3513-7	$29.99
Teach Yourself VISUALLY Photoshop 7	0-7645-3682-6	$29.99
Teach Yourself VISUALLY PowerPoint 2002	0-7645-3660-5	$29.99
Teach Yourself VISUALLY Quicken 2001	0-7645-3526-9	$29.99
Teach Yourself VISUALLY Windows 2000 Server	0-7645-3428-9	$29.99
Teach Yourself VISUALLY Windows Me Millennium Edition	0-7645-3495-5	$29.99
Teach Yourself VISUALLY Windows XP	0-7645-3619-2	$29.99
Teach Yourself VISUALLY Word 2002	0-7645-3587-0	$29.99
Teach Yourself Windows 95 VISUALLY	0-7645-6001-8	$29.99
Teach Yourself Windows 98 VISUALLY	0-7645-6025-5	$29.99
Teach Yourself Windows 2000 Professional VISUALLY	0-7645-6040-9	$29.99
Teach Yourself Windows NT 4 VISUALLY	0-7645-6061-1	$29.99
Teach Yourself Word 97 VISUALLY	0-7645-6032-8	$29.99

For visual learners who want to guide themselves through the basics of any technology topic. *Teach Yourself VISUALLY* offers more expanded coverage than our best-selling *Simplified* series.

The **Visual™**
series is available
wherever books are
sold, or call
1-800-762-2974.
Outside the US, call
317-572-3993.

Did you like this book?

**Teach Yourself VISUALLY
MORE Windows XP**

ISBN: 0-7645-3698-2

If so, pick up a copy of Teach Yourself VISUALLY Windows XP!

**Teach Yourself VISUALLY
Windows XP**

ISBN: 0-7645-3619-2

SOME TOPICS INCLUDE:

- Start a Program Automatically
- Create a Compressed Folder
- Copy Files to a CD
- Copy Pictures from a Digital Camera
- Publish a File to the Web
- Play a Sound or Video
- Listen to Radio Stations on the Internet
- Copy Songs to a CD or Portable Device
- Set Up Multiple Users on Your Computer
- Restore Your Computer
- Get Remote Assistance
- Set Up a Home Network
- Send a File in an Instant Message